SHOEING
THE MODERN HORSE

SHOEING
THE MODERN HORSE

The Horse Owner's Guide
to Farriery and Hoof Care

Steven Kraus, CJF

with Katie Navarra

Foreword by Doug Butler, PhD, CJF, FWCF

Trafalgar Square
North Pomfret, Vermont

First published in 2022 by
Trafalgar Square Books
North Pomfret, Vermont 05053

Copyright © 2022 Steven Kraus and Katie Navarra

All rights reserved. No part of this book may be reproduced, by any means, without written permission of the publisher, except by a reviewer quoting brief excerpts for a review in a magazine, newspaper, or website.

Disclaimer of Liability
The authors and publisher shall have neither liability nor responsibility to any person or entity with respect to any loss or damage caused or alleged to be caused directly or indirectly by the information contained in this book. While the book is as accurate as the authors can make it, there may be errors, omissions, and inaccuracies.

Trafalgar Square Books encourages the use of approved safety helmets in all equestrian sports and activities.

ISBN: 978-1-64601-105-6
Library of Congress Control Number: 2022941667

All photos and illustrations courtesy of Steven Kraus except: figs. I.1, I.2, and 7.4 B from *All Horse Systems Go* by Dr. Nancy Loving and used by permission of the publisher; figs. 1.4 A, 1.6, 1.12, 2.7, 2.8, 5.4, 5.5 B, 5.13, 8.16, 11.6, 14.9, and 15.7 by Katie Navarra; figs. 1.4 B, 2.1, 2.15, 13.17, 4.1, 4.3, 4.4, 4.6, 4.9, 4.10, 4.14, 5.1, 5.2, 5.3, 5.6, 5.10, 5.14, 7.14, 8.17, 11.2, 12.1, 12.2, 12.5 A & B, 13.1, and 14.1 AdobeStock; fig. 2.2 The Vindolanda Trust; fig. 2.9 Hudson Mohawk Industrial Gateway, Burden Iron Works Museum; figs. 3.8 and 6.1 by Gary Gullo, Jr; fig. 3.9 by CSIRO media assets https://www.csiro.au/-/media/News-releases/2013/3D-printed-horseshoe-to-improve-racing-performance/3D-printed-titanium-horseshoes.jpg; figs. 3.10, 8.12, and 12.4 by Sandra Mesrine; figs. 13.15 A–C by Douglas Ehrmann; figs. 5.5 A, 7.1, 13.2, 14.8, and 15.4 A by Jeff Cota for the *American Farriers Journal*; figs. 5.12, 14.2, 14.3, 14.4, 14.5, 14.10, 14.11 A & B, and 14.12 by Jeremy McGovern for the *American Farriers Journal*; figs. 6.6 A, 6.7, and 6.8 A by Butler Publishing from *Shoeing in Your Right Mind*; figs. 6.16 and 6.17 by Mark Caldwell; fig. 8.1 by Kristen Gordeyko for Willow Way Clydesdales; figs. 11.1, 11.4, 13.8, and 15.1 by Christine Hamilton; figs. 11.3, 11.5 A & B, 11.7, and 11.8 by Jochen Schleese from *Suffering in Silence*; fig. 12.3 by Jim Navarra; figs. 14.6 and 14.7 by the *American Farriers Journal*; figs. 14.13 and 14.14 by Lewis Horn for the *American Farriers Journal*; figs. 15.4 B & C by Werkman Black; fig. 15.6 by Prof. Dr. H. Brommer and the farriers J. de Zwaan and G. Bronkhorst, Utrecht University, The Netherlands

Book design by Lauryl Eddlemon
Cover design by RM Didier
Index by Andrea Jones (JonesLiteraryServices.com)

Printed in China

10 9 8 7 6 5 4 3 2 1

This book is dedicated to Gloria,
my mother, Kermit, my father, and to
all the horses who taught me so much.

Contents

Foreword by Doug Butler, PhD, CJF, FWCF   xi

Introduction   1

Chapter 1: To Shoe or Not to Shoe?   4

An Objective Way to Determine Hoof Care   4
    Making Objective Observations   5
Shoes vs. Barefoot—Common Questions   10
    Can Horseshoes Harm My Horse's Feet?   10
    Does My Horse Need Shoes?   10
    Can My Horse's Shoes Just Be Reset?   12
    What Should I Know About Going Barefoot?   14
Digging Deeper into Barefoot Trimming   16
    Putting Barefoot to the Test   17
    The Debate Continues   19
From the Forge: The Birth of the WIDTH Protocol   20

Chapter 2: The Evolution of the Modern Horseshoe   21

Shoe Style and Materials Used   23
    Glue-On Shoes   25
    Manufactured vs. Handmade Horseshoes   28
More Than Meets the Eye: Shoe Design   30
    Horseshoe Cross-Sections: Flat vs. Rim Styles   30
    Horseshoe Modifications   32
Horseshoe Accessories   41
    Pads   41
    Traction Control   43

Largely Unchanged   44
From the Forge: Can Glue-On Shoes Replace Nails?   45

Chapter 3: Modern Horseshoe Styles   46

Modern Shoe Modifications   49
    Straight Bar Shoe   49
    Egg Bar   49
    Heart Bar   50
    Z-Bar   50

Hospital Plate	51
Wedges	51
Pharoah Plate	52
3D-Printed Horseshoes	53
Glue-On Shoes	53
Additional Modern Shoe Alternatives	57
Hoof Taps	58
Hoof Boots	58
From the Forge: A Modern Approach for Hard-to- Shoe Horses	*60*

Chapter 4: Horseshoes for Specific Uses and Sports   61

Horseshoes by Discipline	63
Rules and Regulations	65
Outside USEF Jurisdiction	67
Shoeing for Performance	71
From the Forge: What Hoofprints Tell Us	*72*

Chapter 5: Hot Shoeing vs. Cold Shoeing   73

Hot-Fit Basics	75
Cold-Fit Basics	77
Why Hot-Fit Shoes?	77
Disadvantages of Hot-Fitting	80
Training Horses for Hot-Fitting	81
Going without Heat	82

Chapter 6: How Conformation Determines Soundness and Performance   85

Where Do Conformation Defects Start?	85
Defining the Level of Conformational Issues	87
An Objective Evaluation Method	89
Consequences of Conformational Defects—Front End	94
X-Axis Front-End Defects	94
Y-Axis Front-End Defects	95
Z-Axis Front-End Defects	96
Consequences of Conformational Defects—Hind End	96
X-Axis Hind-End Defects	96
X- and Y-Axis Hind-End Defects	97
Z-Axis Hind-End Defects	97
Management of Conformation Defects with Farriery	98
Trimming	98
The Whole Picture	99
From the Forge: Having Courage	*100*

Chapter 7: Hoof Conditions and Diseases   101

Abscess	102
Bony Growths	103
Canker	104
Coffin Bone Fractures	105
Contracted Heels	106
Corns	107
Coronitis	108
Cracks	109
Interbulbular Dermatitis	110
Keratoma	111
Laminitis	111
Navicular Disease	113
Pedal Osteitis	114
Punctures	115

Osteomyelitis	115
White Line Disease	116
Thrush	117
High/Low Syndrome (Mismatched Front Feet)	118
The Vet/Farrier Partnership	118
The Lameness Exam	119
The Bottom Line	121
From the Forge: Meeting Burney Chapman and Learning About Laminitis Treatment	*121*

Chapter 8: Hoof Care for Foals — 122

Early Observation and Recognition of Problems	123
Angular Limb Deformities	125
Flexor Tendon Flaccidity	126
Flexural Deformities (Contracted Tendons)	127
Knock Knees (Carpal Valgus)	127
Consequences of Inaction	131
The Role of Nutrition	132
Hoof Quality Determined Before Birth	132
From the Forge: The Case for Farrier Visits for Foals	*135*

Chapter 9: What Can Possibly Go Wrong? — 136

Common Farrier Mistakes	137
Incorrect Angles	137
Trimmed Too Short	138
Not Trimmed Enough	140
Excessive Heel Length	140
Misalignment of Angles	140
Nail Too Deep	141
Wrong Shoe Size	141
Fixing What Isn't Broken	142

Chapter 10: Why Horses Lose Shoes and How to Limit Thrown Shoes — 144

Shoeing Schedule	144
What Does a Proper Shoeing Look Like?	145
Rider/Owner Errors and Environmental Factors That Lead to Shoe Loss	146
Horse-Caused Shoe Loss	149
Farrier Errors Causing Shoe Loss	150
Being Proactive	152
From the Forge: A Rider's Influence	*154*

Chapter 11: The Horse Owner's Role in Hoof and Shoeing Problems — 155

Understanding Saddle Fit	155
Saddle Position	157
Wither Clearance	158
Panel Pressure and Contact	158
Pommel-to-Cantle Relationship	158
Saddle Balance	158
Channel Clearance and Gullet Width	159
Saddle Length	159
Tree Angle	160
Signs That Signal Saddle-Fit Issues	160
Improving Saddle Fit	160
The Rider's Role in Hoof Problems	162
Weight Considerations	163
Consider the Whole Picture	163
From the Forge: Watching a Client Ride	*164*

Chapter 12: Horse Behavior and Handling for Farriery — 165

What Happens When a Horse Doesn't Stand for the Farrier? — 165
Create Positive Farrier Experiences — 167
Common Causes of "Bad Behavior" — 168
   Is It Pain? — 168
   Owner Actions That Cause Behavioral Problems — 169
   Barn Management That Contributes to Behavioral Problems — 169
   Farrier Attitude That Causes Behavioral Problems — 169
   Sedative Solutions — 169
A Horse-First Approach — 171
   Training Horses for Shoeing — 172
From the Forge: Tales from the Field — *174*

Chapter 13: Becoming a Better Consumer of Farriery — 175

Dangerous Conditions or Badly Behaved Horses — 175
Know-It-All Clients Who Micromanage — 176
No, Slow, or Poor Payment — 176
Loose Horses — 176
Muddy Horses — 176
Poor Working Conditions — 177
Inconsistency — 178
Skipping Management Recommendations — 179
Switching Farriers Often — 179
What You Can Expect — 180
   Prompt, Clear Communication — 180
   Lateness — 180
   Poor Horse Handling Skills — 180
   Unprepared — 180
   Disinterest in Continuing Education — 181
   Quality of Work — 181
Basic Hoof Care Skills for Horse Owners — 182
   Pulling a Shoe — 183
   Rasping a Hoof — 185

Chapter 14: Who Is the Modern Farrier and What Training is Required? — 187

What Training Do Farriers Receive? — 188
What Does It Take to Be a Farrier? — 190
Advanced Training — 190
   Equine Podiatry Specialty — 192
From the Forge: Eye of the Beholder — *192*
   Farrier Competitions — 193
The Cost of Shoeing — 194
Who Is the Modern Farrier? — 194
Female Farriers — 195
What Farrier Training Means to Horse Owners — 197
From the Forge: How Shoeing May Have Saved My Life — *200*

Chapter 15: The Future of Farriery — 201

The Rise of Technology in Shoeing the Modern Horse — 202
   Predictions for the Future — 204
From the Forge: My Why — *207*

Additional Resources — **209**
Bibliography — **211**
Acknowledgements — **213**
Index — **215**

Foreword

As an experienced farrier, life-time horse owner, and retired college professor, it gives me great pleasure to have the honor to write a foreword to this important book by my friend Steve Kraus. I have known Steve for more than 50 years and have had enough experience with him to know he can be relied upon for sensible, factual information.

Steve has ideas and opinions, as we all do. These are based on his considerable experience. He has shared these with horse owners, farriers, and veterinarians for many years. He is a competent horseman who began his learner's journey working summers at riding stables in the Northeast. He went on to become a rated polo player and university polo team coach, as well as a respected clinician.

In the mid-1970s, after I published my book, *Principles of Horseshoeing,* and while I was a graduate student at Cornell University, Mustad's Karl Maum contacted me about being their American representative. I invited Steve to a meeting at my home and suggested Steve would be better suited to do what needed to be done to introduce their nails to the American market. Steve served as a consultant to them for many years. He also ran a farrier supply business.

We did many farrier clinics together during those early years, along with Harold Mower, Marshall (Buster) Conklin, and Doug Pokorney. Later, he worked for my mother, who raised champion registered Welsh ponies in Ithaca, New York, while I was teaching at universities in the West.

Farriery is more of an art than a science. However, science is an essential component to good horse management and understanding farrier work. Experience is king in farrier work. Some gray hair is necessary to get it right. Even though Steve has no hair, he has the experience to get it right!

I know that Steve seeks excellence in all that he does. He became interested in the martial arts and desired to excel in that as well as horsemanship and farrier work. We have worked together to solve difficult farrier problems. You can trust him. His earnest desire is to help your horses and you.

Doug Butler PhD, CJF, FWCF
Butler Professional Farrier School
The trusted name in farrier education

Introduction

How do we define the "modern horse"? The "modern horse" is the recreational and competitive horse that emerged in the post-World War II era. Before that, horses were mainly work or military animals. Only the wealthy could afford the luxury of horses for the sole purpose of enjoyment.

The five decades spanning the early 1900s to the 1950s brought a significant transition in the horse industry. Cars, trucks, and tractors replaced four-legged horsepower, and the end of WWII ushered in a new era of horse ownership—one that was widely accessible to the average household.

Since then, horse owners, veterinarians, farriers, trainers, and other professionals have advanced the care for and use of horses to where we are today.

The basic principles of farriery have changed very little in hundreds of years. What has shifted is the ownership and needs of today's horses. The purpose of this book is to inform horse owners, farriers, and enthusiasts, with the information needed for a better understanding of hoof care and farriery for today's modern horse.

Numerous farriery textbooks have done an excellent job explaining how to shoe different horses, but the content is geared to the hoof-care professional. Horse owners must also become more knowledgeable about their horses to be better consumers of farrier services. Reading this book provides tips and advice for achieving this goal.

The idea here is not to teach a horse owner how to shoe or trim. Instead, it is to help an owner have a better understand of shoeing and hoof-care requirements for the modern horse to create more informed conversations with a farrier. It still remains that a well-trained farrier usually knows what is best for individual horses.

This book will start with an objective way to sort out an individual horse's needs to either wear shoes or remain shoeless. To provide some background, I will continue with the evolution of horseshoes. You'll get a detailed look at how the first horseshoes evolved into modern materials and the adhesives used today. Despite the changes, the purpose of horseshoes has remained the same for thousands of years—to protect the hoof, provide traction, and offer hoof support based on the individual horse's needs.

Just like footwear for humans, our equines need specific horseshoes to do their best in their various sports and work. Variations in horseshoe styles have specific uses that range from increasing performance for equine athletes, to assisting injured feet, and managing conformation problems.

The hoof-care profession is a blend of centuries-old skills combined with new research findings and technology that emerges. During the age of the modern horse, many new technologies have arisen to augment the existing art of farriery. Nevertheless, the connection between the horse and those who provide hoof care are linked forever.

The foundation to proper shoeing and trimming begins with understanding conformation. Learning to recognize conformation faults helps farriers provide the best trim- and shoe-selection protocols. Likewise, horse owners will benefit from understanding conformation to select problem-free horses, which can be helpful when thinking about acquiring a young horse or raising a foal (figs. I.1 and I.2).

There are many things to know to protect this investment of time and money. To produce a useful sound horse, you must be aware of the role farriery plays in this endeavor. When it comes to hoof injuries and diseases, the knowledge you gain will take the mystery out of these unfortunate circumstances. When a horse becomes lame, there is always a reason, so this book includes definitions and possible management of lameness. The management, riding, and saddling of horses also affect soundness and horseshoe retention. Learning the horse owner's role in avoiding shoe loss is critical to preventing these problems.

Horse behavior while being worked on is also an owner's responsibility. Learn what you can do to provide the best possible behavior for your farrier. And, farriers may not always be available, so learning the basics of emergency hoof care and shoeing problems is included within these pages along with tips for regular maintenance.

I.1 The hoof may look like a simple structure but a healthy hoof is comprised of multiple structures that influence how a horse is trimmed and shod.

I.2 Farriers take into account the bones, tendons and ligaments that extend from the hoof up into the leg before trimming and shoeing.

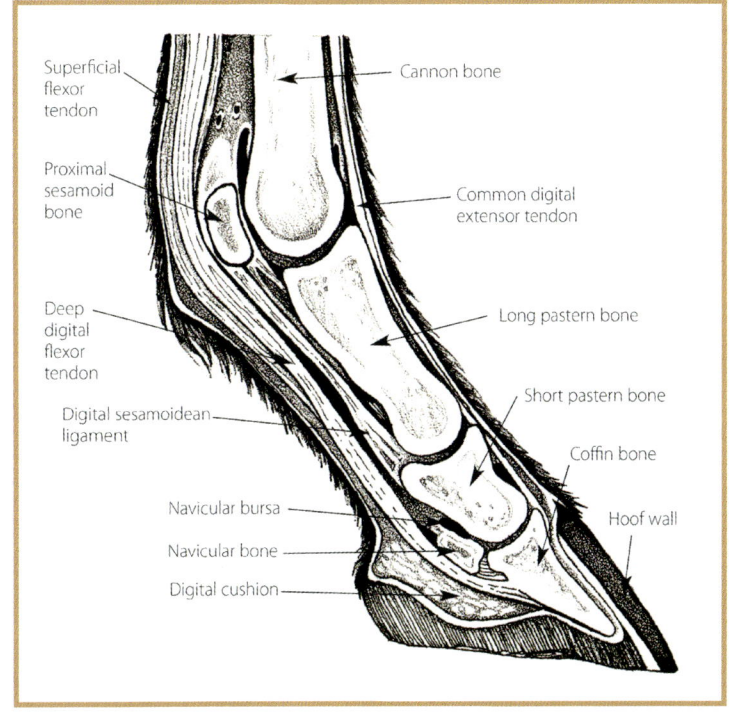

Many horse owners are unaware of how farriers learn the trade. You'll get an inside look at the many ways education occurs. You'll also learn that there are no enforceable professional standards in the United States. Fortunately, several associations administer certifications and accreditations. I will outline what all these titles mean to the horse owners hiring farriers.

As a "baby boomer," my involvement with horses began early in the 1950s, so maybe that also makes me a modern horseman. From the first time I saw a horse, I wanted to learn as much about horses as possible and become a well-rounded horseman. That quest to gain knowledge led me to the farriery world.

I have spent most of my life underneath horses working on their feet or on their backs, enjoying them! Possibly, it was my destiny because the path that appeared to me had the many opportunities that brought me to where I am today. But maybe I just had no choice in the matter because my desire to work with horses and farriery was irresistible.

In this book, I share real-life experiences and personal stories from more than 50 years in the horse business in the sidebars called: "From the Forge." I've invited a handful of farriers and veterinarians to contribute their expertise within these pages to enhance creating topics. These sidebars sprinkled throughout the text illustrate the translation between theory and real-life scenarios.

As you can see, there is a lot more to hoof care than trimming some hoof material and nailing on a horseshoe. My goal in writing this book for you, the horse owner, is to provide you with a firm understanding of farriery and hoof care, not to dictate to professionals, but to have enough knowledge to make informed decisions and have intelligent conversations for the benefit of the horse.

CHAPTER 1

To Shoe or Not to Shoe

An Objective Way to Determine Hoof Care

To shoe or not to shoe? If you've ever wondered which is better for your horse, you're not alone. The internet is full of opinions for you to consider. People have strong beliefs on both sides of the debate, which has created confusion and philosophical disputes rather than focusing on what is best for the modern horse.

Rather than ask, *Are shoes necessary?* or *Is going barefoot better than being shod?*, think of each horse as an individual. You will find the best answer for any horse when you take this approach. Horses live in diverse environments and are in many types of work, which contribute to deciding the best option for each horse (figs. 1.1 & 1.2).

With that in mind, it's impractical to think that one method of hoof care is the only way to take care of all horses' feet. Horseshoes may all look the same in the back of your farrier's truck, but there is no such thing as one

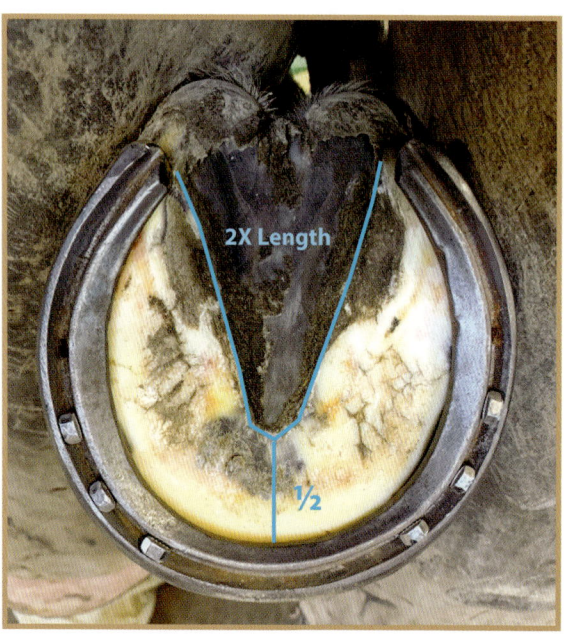

1.1 A shoe should cover the heels of the foot and be placed so it fits the perimeter of the normal hoof after trimming away any distortion. The length of the frog is twice the distance from the frog apex to the front of the shoe. This symmetry is called the "Golden Ratio" proportion.

method or one horseshoe for all horses. "Cookie cutter" style shoeing or trimming does not work. Whether you choose to leave a horse barefoot, or use a shoe, trimming is the foundation of your horse's hoof care.

Making Objective Observations

Observation and analysis of each horse, and not emotions, must guide the decision-making process to determine the best management of any horse. Good horsemanship, such as knowing the horse, his function, how to properly train, care for and use him offers the best answer in the barefoot versus shoeing debate.

Often, there is more than one solution to consider, and the decision of which method to use should be based on facts and data. The **WIDTH** Protocol can establish if any horse is a good candidate to remain barefoot or is better served with horseshoes from an objective rather than subjective point of view. This protocol was developed using my observations working on horses in the central New York State region, shoeing almost 250,000 hooves over a nearly 50-year career (see also Story from the Forge, p. 20). Ask yourself the following questions:

> 1 **W**ork—What does the horse do?
>
> 2 **I**ntensity—How much power does this horse have to transmit to the ground during work?
>
> 3 **D**uration—How many hours or miles does the horse work?
>
> 4 **T**errain—How hard or forgiving is the working surface? Is traction needed to be safe while working or being competitive?
>
> 5 **H**orse—What is the breed? Conformation? Any health issues? How will the horse be used, and what care will he receive?

Let's take a closer look at each one of these criteria to gain an understanding of how to use these principles to determine if your horse is a good candidate for staying barefoot or if he should have shoes.

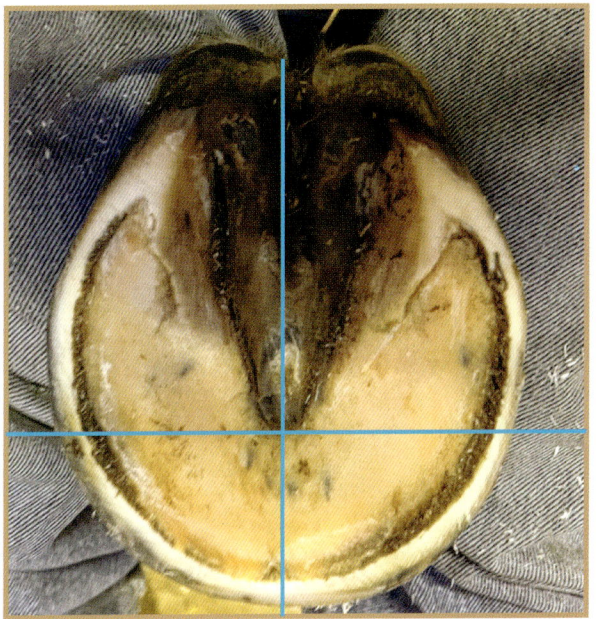

1.2 The hoof-wall thickness is uniform around the whole foot. The widest part of the foot divides the hoof into equal parts. The points of the heels align with the highest, widest part of the frog.

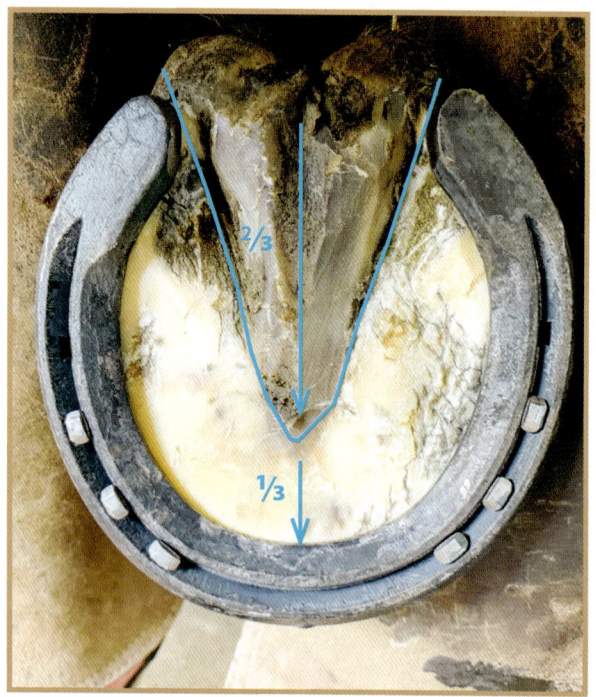

1.3 A A wide-web rim-style shoe, popular with Western performance horses and larger-footed polo horses. The groove or "V" crease digs into the ground providing stability at speed. Notice the 1/3 to 2/3 proportion from the apex of the frog forward to the distance to heel support.

1.3 B Horseshoe features vary based on the discipline. Typically, a polo horse, for example, wears shoes that include heel calks on the hind shoes to provide traction, stability, and safety while stopping and turning at speed on grass (B).

Work: What Does the Horse Do?

There are a multitude of ways horses are kept and used. Some are highly competitive, others perform in harsh environments, and some spend most of their time on turnout doing nothing at all. Most horses live somewhere between. Considering how often the horse works, the surface he works on, and his natural hoof quality are all part of the equation (figs. 1.3 A & B).

Intensity: How Hard Does the Horse Regularly Work?

Intensity refers to force or power transmitted to the ground for propulsion. Think of intensity as tires on a tractor. Smooth tires don't get as good grip as those with lugs. The same is true for shoes. A dressage horse working in collection, a barrel racer running a pattern, or a draft horse pulling a cart all need traction. Remaining barefoot doesn't transfer horsepower to the ground as well as shoes.

Duration: How Many Hours or Miles Does the Horse Regularly Work?

The frequency and length of rides help determine if a horse needs shoes. Those in regular training and competition, or endurance horses that cover a lot of ground, may need shoes to prevent the hooves from wearing too quickly between visits. It's important to ask, "Will a horse wear his feet faster than he can push out new growth to replace that worn hoof?"

Terrain: How Hard Is the Surface and Is Traction Needed?

Climate and geography make for a wide range of soil types and moisture conditions that affect hooves. A horse's hooves can adapt to the environment he lives in, but it is gradual. Some environments change too rapidly for a horse's foot to adjust on its own. Those could be seasonal weather variations such as extremely dry to exceptionally wet ground or frequent changes in performance venues with varied footing types. Horses that wear shoes while living in snowy, icy climates can have traction devices added to the shoe to limit slipping (see also Traction Control, p. 43).

Horse: What's the Breed, Conformation, Health, Care, and Use?

Heavier-boned horses tend to be thicker-skinned and have tougher feet whereas some light-boned breeds have genetic predispositions for hoof problems. For example, the lighter bone structure that gives Thoroughbreds speed is a finer structure but makes racehorses more susceptible to fractures than breeds with denser bones.

Breeding choices significantly impact the strength of the hoof and its structures. Horses with poor conformation are likely to need support beyond trimming to prevent soft-tissue damage. Ignoring conformational defects in favor of achieving specific traits, such as color or athletic ability, carries through to offspring and can perpetuate bone and joint issues.

The individual horse's conformation also impacts how forces from working are distributed up the legs. Crooked legs do not absorb impact as well as straight legs. These uneven forces can damage unprotected hooves in predictable ways and lead to the breakdown of bones and joints.

There are exceptions to every rule. There will always be a horse that does well barefoot regardless of his circumstances, but this animal is in the minority. A combination of good genetics, suitable habitat, and compatible selection for the activity allows certain horses to function well without shoes. However, missing even one of these criteria may be a deal-breaker for going shoeless.

A mechanically correct trimming paired with a well-fitted shoe has a multiplier effect where the result is greater than a factor of one plus one equaling two. The combination offers exponential benefits that allow the horse to load evenly, move well, and remain sound.

WIDTH Protocol Results

Based on the WIDTH Protocol we just discussed, these types of horses are candidates for going barefoot (fig. 1.4 A):

- ∪ A ranch-style Quarter horse, checking cows on the prairie.

1.4 A A recreational trail horse that regularly travel on soft, sandy trails may be able to go barefoot if he has good conformation and the hoof is healthy.

- A sturdy Arabian used for trail riding on sandy or clay soils.
- A horse that is not in work with solid hooves and good conformation.

Based on the same WIDTH criteria, these horses are likely to need shoes (fig. 1.4 B):

- An off-the-track Thoroughbred training as a field hunter in a moderate work schedule on hard ground.
- A polo pony. He will not likely damage his hooves on a well-maintained polo field but typically needs shoes for traction while running on grass.
- A rescued Thoroughbred racehorse in poor condition, turned out to pasture during fly season but never ridden. Weak hoof structures are prone to chipping and breaking from excessive stomping.
- A Morgan horse with good conformation. He may be training well without shoes but will not place in the show ring without weighted shoes to enhance his gaits.
- A Standardbred pacer training 5 miles per day on a stone dust track. The surface is like an emery board or nail file, and as a result he will wear his hooves faster than the structure will grow. The shoes will not only protect his feet but also balance his gait and improve racing speed.
- A horse with a moderate case of laminitis. Shoes with properly applied frog support can keep him more comfortable than if he were barefoot.

1.4 B A horse in regular work on a hard surface likely needs shoes to keep his feet from wearing too quickly.

There are exceptions to every rule, so it is critical to consider the whole horse. As a horse ages, his needs may change too. For example, a straight-legged young Warmblood in early training, in good footing and managed turnout, will not need hind shoes until the rider asks for more collection to move up the levels in competition. Another scenario: a crossbred endurance horse with good hooves may need shoes to be competitive in certain venues.

These are just snapshots of situations that indicate whether or not a horse may need shoes. It's the horse owner's responsibility to communicate with her farrier about all the factors that affect her horse's life and work so he can choose the options that fit the horse. Shoeing all horses the same way, or making an emotional decision about your horse's needs can be counterproductive. Knowledge and experience should prevail to determine the best management strategy. Both good horseshoeing and barefoot management practices produce positive results when applied appropriately.

Shoes vs. Barefoot—Common Questions

An understanding of the WIDTH protocol can answer the question, "Does my horse need shoes or can he go barefoot?" These are a few other common questions horse owners ask about shoes and barefoot trims.

Can Horseshoes Harm My Horse's Feet?

When applied improperly, yes. Just like anything we do with horses—training, veterinary care, trailering, for example—shoeing can hurt a horse when it's done incorrectly. Done appropriately, and for the right reasons, shoes offer support to the hoof structures, enhance motion, prevent cracking, and protect the hoof from hard terrain. Therapeutic shoes can even help lame horses become and stay sound (fig. 1.5). Shoes designed for particular sports or work also enhance a horse's performance ability.

Does My Horse Need Shoes?

It depends. Natural models work well for wild horses. Constant roaming adequately wears the hoof, and the foot adapts to the varied landscape (fig. 1.6). A feral horse either adjusts to his environment or does not live to reproduce. Nature culls those with poor hooves; humans do not. Some domestic horses can also go barefoot. For example, a horse that wears shoes in the summer while in heavy work often has his shoes removed in the fall and is left barefoot when not being ridden through the winter. Other horses are comfortable and sound under saddle without shoes all year round.

It's okay to be curious about how shoes might support your riding goals. Just because a horse isn't lame or is working reasonably well barefoot doesn't mean he is performing to the best of his ability. A horse that needs shoes to do his job but is denied them will underperform or suffer. Shoes give horses competitive advantages,

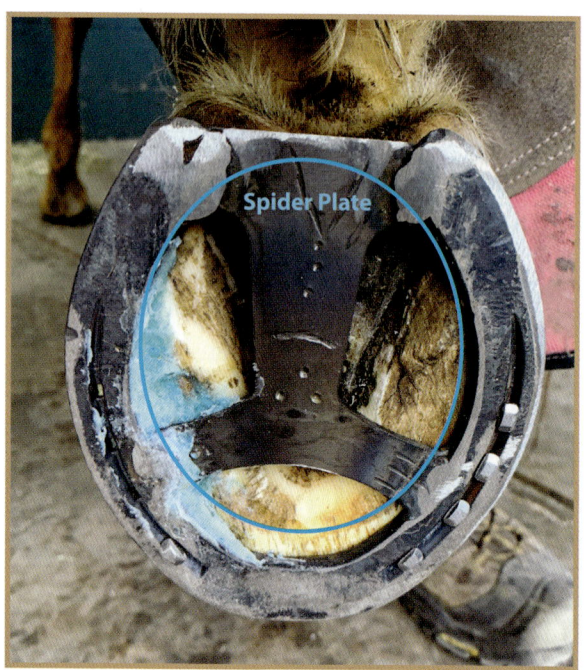

1.5 Horseshoes are configured in many ways to protect and heal injured or diseased hooves. A shoe with "spider plate," an extra piece of steel that protects the frogs and attaches to the sides of the shoe, helps to restore a damaged hoof.

1.6 Roaming on varied terrain that includes hard surfaces naturally wears down the hoof. Feral horses that need shoes or hoof care do not survive.

such as traction, gait correction, and enhancement. To get a better understanding, consider asking your farrier these questions:

- What makes my horse a good candidate for shoes?
- How might shoes help my horse?
- How do shoes support peak performance in my discipline?

Appropriate, skillful farriery is a combination of *trimming* and *shoeing* with decisions made based on the individual horse, rather than taking a one-size-fits-all approach.

Farriers consider multiple factors but recognize that trimming is the first step to deciding whether to leave a horse barefoot or to use a shoe. Regardless of the farrier's skills in shaping a shoe, when the hoof isn't trimmed correctly, the shoe will not be compatible (fig. 1.7). Essentially, the trim creates the blueprint for a shoe. Think about your own footwear—if you wear size 9, size 8 is never going to fit. At a minimum, poorly fitted shoes are uncomfortable. Worn for extended periods of

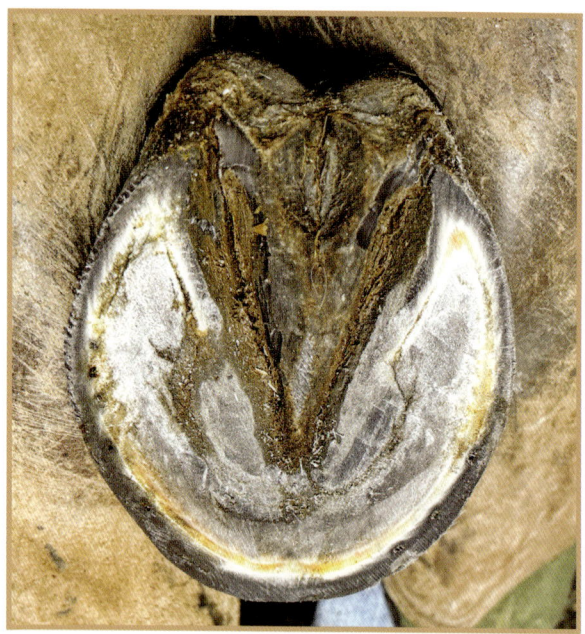

1.7 A well-trimmed, balanced hoof creates a blueprint for a shoe.

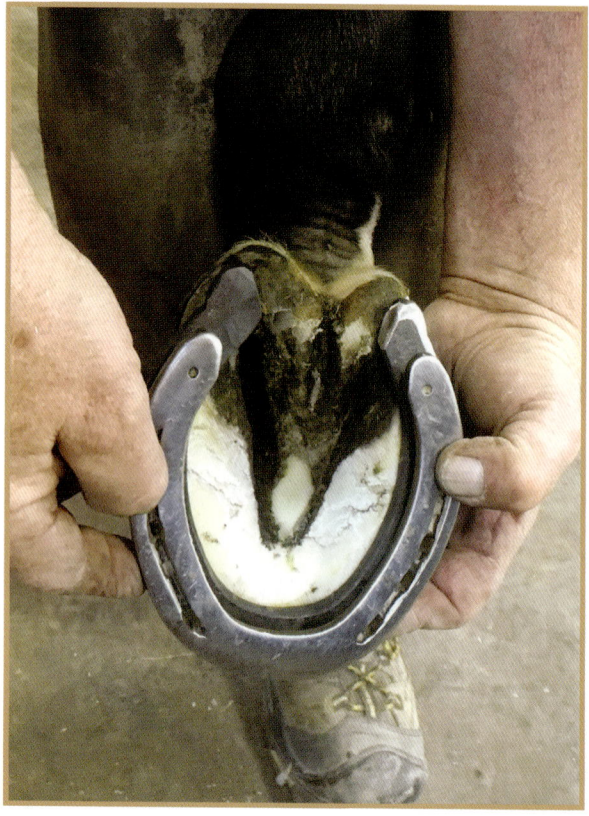

1.8 The shoe being held on top was on this foot before the one you see beneath it. Notice the increased heel support with the new shoe now on the foot when proper fit is achieved.

time they can leave blisters and potentially lead to larger issues in your feet and legs.

The same is true in horses. Improperly fitted shoes interfere with a horse's gait and add unnecessary strain on the hoof wall, which can lead to problems (fig. 1.8). A horse with poorly fitting or inappropriate shoes is better off without them.

Can My Horse's Shoes Just Be Reset?

Since horseshoes are durable, it is possible to reuse the same pair or set on a horse multiple times. The amount of work a horse does and his individual conformation establish how quickly shoes need to be replaced. There is no benefit using new shoes at each shoeing when the last set is in good condition. In fact, some horses appreciate the wear pattern that has developed in the old shoes.

If a horseshoe is not worn much and fits properly after trimming, the farrier will make sure the shoe is flat and nail it back on. When the same shoes are applied again it is called *resetting* or *refitting*. A farrier may even use the wear patterns on old shoes as a guide for producing new shoes. Uneven shoe wear patterns can suggest a necessary alignment change through trimming. The exception is that a lame horse breaks in the shoe to be comfortable to his foot—much like your sneakers or boots mold to your footfall.

CASE STUDY
How Two Horses Handled Barefoot Trimming

Unfortunately, it's the horse that suffers most when thinking of shoeing versus barefoot as absolutes.

A couple took a Paint Horse to the equine hospital at Cornell University. The horse was lame in both front feet, but standard lameness exams including observation of gait, hoof testing, flexion tests, and radiographs, didn't indicate the cause.

I immediately noticed beveled hoof walls resulting from a barefoot-style trimming method. This average-sized (1,100 pound) horse had less than a 3-inch toe length rather than the 3½ inches that is more appropriate for the horse's size (fig. 1.9). I commented that the feet were too short, and this horse could just be footsore. The radiographs indicated how little sole thickness this horse had, and my conclusion was the short toes and lack of sole depth were causing the lameness.

Shoes and pads could immediately make this horse sound, and rideable. However, the owners responded, "We do not believe in shoes. We will only use boots!" The boots clearly weren't working for this horse, but regardless of the evidence, the owners refused shoes and left with an uncomfortable horse. This horse could have felt instant comfort in shoes that offered sole relief by using frog support and rim pads or full pads.

Conversely, I was able to convince another client that her horse would be better served with shoes. She owned a nice gelding and was working toward lower-level eventing. He was a heavy-boned horse with large feet, and thick hoof walls and soles. His feet were perfect without shoes and his rider preferred keeping him barefoot since he was never sore. Then, as his training progressed, he plateaued.

Even though this horse had tough feet that were in good shape, his right front and right hind feet were imbalanced, and both were excessively worn down on their lateral sides. This impacted his ability to carry himself, especially when circling to the right. A few days after shoeing this horse with wider-fitting lateral branch shoes, the rider called to report the horse was performing the dressage movements previously impossible (fig. 1.10).

Shoeing horses is not just about protecting feet or relieving soreness; when done well, shoes provide support for horses to use themselves properly.

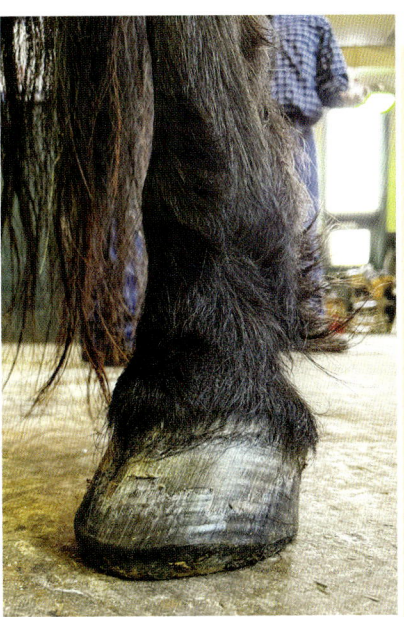

1.9 Here is a foot that has been over-trimmed and beveled so there is almost no weightbearing on the hoof wall. As a result, the horse was sore.

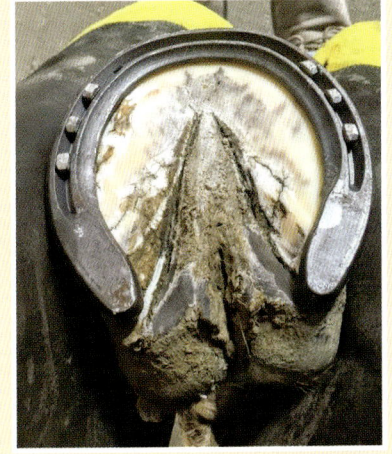

1.10 A wide-web rim shoe showing proper heel coverage and support.

Horseshoes with *Borium* made of tungsten carbide (see p. 00) or Drill-Tech studs are reset many times and often the nail holes wear before the actual shoe. Shoes made of lighter-weight materials wear sooner and may not be able to be reset even once. In some parts of the United States, the ground conditions are so abrasive that shoes become too worn in one shoeing cycle to reset. Some horses are extra hard on shoes and wear them out quickly while others produce no wear at all.

Resetting shoes is practical for making the most out of the materials used. In some cases, new horseshoes at every visit—especially those with modifications—can increase the cost unnecessarily.

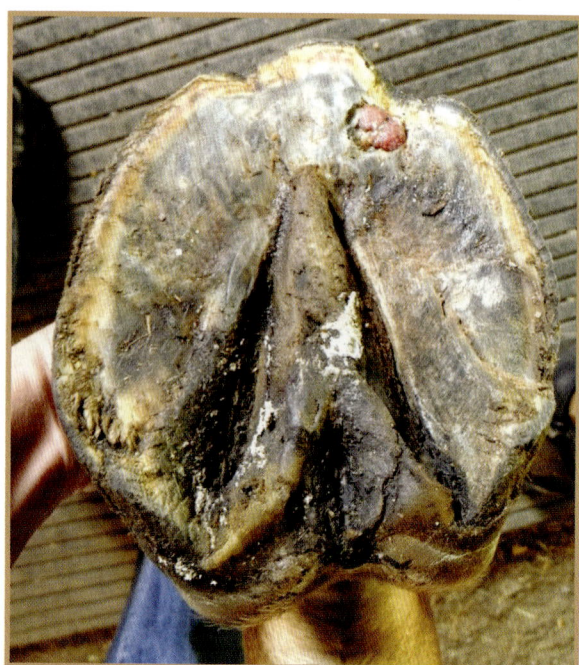

1.11 This horse had extremely thin walls and the sole eventually wore down from excessive stomping while he was turned out during fly season.

What Should I Know About Going Barefoot?

Not all horses wear horseshoes. In fact, with approximately nine million horses in the United States, fewer than two million are shod regularly every year. Barefoot (shoeless hoof management) has gained popularity for a variety of reasons. One is the expense of shoeing. Competitive riders can pay over $150 every five to six weeks to maintain properly fitted shoes. Over a year's time that can add up, so sometimes leaving a horse barefoot is viewed as a cost savings. However, skipping the shoes based on budget alone may lead to more costly expenses if the horse physically needs shoes.

Barefoot trimming has also become popular in recent times as horse owners are increasingly interested in keeping horses in a natural state, but many horse activities are unnatural to horses: riding disciplines and stabling conditions are not what would be found in the wild.

The decision to permanently maintain a barefoot horse requires a plan rather than simply deciding to leave shoes off. Working with a farrier who understands your horse's feet will help assess the horse's hoof condition and whether he can be left barefoot. Horses with naturally thick soles and hoof walls are more likely able to produce enough hoof material to sustain being shoeless. Correct conformation is also necessary to keep the hoof wear in balance.

The worst candidates for going shoeless while working are those with thin soles and hoof walls and horses with poor conformation. Often, these horses have coffin bone defects from an inherent weakness that typically emerge as persistent hoof wall cracks (fig. 1.11).

Going shoeless should not be done on a whim, especially if your horse has worn shoes for some time.

There needs to be an assessment to see if the horse is a good candidate and a plan must be created to achieve the desired results. It's important to ask, "What am I gaining or losing by going with this option?"

The transition from shod to barefoot is best accomplished at the end of a normal shoeing cycle. After removing the shoes, the farrier trims the hoof longer than he would if resetting a shoe. Leaving a little extra sole and hoof wall helps the horse adjust to being shoeless.

Many riders in colder climates tend to remove a horse's shoes at the end of a riding or showing season, usually before winter sets in. The idea is to "give the hooves a rest." There is nothing wrong with doing this (fig. 1.12). However, weather conditions differ year to year. The best winter scenario for maintaining healthy feet is a constant snowpack. When this happens, most horses do remarkably well barefoot.

Inconsistent winters with frequent freeze/thaw cycles are not barefoot friendly. Neither is bare, frozen ground. In this scenario, there is excessive wear on hooves and severe impact on internal structures. When a long hard freeze stiffens up the ground, farriers are often called to put shoes back on these sore-footed horses. In the worst-case scenario, coffin bone fractures and ligament tears can occur simply by a horse walking on rough frozen mud. The wet conditions are also more likely to cause thrush and lead to softer hoof walls, which will be more susceptible to large tears when the wintry mix freezes.

Some horses require extra attention to shift from wearing shoes to going without, and the

1.12 This Quarter Horse mare wears shoes throughout the summer while in work as a ranch-type show horse and is comfortable barefoot in snowy, frozen conditions.

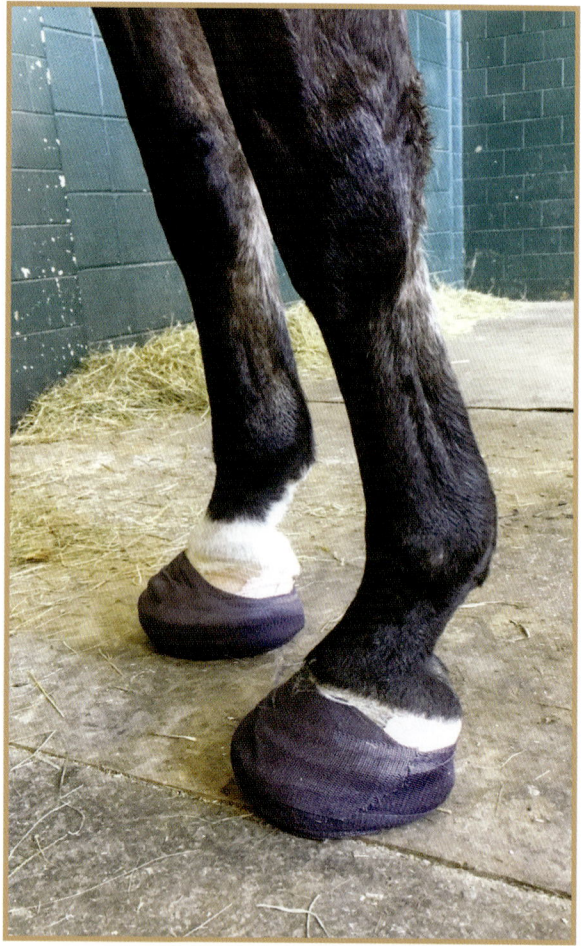

1.13 A temporary hoof cast can help build stronger hooves during the transition from being shod to going barefoot.

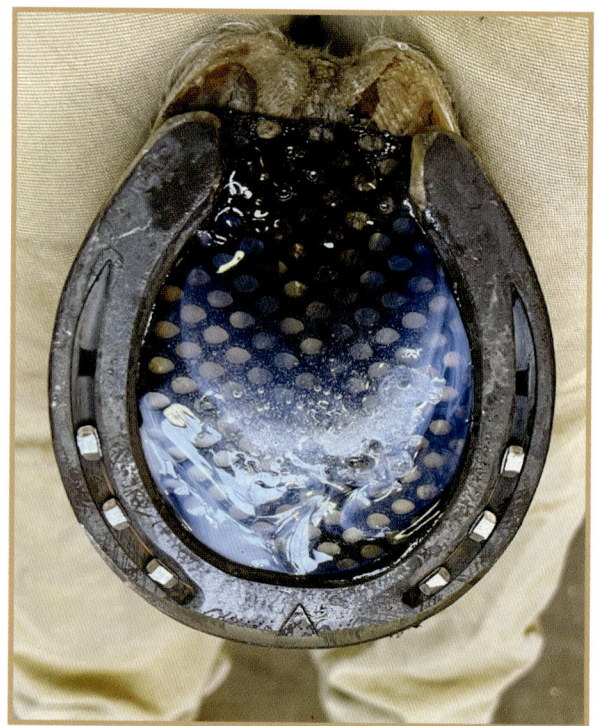

1.14 Tender-footed horses can benefit from a pour-in pad like the one pictured here.

process may take six months to one year. Hoof casts and nutritional changes can be used to build hoof strength (fig. 1.13). It may take several applications with proper trimming to develop a proper barefoot hoof.

Another way to help a sore-footed barefoot horse is using a polyurethane or methyl methacrylate sole pad. These products are poured into the sole cavity of the foot to add an artificial sole thickness. These "pour-in pads" are temporary but can support the growth of a thicker sole (fig. 1.14).

Whichever method is used to temporarily--or permanently—have a horse go barefoot, planning and adhering to a process that will enable success without causing discomfort is the goal. Being shoeless does not mean that you never provide hoof care.

Digging Deeper into Barefoot Trimming

An attachment to a horse can override an owner's ability to consider the bigger picture. As we discussed at the beginning of this chapter, decisions about hoof care must be objective and based on critical analysis.

Scientific methods use observation and data to draw conclusions, but most information regarding shoeing or keeping horses without horseshoes is anecdotal. An exception is the book, *The Mirage of the Natural Foot* by Michael E. Miller, MD, CJF, FWCF. He followed scientific methods to study barefoot hoof management theories. Published in 2010, this is a one-of-a-kind comparison of natural barefoot management to traditional practices. The study results found that specialized "natural trimming" methods had no noteworthy effect over normal trimming.

Misinformation about barefoot trimming is rampant on the internet and perpetuates misconceptions. This is one example of a social media account promoting only barefoot practices that shared scientifically unsubstantiated claims.

"Just remember, shoes don't make your horse's feet healthy; they make them dead. Not to mention the necrotic burden on the horse's liver, heart, and kidneys. Dead hooves are insensitive so if you shoe them, they become numb first and eventually, without circulation, the tissues beneath the horn, the corium, strangulates and dies. There are so many new boots out there that there is no excuse for nailing a piece of metal on one of the most vascular parts of the horse's anatomy."

Zero scientific studies have produced results confirming this claim. Horses are individuals and thus the decision to shoe or go barefoot is best made using the WIDTH method described on the pages prior.

Putting Barefoot to the Test

From 1983 until its closure in 2010, I conducted an anecdotal study on barefoot trimming as part of my role as the farrier in charge of horses included in the Equine Drug Testing (EDT) program at Cornell University. The program was designed to establish better control over illegal drug use in the horse racing industry and findings were later adopted by other competitive organizations.

Twelve Standardbred racehorses were initially donated for the study. The intent was to develop tests to detect banned substances to either enhance performance or mask pain. While in the study, the horses received regular health and hoof care, which provided the perfect opportunity for experimentation and observation.

The original horses kept in training on a stone dust track were all shod with typical Standardbred racing shoes and stayed in training as if on the racetrack. Over time the herd swelled to 40-plus horses, approximately one-third Standardbreds and two-thirds Thoroughbreds. The Thoroughbreds were also shod and galloped regularly to maintain racing conditions to allow for the development of accurate blood testing for detecting banned substances.

The program lasted nearly two decades until computer modeling was developed to simulate the blood chemistry of racehorses in training. At this time, it was no longer necessary to keep these horses in training to properly test for illegal drugs, so I pulled all their shoes and continued to provide proper care and regular trimming.

About the same time barefoot hoof care was gaining popularity, so I started using the suggested barefoot

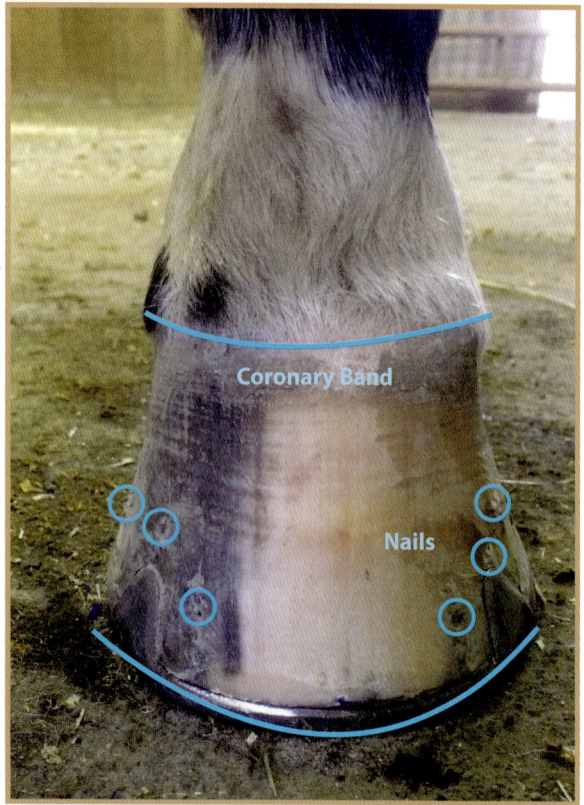

1.15 A well-shod front foot that shows best practices: The coronary band should be parallel to the ground with a gentle, sloping angle to the toe; the perimeter of the shoe maintains the same curve as the coronary band; the nails are approximately 1/3 the hoof-wall height, and the clinches are smooth and short.

trimming techniques with this group of horses. The consistent conditions offered an opportunity to study those feet using barefoot trimming protocols.

When we stopped training the Standardbreds and pulled their shoes, we never found a need to shoe any of those horses again. Not one trim style produced any special or different results compared to a generic, sensible trim. *A good trim* removes the flakey sole by trimming to leave concavity between the sole and ground, rolling or beveling all edges, slightly blunting the toe, and slightly unloading the quarters.

As for the Thoroughbreds, the results were quite different. No matter what trimming method I employed, there was no advantage. However, about one-third of the Thoroughbred group always needed to have front shoes to maintain pasture soundness, while the rest of the group grew sound hooves. One horse had the best hooves in the facility requiring the least amount of trimming. It was likely due to good genes for feet and compatibility with the environment and nothing to do with what I did.

Although it was not a scientifically controlled program, the conditions were consistent, and my findings closely aligned with Miller's. Based on the regular hoof care these observations stuck with me:

- Heavier-boned horses like Standardbreds have thicker hoof walls and soles and do well without shoes if not training on stone dust.

- Lighter-boned horses like Thoroughbreds have thinner hoof walls and soles and are more likely to need shoes for comfort.

- Thoroughbreds are more sensitive to flies so damage their hooves with excessive stomping, no matter what trimming protocol is used.

- Conformational issues and hoof injuries require shoeing even on an out-of-work horse.

- None of the widely promoted barefoot-trimming methods offered any better hoof management over an appropriate generic trim.

- Occasionally, some horses have good feet despite what we do or do not do for them.

- Barefoot does not work on all horses.

The Debate Continues

So, in conclusion, this remains a controversial topic. Websites or magazine articles condemning horseshoes for hurting horses or causing diseased hooves are making claims without scientific data. A balanced approach based on an individual horse, and his conditions, is always the best place to start. Applying an objective evaluation as proposed in the WIDTH Protocol I describe in this chapter will help take emotion out of the decision-making process (fig. 1.15).

The number of negative outcomes from nailing shoes on is insignificantly small, especially with well-trained farriers. I have shod countless horses from their first set of shoes to their retirement, some in their late twenties. Many wore shoes year-round. These horses worked hard, were always sound and had consistently healthy feet for their entire lifetime. The number of horses that have been helped with nailed-on shoes has been significant when used at the right time for the right reasons. Many other farriers could make the same claim.

FROM THE FORGE
The Birth of the WIDTH Protocol

As a practicing farrier and technical consultant for Mustad Hoofcare Group, I sought ways to learn about horseshoeing and hoof care trends. I eagerly awaited issues of the *American Farriers Journal* and always sought out the latest hoof-care articles featured in equine publications.

In the late 1980s, I noticed articles about "natural hoof care" appearing more frequently. Although interesting, these articles were mostly one-sided, claiming horseshoes were bad and unnecessary. The authors said that since wild horses did not wear shoes, domestic horses did not need them either.

The articles and pictures presented showed only the most horrible shoeing jobs. Certainly, the shoes shown were damaging the hooves and harming horses. However, my work (and others) did not look like that! The horses that I regularly shod were sound and competitive during long-lasting careers.

As the anti-horseshoe rhetoric increased, I submitted counterpoint letters to the editors, and boy, did I receive vicious replies from authors. One leading anti-horseshoe advocate was speaking at a hoof-care symposium, so I went to learn more and study the methods.

While circulating amongst the horse owners and hoof-care providers I discovered that the farrier profession lacked enough skilled farriers. Most of the attendees had bad experiences with farriers and poorly shod feet, so were looking for alternatives. In their minds, it was the shoes that were bad.

During the hands-on portion of the symposium, the presenter demonstrated radical trimming methods that included completely removing the bars and trimming excessive amounts of hoof wall. This was performed on what I considered a normal, healthy hoof. I was horrified to see a horse's hooves trimmed in such a destructive manner. The speaker promoted this method as improving hooves after a long period of lameness.

This did not make any sense to me. Supposedly, this trimming method would bring forth a better hoof that did not need shoes. I was especially skeptical that she said the horse needed a long period of recovery before the horse could be ridden again. I tried to play the devil's advocate and asked deliberate questions about how working or performance horses can succeed shoeless. The answer was, "If they need horseshoes to do their work, they are not fit for their job!"

I began receiving phone calls from new clients asking if I was qualified to trim their horses with barefoot-only methods like the "Mustang Roll" or the "Natural Trim." Simultaneously, horse owners called saying a barefoot trimmer had removed a horse's shoes and the horse was too sore-footed to be ridden weeks later. Each wanted to know how long it would take to transition to being barefoot and my answer was, "Usually, forever."

It occurred to me that the way to counteract the misinformation floating around was to develop a factual, logical, unemotional way of determining the best hoof care for individual horses. After some thought, the WIDTH Protocol took shape in my mind.

As time went on, the controversy of barefoot versus shod seemed to become more divisive, closely resembling politics. Horse owners were being told that farriers only want to shoe horses and that horseshoes only harm feet. Although, that may be true in some cases, it is certainly not true for all, and dedicated farriers like myself were offended.

Several years later, the topic came up at the International Hoof Care Summit in a round table session. The moderator asked a simple question, "How are barefoot-only trimming methods working in your business?"

Many barefoot-only trimmers attended the discussion group; however, many traditional farriers were there also to voice dismay with being criticized for nailing on shoes.

The discussion escalated into a shouting match. The moderator, who was a friend, looked at me for help. She whistled to quiet the room down and I asked the audience to listen to my description of the WIDTH Protocol.

The room became dead silent. As I finished, someone asked if I could go through it again only slower so he could write it down. As I repeated it, I looked up and everyone was writing!

The following year I published this in an article for the *American Farriers Journal* and subsequently produced a lecture for the International Hoof Care Summit. And now, I am sharing it with you in this book.

CHAPTER 2

The Evolution of the Modern Horseshoe

The wheel is one of humankind's greatest inventions. It made it easier to travel farther and move heavier loads with less effort. The design has evolved over thousands of years, but the fundamental concepts have never changed (fig. 2.1). The same is true for the horseshoe. Like the wheel, the horseshoe improved mobility and enabled horses' longevity in work. In fact, the advancement of our entire civilization has been made possible by both devices.

Basic horseshoes are not much different today than when they were first developed around 400 BC. Historical evidence suggests that the Romans produced horseshoes 2,500 years ago, which coincided with the early civilization's quest to conquer the unknown world (fig. 2.2). To do so, the Roman Empire relied on horses and knew that the horse's usefulness could be extended by protecting the horse's hooves.

By itself, the horseshoe is nothing more than a paperweight or an interesting wall ornament. On the hoof, it serves the simple purpose of providing protection, traction, and support for a horse's feet and legs. At first, horseshoes were invented only to protect

2.1 The ancient wheel changed civilization yet its fundamental design remains the same thousands of years later.

a horse's hooves from excessive wear. Over time, farriers began to realize that the horseshoe could do more. By studying the horse's anatomy and movement, they discovered the simple shoe could enhance a horse's performance or address an issue.

When the right horseshoes are correctly fitted to properly trimmed hooves, the synergy allows the horse and human to accomplish more than either method could do individually.

Shoe Style and Materials Used

Just like in human shoe selections, many types of materials are used, and it is the same for horseshoes. The earliest metal horseshoes may have been made from copper, bronze, and iron. Over time, ironworkers began adding carbon to iron, a process that turns the combined metals into steel, a more durable, longer-lasting metal. Blacksmiths and farriers brought that knowledge into the horse industry.

Today's horseshoe steel is called "mild steel"—a material that is easier to work with and has relatively low levels of carbon. This is why lighter horseshoes can be fitted without being heated. Steel with higher levels of carbon is used for making knives and tools and is only malleable with heating.

Modern mass-produced steel horseshoes remain the most common option and the shoes are available in a variety of widths and thicknesses. Modern materials have been incorporated into this ancient invention with options that include polyurethane, rubber, composites, carbon fiber, and 3D printed shoes. Even copper is used to make shoes for the hooves of coal-mining

2.2 Some early horseshoes had a "strap" that made them look like a sandal.

carthorses to prevent a random spark from setting off a methane explosion.

The horse's work and conformation determine what style of shoe is needed. For example, a racehorse wears aluminum rather than steel to eliminate weight that could slow him down. Weighing one-third the weight of steel, aluminum provides hoof protection and traction with less weight to interfere with movement (fig. 2.3).

While seen most often on the racetrack, aluminum shoes are also used on show horses. The lighter shoes reduce the "pendulum effect," resulting in a less animated stride when desired. This swinging leg action is common with Western Pleasure horses, show hunters, and equitation horses, which are judged positively for having a flatter stride. Aluminum is more expensive than steel and is not as durable. These shoes are a poor choice for trail riding or work on abrasive surfaces because the material wears too quickly.

Looking Back to Understand Hoof Care for the Modern Horse

Horses have been partners with humans for thousands of years. Throughout the history of this partnership, the caretakers of horses have recognized that there is a need for hoof care. Rudimentary hoof care was likely a trial-and-error process at first—and it still can be in less developed places around the world.

The individuals who first domesticated the horse probably had no idea of how important the horse would become to the development of future civilization. As horses were first used for transportation, then other forms of work and battle, the need for hoof care became more apparent to extend the usability of these magnificent animals. The Romans and the Celts are credited with early nailed-on metal horseshoes 2,000 years ago; however, there is historical evidence that other forms of hoof protection were employed before those times.

The development of hoof care, breeding, and husbandry practices closely follows the development of many societies. As various societies developed more specialized horses for their needs, hoof care became particular to these horses. For example, to conquer parts of the world that had hard stony ground, the Romans developed large war horses to pull chariots. Those horses needed some of the first metal shoes. In contrast, the Mongolian horses used in other parts of the world were shoeless.

For hundreds of years horses were carefully developed around the world for uses in transportation, work, and battle. Breeding theories, as well as training and care techniques, were closely guarded secrets. The iron-working trade was protected similarly. As the need for metal horseshoes became valued, the traditional blacksmiths who worked metal for other reasons assumed the role as "the horseshoers," thus the two trades became intertwined. The military became the one of the largest trainers of shoeing smiths, who eventually became known as "farriers."

The horse was found to be an excellent choice as a partner in sports, some of which developed around its original uses in the military. The need for standardization of hoof care arose as societies developed private ownership of horses. In 1356, The Worshipful Company of Farriers was founded "to manage those involved with the craft of farriery and to uphold the welfare of the horse through good practice." They are still active today.

The modern horse living in affluent societies is now mostly used for recreation and sport. For many, horse ownership has become a hobby instead of a need. General horse management is often contracted out to grooms and trainers, and hoof care is taken care of by professional farriers to the point of owner ignorance of the subject.

Not all horses are the same and not all hoof management is the same. Not all horses need shoes, but all horses need some kind of hoof care. I have spent most of my life learning and practicing many forms of hoof care. In the past 50 years, I have had the opportunity to travel the world, and meet many fine farriers and horse owners to gain a diverse perspective. No matter where I travel, or the type of horse I work on, the one constant remains—there is always something new to learn and there is more than one way to approach both common and uncommon conditions.

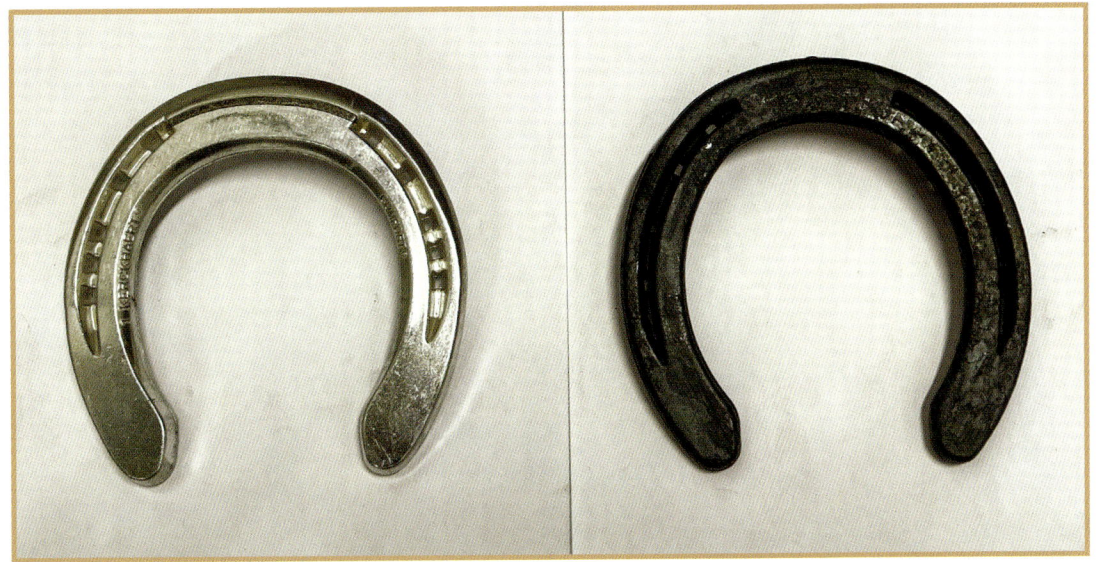

2.3 The aluminum shoe on the left is one third the weight of the steel shoe on the right. Aluminum is preferred when the upward motion of the hoof flight needs to be kept to a minimum for show hunters and Western pleasure horses.

Titanium is lightweight and stronger than steel, so some manufacturers thought it could replace aluminum. The assumption was that the longer-lasting quality of the metal would offset its higher cost. However, horses shod with titanium shoes became sore.

Aluminum shoes wear away the toe at a similar rate of hoof growth. Titanium did not wear in the same way, changing leverage in the hoof and leg, which led to lameness. The strength of titanium also transmits more vibrational forces to the foot, which contribute to soreness. So, a limited number of titanium horseshoe styles still exist but have never been a popular item.

We take for granted that nails hold the shoes onto the hoof. Some of the earliest horseshoes looked more like a sandal with straps to secure it, a concept you can see today in hoof boots.

Glue-On Shoes

Through research and innovation, new materials like glue-on shoes are now available. The term "glue-on" is widely misunderstood by horse owners and uninitiated farriers. Adhesives are regularly used to secure the therapeutic as well as normal shoes to the hoof. These alternatives are used in a range of cases that may include chronic laminitis, white line disease, heel pain, chronic bruising from flat-footed conformation, poor hoof-wall quality, and surgery. Just like regular horseshoes, glue-on shoes have advantages and drawbacks.

Reasons to Use Glue-On Shoes

- The hoof wall is too damaged or too thin to hold horseshoe nails.
- The hooves are too sore to tolerate nailing.
- The need to enhance shock absorption.

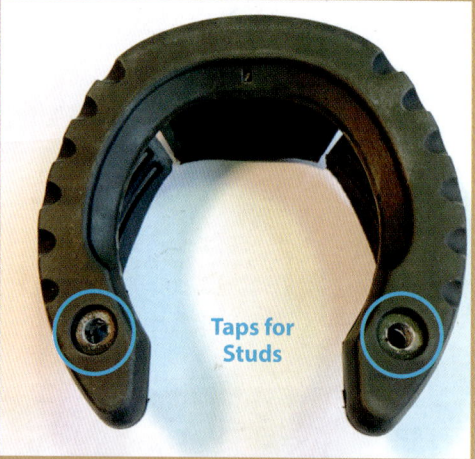

2.4 A The GluShu cuff-style, front glue-on shoe has an aluminum core that can also be tapped for studs.

2.4 B The steel-wire spine inside holds the desired shape of the PolyFlex direct glue-on front shoe. The design allows the shoe to flex with the foot.

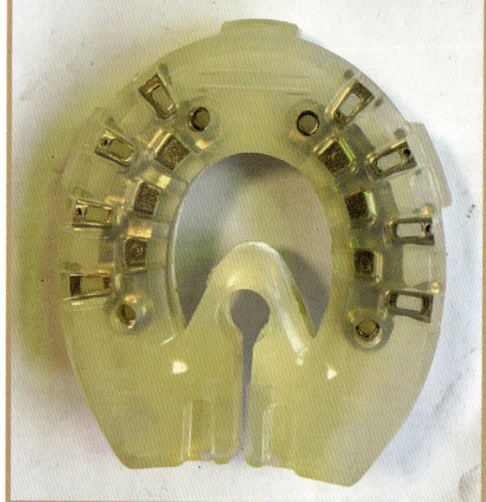

2.5 The EasyShoe Performance N/G can either be glued or nailed on, and is designed to provide support on and around the frog. The shoe includes three toe clips to help keep the shoes in place.

U The ease of fitting to the hoof.

U The horse needs custom support after a surgical procedure.

Disadvantages of Glue-On Shoes

Cost: the shoes and adhesives are pricier than steel shoes and nails, and the extra time it takes to apply the shoes also adds to the expense.

Learning curve: the application requires a farrier to learn a new method.

Weather: adhesives are sensitive to heat and cold, which can affect the application.

Hoof preparation: extra attention to hoof cleanliness and preparation is required.

Horse behavior: for the shoe adhesive to properly set, the horse must be patient and stand. Pulling a foot away and stomping it down can shift the shoe as the glue is setting up. This can attach the shoe in the wrong place or ruin the bond.

Glue does not guarantee a shoe will stay on as the glue-on shoes are not a fix for overreaching (often the cause of a "stepped-off" shoe) since the glue-on shoes do not change the horse's gait. They can be helpful when working on damaged hooves and on young foals with hooves too tender for nails (figs. 2.4 A & B, 2.5, and 2.7).

Handmade Nails

Before the rise of manufacturing, a farrier also made his own horseshoe nails or specialized tradesmen traveled from shop to shop making nails. Like horseshoes, today, pre-made nails are available in varying dimensions and shapes. Nails are classified with a number that describes the size (length) and shape of the nail head, which range from the smallest "3" to the largest "16."

There are three American go-to nail styles that most farriers work with—*city head, regular head*, and *race head* nails (fig. 2.6). Originally, the *regular head* was the most popular nail because the head was designed to protrude above the surface of the horseshoe, providing some traction on dirt roads and farm fields.

As horses moved into the paved streets of the cities, the protruding regular head wore off on the hard surface. The *city head* was created to sit flusher in the crease, and this nail is by far the most popular option today.

The *race head nail* is designed for use with racing plates. Race nails are the smallest, thinnest, lightest nails and are designed for the shortest shoeing cycles and the lightest horseshoes.

With the global marketing of horseshoes and nails, many European products have made it to the United States and vice versa. European manufactured horseshoes are punched for a square, tapered head nail called an *"E" nail*.

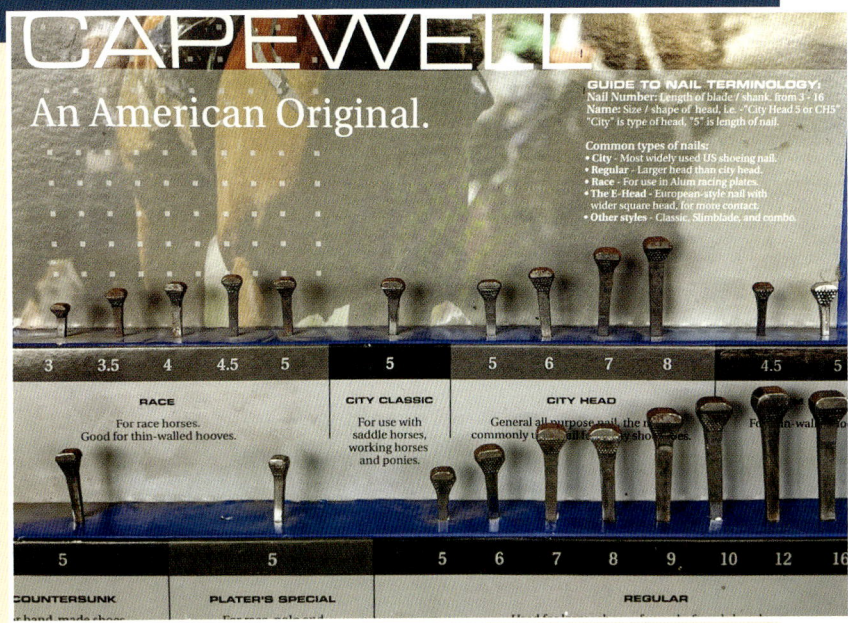

2.6 This display of nails is from the Capewell Horse Nail Company. It shows a variety of styles used for specific situations.

Up until the late 1970s, only standard shanks were available from manufacturers. In 1978, working as the technical consultant for Mustad Hoofcare Group, I created a slimmer shanked version of the popular size 5 city head. This new nail featured a slimmer shank on a standard city head, which would be helpful for thin-walled horses. Eventually, the slim shank version was adapted to other nail styles, including those nails made for European shoes.

Manufacturers that serve the global markets have developed many other nail styles for specific shoes. Farriers from many different countries have traditional nail styles that they are accustomed to.

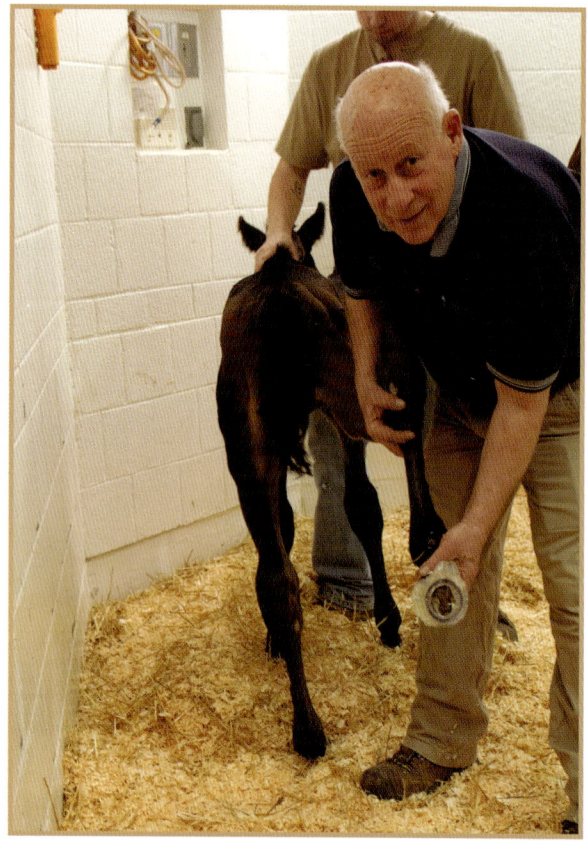

2.7 Glue-on shoes on this foal provided support to his hind end at a time when his hoof walls were not thick enough for nails.

2.8 Before manufactured shoes the only way to make a shoe was by hand. This process is still used to make custom shoes, or it may be a farrier's preferred process.

Manufactured vs. Handmade Horseshoes

Up until the 1800s, blacksmiths forged every shoe by hand (fig. 2.8). First, a farrier heated a bar of iron and hammered it, bending it around the horn of an anvil. Next, he forged the grooves or creases by hammering on the shoe with a tool called a creaser.

Then he worked on the heels. If more traction was needed, he left extra length in the heels and bent the excess metal to create a heel calk to better grip the ground. If calks weren't needed, he trimmed off any excess length of the shoe. Finally, he punched the nail holes by hand.

In 1835, Henry Burden invented a horseshoe machine that could make 60 horseshoes per minute (fig. 2.9). His Troy, New York, company supplied horseshoes to the entire Union Army during the Civil War. Burden is credited with influencing the outcome of the war because an army with well-shod horses could more efficiently cover greater territory than barefoot horses.

Before the invention of tanks and fighter

planes, blacksmiths were the equivalent of today's mechanics. Special training was provided, and good horseshoeing was a priority for building a successful calvary. As gas-powered vehicles replaced horsepower, the horse population decreased, and so, too, did horseshoe manufacturers. After World War II, baby boomers rediscovered horses for sport and recreation, effectively revitalizing the horseshoe industry.

While many farriers use pre-manufactured shoes, some still choose to hand-forge. Does it mean your horse is getting shod better if his shoes are hand-forged? Not necessarily. Farriers who hand-forge shoes can create a shoe that is custom-fit and tailored to the horse. Forging offers control over the width and thickness of the shoe rather than having to work within the parameters of a manufactured shoe. The process also allows for opportunities to build specialized shoes for foot problems. Even high-quality manufactured shoes need adjustments to fit well, so a pre-made shoe still needs some shaping.

To forge or not to forge shoes from scratch: this decision often comes down to a farrier's personal preference and business model. These are a few of the reasons farriers choose one over the other.

Advantages of Hand-Forged Shoes

- Less inventory to carry.
- Can be customized to any horse in any configuration of width and thickness.
- Can produce special shoes unavailable as manufactured styles.
- Can provide personal satisfaction.

2.9 Henry Burden revolutionized horseshoes when he designed the first machine to manufacture them.

Disadvantages of Hand-Forged Shoes
- Requires more skill to attain proficiency.
- Takes more time and physical effort to produce.
- Increases opportunities for errors.
- Not necessarily better than machine-made.

Advantages of Manufactured Shoes
- Wide selection of sizes and styles. Front and hind patterns are available, requiring less shaping effort.
- Factory clips are available for less forge work.
- Readily available.
- Less work to shoe the horse.
- Relatively inexpensive.

Disadvantages of Manufactured Horseshoes
- Larger inventory is required.
- Allows unqualified practitioners to operate.
- Skill is still needed to fit properly. There is no guarantee of proper fit when simply used off the shelf.

More Than Meets the Eye: Shoe Design

Horseshoes seem simple. At first glance, the common horseshoe is just a flat piece of steel in the shape of a horse's hoof (fig. 2.10). Initially, there were no differences between front or rear pre-manufactured shoes. The pattern was referred to as "generic"; however, farriers called

2.10 The basic horseshoe follows a generic pattern that can be shaped to either front or hind feet.

these shoes "frinds." As companies became more competitive, front, and hind pattern shoes emerged.

The front feet are rounder than the hind; thus, the front shoe is made to follow the natural contour of the hoof to provide greater support. The hind feet are more pointed at the toe to aid with propulsion; hence a premade hind shoe reflects this difference.

Horseshoe Cross-Sections: Flat vs. Rim Styles

Flat horseshoes have a cross section that is in proportionate dimensions to the steel bars used to make them. Common examples are: ¼ inches by ⅝ inches, 5/16 inches by ¾ inches, and ⅜ inches by ⅞ inches.

Rim shoes have an additional feature—a continuous groove from heel to heel, in the center of the width of the shoe. This groove has two purposes: the groove lightens a shoe's weight and allows the shoe to penetrate

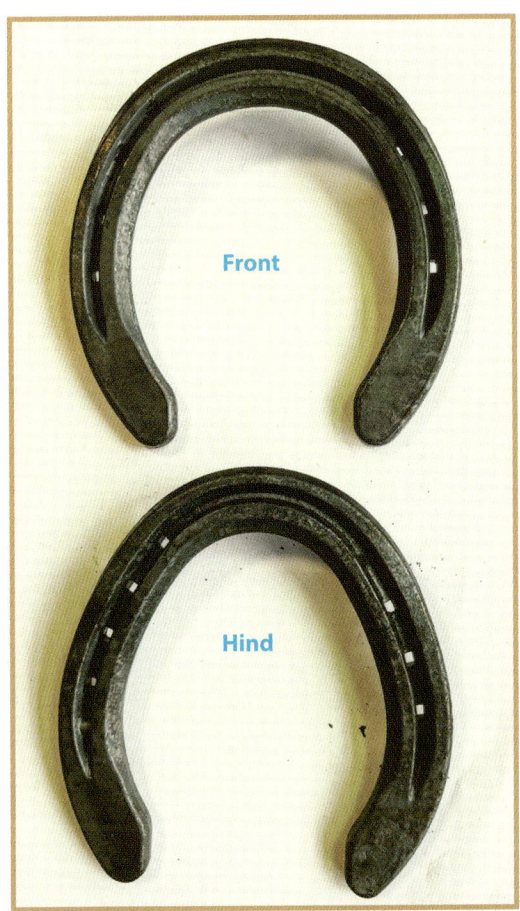

2.11 A Horseshoes start as a generic shape but are modified for different disciplines. This is an Eventer Plus front and hind wide-rim shoe that feature solid heels. Farriers can drill holes in the heels in which threaded studs can be added or removed for greater or lesser traction.

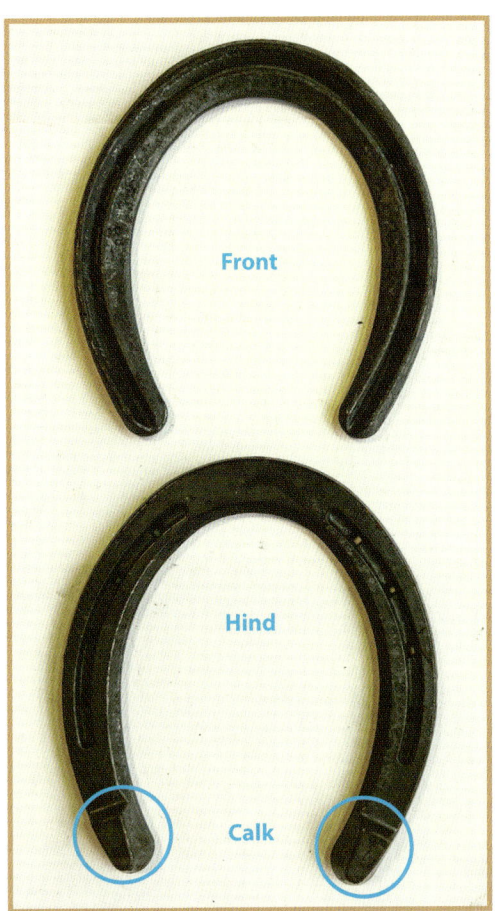

2.11 B A polo pony tends to wear slightly different shoes on the front and hind feet. On the fronts it is common to use the lite rim shoe (top horseshoe), the hind is called a lite heeled shoe. The hind shoes need the heel calks for traction when stopping and turning at speed.

the ground for increased traction. Conversely, flat shoes tend to "float" on top of the ground and have less traction. Variations of this are "concave" and "eventer" styles. These are popular for polo, Western, and eventing horses.

The average horse has a ⅜-inch-wide hoof wall and is shod with a standard width shoe that is ¾ inch wide—twice the hoof-wall width. Hoof-wall thickness varies between breeds and individual horses, so the goal is to choose a *web size* that covers the hoof wall so that the nail holes line the border of the white line (figs. 2.11 A & B). The web size refers to the dimensions of the material used to make the shoe. A *narrow* web shoe reduces the surface area of the hoof as it strikes the ground, allowing the hoof to sink deeper into the surface (figs. 2.12 A & B). *Wider* webbed shoes increase the contact made with the ground. Similar to snowshoes, wide-web shoes create a "floating" effect, allowing the hoof to stay on top of the footing surface. A wide-web shoe covers more of the hoof while a *lite* or narrow-web shoe covers less surface area.

Dressage horses and show hunters are often shod in wider Standard web shoes to encourage flotation on footings common to the sports. When the horse's feet penetrate deeper into the surface, it inhibits the gait causing the horse to exert more effort. Wider web shoes limit that by keeping the horse on top of the footing.

The basic shoe is made in several thicknesses. Generally, as the width increases, so does the thickness, which increases the longevity of the shoe. This chart lists the most common horseshoe sizes and the disciplines in which each is commonly used. The thicker the shoe, the longer it lasts.

2.12 A & B Photo A is an example of a wide-web aluminum horseshoe. Though not visible in this image, the shoe includes a rolled toe and side clips. Both shoes in Photo B are wide-web shoes used for Warmblood-type horses. The shoe on the left is a right-hind pattern; the shoe on the right is a left-front pattern.

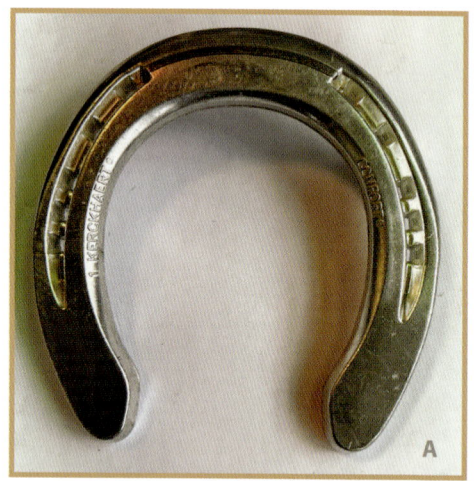

\multicolumn{3}{c}{Common Shoe Sizes and Uses}
Type	Thickness	Use
Lite	¼ inch (7mm)	Racehorses, ponies, smaller-footed horses
Standard	5/16 inch (8mm)	Most average horses
Wide-web	5/16 inch and 3/8 inch (10mm)	Dressage, show hunters, bigger hooves, and thicker hoof walls

Horseshoe Modifications

The standard horseshoe is like a blank painter's canvas. It offers a starting place, parameters to stay within but with the flexibility to become what is the artist's vision. Farriers start with a basic shoe as a template and make any number of modifications to craft the perfect fit for the horse. Here is a look at alterations you might notice.

Clips

Clips are one of the most misunderstood horseshoe modifications (fig. 2.13). Farriers and horse owners alike either hate or love clips. Clips emerged to help limit the shearing forces on the nails when a horse is in work. Traditionally, toe clips were used on the front or rear feet of draft/street horses to counteract the shear forces—without clips, the concussion of the shoe striking a hard surface shifted the shoes forward and rearward as the horse used his toes to propel himself, thus exerting

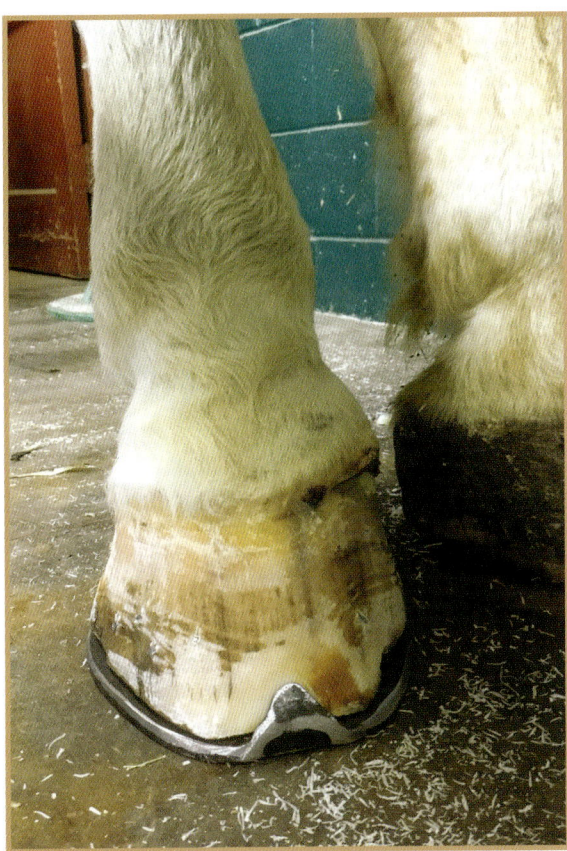

2.13 A toe clip is used to prevent the shearing forces on the nails from moving the shoe rearward.

When a Big Horse Needs Light Shoes

A former surgical resident at Cornell University's Equine Hospital called me because, he said, "one of his client's horses needed me." We had worked closely on a number of horses before he joined a private practice in Arizona.

The purebred Shire gelding was being used for dressage and the veterinarian felt the horse was moving poorly. He attributed this to pre-manufactured draft horseshoes that were too heavy but not sized large enough to properly support the limbs of this big guy. Typical draft horseshoes are a half-inch thick, not quite big enough to support this particular horse. And the excessive weight produced a choppy gait.

I had the vet pick up the hoof, place a ruler across the foot and take pictures. These feet were almost 9 inches across! My plan was to forge these big shoes out of thinner steel to reduce the weight but with enough length to provide the needed support.

With the shoes made, I boarded a flight to Phoenix. We arranged for the local farrier to be on-site too. With some small adjustments on the fit, the shoes went on easily. Afterward, I watched the rider put the horse to work—the result was smooth gaits with ample extension. The pair went on to successfully compete in regional- and national-level dressage competitions. Picking the right cross-section makes a big difference!

greater force on the hoof tissue. Clips absorb this force, securely holding the shoe in place.

As horses were used for more than transportation, such as in the military and fox hunting, "work" began to include a combination of cross-country and jumping. Clips became necessary to prevent shoes from shifting under the strains of galloping and jumping with added traction.

By the late 1800s, horseshoe manufacturers produced pre-clipped horseshoes in many varieties, but after World War II, as the horse population dwindled, there were not any pre-clipped horseshoes available in the United States market.

If a farrier could forge some clips on the limited standard horseshoes available, he was considered an expert. Therefore, using clipped horseshoes became a sign of superior workmanship. Many of today's farriers use pre-clipped horseshoes to not only reduce shear forces but also to make it easier to hold a shoe in place when nailing.

Clips are added in one of three places—the toe, quarter, or side of the hoof. The weight of a 1,000-plus pound animal moving at speed creates a lot of shear forces on the nails. The clips reduce that strain and may help reduce shoe loss (fig. 2.14). Add jumping, changing direction, or sudden stops to the equation, and the shear forces on the nails multiply and can weaken nails without clips to secure the shoe to the hoof. Many people think that clips prevent shoes from being stepped off, but that is not the case.

It is recommended that clipped shoes are "hot fit" to ensure the proper placement of the shoe and clip. When clipped shoes are not hot fit properly, the thickness of the clip keeps the shoe from setting in the right place, and this can interfere with the horse's gait and soundness.

On the plus side, clips provide shoe stability when horses are in hard work, especially on shoes with traction devices. On the flip side, improperly fitted clips can put the shoe out of position or may restrict needed hoof expansion. Also, if a horse partially steps a shoe off, twisting it, he can step on the clip, penetrating the sole.

2.14 You can see the toe clip on the lower front shoe. Compare it with the position of quarter clips as seen on the upper hind shoe.

Clip Uses	
Clip Location	**Use**
Front-foot toe clips	Keep the front to back forces from shearing nails when landing after a fence.
Side Clips	Positioned on either side of the toe, the side clip helps secure the shoe to the hoof.
Hind foot quarter clips	Limit twisting forces from shearing nails as the horse thrusts forward.

Toe Modifications

Changes to the toe of the shoe are often made to influence *breakover*. Breakover in horses is widely talked about but one of the least defined concepts in print. The start of breakover is an important part of a horse's stride, making it, in essence, a process not an exact moment in time. It's often concentrated at the horse's toe, but to some degree, breakover also occurs off center, depending upon the horse's conformation.

Ideally, the breakover point on a foot is an extension of the *coffin bone* (see p. 3) through the sole to the point where the hoof hits the ground. As a horse moves, his heels should lift off first. As the coffin bone (and foot) rotate upward, the fetlock descends, storing energy. When the foot reaches its end of the upward rotation, the toe digs into the ground to propel the horse forward, creating the point of breakover.

Maximizing breakover supports optimal performance while also supporting the horse's build. The point where breakover occurs can be manipulated with shoes, but placing breakover too far forward or too far back can have detrimental effects.

Breakover changes should be based on footing, the horse's conformation, shoe placement, and any existing hoof problems. Trimming and shoeing decisions that impact breakover are based on a geometric balance known as the *Golden Ratio*. Ancient Greek mathematicians first studied what is called the Golden Ratio because it frequently appeared in geometry. Sometimes called the "Most Beautiful Number in the Universe," the Golden Ratio Phi (φ)= 1.61803398874 is found everywhere—in architecture, art, and nature (fig. 2.15).

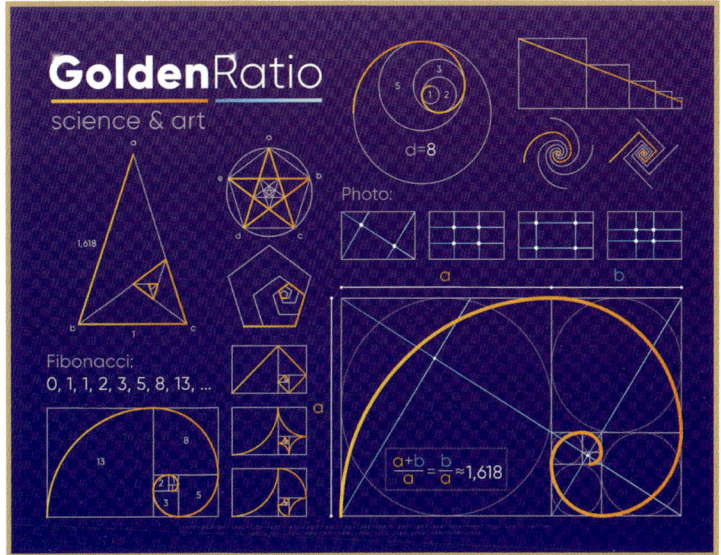

2.15 The Golden Ratio can be seen in all aspects of life, and it creates a natural balance.

"Euclid's Elements," the first written definition dating to the 1500s, explains the Golden Ratio as, "A straight line is said to have been cut in extreme and mean ratio when, as the whole line is to the greater segment, so is the greater to the lesser." The ratio represents proportional balance, and it surrounds everything in life. The pyramids were built using this theory. Look at the shape of a leaf and you'll see it. You can see it in the human body. Even though people are different sizes, the proportion of individual body parts remain the same.

Consider this:

U Measure the length between your head and toe and divide that by the distance from your belly button to toe. The result is close to φ.

U Divide the length from the top of your head to your shoulder by the length from your top of the head to your chin; φ again.

The Golden Ratio in Practice

Whenever someone asks me how to trim feet correctly or how I am able to teach students this crucial part of hoof care, I explain the principles of the *Golden Ratio*. The Golden Ratio is a method of describing symmetry and predictable patterns that occur in nature. Natural phenomena in this ratio maintain balance and proportion on everything from atoms to stars.

The ratio stems from the *Fibonacci sequence*, named after its Italian founder, Leonardo Fibonacci. The Fibonacci sequence is a listing of numbers where each subsequent number is the sum of the previous two. For example: 0, 1, 1, 2, 3, 5, 8, 13, 21—and so on. The series is never-ending, so it is often written as 1.618 for shorthand while the full sequence is noted as 1.61803…, with the … to signal that numerals continue into infinity. The real magic unfolds in the ratios of sequential Fibonacci numbers. When each is divided (2/1, 3/2, 5/3, and so on) the resulting calculation approaches the "Golden Proportion," which is 1.618.

So, where do horses fit in here? Let's first look at humans. When key anatomical points are located and compared to each other, they should fall into Golden Ratio proportions. Bone lengths in hands, arms, and legs will usually have these relationships, especially in top athletes. Plastic surgeons use this concept in the "Beauty Equation" to bring proper proportion to the faces of accident victims or movie stars.

In order for horses to be athletes and move efficiently, their bones and body proportions, including legs and hooves, need to follow these same Golden Ratio proportions. There are few perfect humans or horses. However, many top athletes of either species have Golden Ratio characteristics in their anatomy and structure (figs. 2.16 A & B).

Let's start at the bottom of the horse's front leg. As the horse's foot strikes the ground, it bears the horse's weight and drives propulsion. When the ground side of the hoof follows Golden Ratio proportions, the structure provides optimum loading and propulsion. Trimming hooves to Golden Ratio proportions is easy on horses within the "normal" range of conformation. However, distorted hooves or feet of conformationally challenged horses wear or grow outside Golden Ration parameters. When trimming, the Golden Ratio becomes a guideline for trimming these feet as close to ideal as possible. To compensate where Golden Ratio proportions cannot be met, farriers use horseshoe modifications to achieve the correct proportions.

You can find these proportions throughout the horse's entire body. For example, the short pastern bone should be in the ratio of one-third to two-thirds in size to the long pastern bone above it. Moving up the leg, the long pastern bone compared to the cannon bone is also in the same ratio, and so on. When there are disparities in bone lengths that do not fit in these proportions, a horse's movement efficiency is compromised. The added stress can cause injury or lameness, or reduce the horse's athletic ability.

Several years ago, the Cornell University and Veterinary College Board of Trustees asked me to teach a lesson from the farriery program. I chose the Golden Ratio, my favorite demonstration, and one that I give at every continuing education program.

A horse with long toes and underrun heels was brought in for the presentation. I put a dot behind the apex of the frog, a space that is referred to as "Duckett's Dot." This point aligns exactly below the intersections of the extensor and deep flexor tendons, the main tendons that flex and extend the leg.

After trimming the frog and sole, I drew a perpendicular line from Duckett's Dot to the outside of the hoof and another from the point of the untrimmed. With the foot on the mat, I drew lines at a right angle and then added lines at the toe and at the heel bulbs. The result: the lines show no Golden Ratio proportion.

Next, I sketched a straight line across the highest and widest point on the back of the frog and began trimming the foot from that point around to the same point on the opposite heel. After some quick rasping to smooth up the edges and create uniform hoof-wall thickness, I put the foot down and redrew the lines. The new marks perfectly followed the Golden Ratio proportion where the toe length was the same as the distance from the tip of the frog to the heels. This is also known as *geometric balance*, and it improved the horse's stance by placing the foot squarely under the horse's leg. Farriers can only change the line at the toe and the heel, so it's important to recognize the other two lines are unchangeable landmarks.

The Board of Trustees, some of whom were veterinarians from the Veterinary College, shared they had learned more about horse's feet in my 45-minute demonstration than in all their time in vet school.

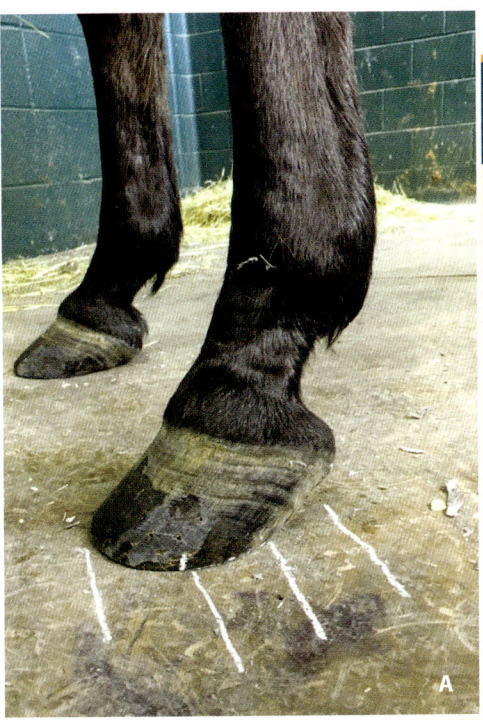 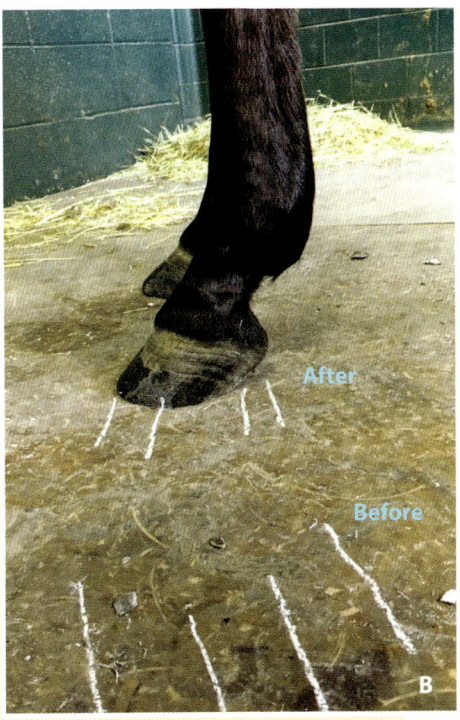

2.16 A & B This foot, before trimming (A), shows the Golden Ratio is reversed with too much foot in front of the frog. By drawing chalk marks on the ground, farriers can create a visual aid for checking hoof angles before beginning to trim or shoe. The lines drawn here highlight that the dimensions of this hoof do not follow the correct ratios from heel to toe. The chalk lines drawn in B highlight that the proportions at the heel and the toe are equal rather than in an ideal ⅓ to ⅔ ratio. Here you see a proper trim where the lines at the toes and the heels exhibit the Golden Ratio.

2: THE EVOLUTION OF THE MODERN HORSESHOE

2.17 The upward slope at the toe is called a "rocker toe." The modification adds mechanical assistance to the forward breakover when conformational or arthritic problems need help.

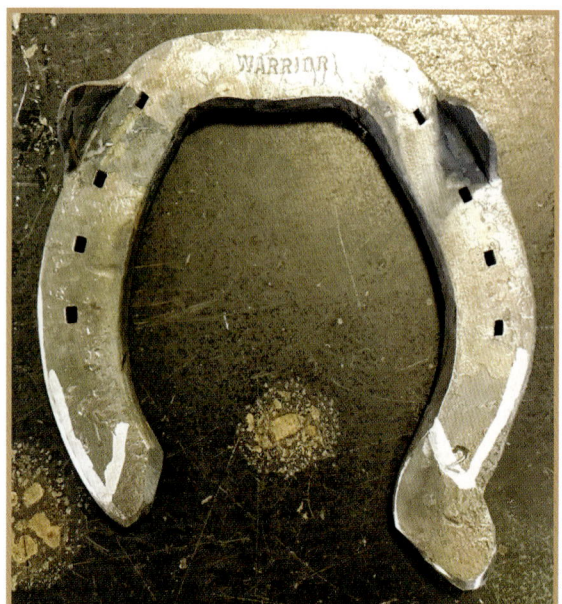

2.18 This is a "square toe" shoe with a "lateral trailer" and quarter clips. The square toe encourages straighter movement; the trailer is used to prevent interference from a base-wide conformation.

Horse hooves follow the same proportional balance. Using the Golden Ratio while measuring the hoof walls and the heels can indicate the coffin bone's location within 1 or 2 millimeters.

Rolled Toe

A *rolled-toe* horseshoe is one modification farriers use to reduce the leverage on a horse's joints. This adjustment places breakover at an ideal point when basic trimming and shoeing aren't enough. The edge of the shoe is hammered or ground at an angle to achieve this outcome. Manufacturers produce horseshoes that come with rolled toes, but most farriers start with a basic horseshoe and add the rolled toe.

Rocker Toe

Another variation farriers use is known as a *rocker toe*. In this application, farriers form a sharp upward bend at the toe (fig. 2.17). The ski-like shape increases the pivot point, thus, enhancing breakover. A horse that stabs his toes or has unusually high-angled feet may benefit from rocker toes. Horses with stiff coffin joints due to arthritis or laminitis may also be candidates for this style of shoe.

Square Toe

The *square shoe* is another toe alteration. Instead of following a rounded path around the toe, the shoe is shaped into a straight line (fig. 2.18). This style is often used to straighten a sloppy horse's gait. The square edge encourages straighter movement where a horse's conformation is less than perfect and there are interference problems. Square-toed shoes may also be used on hind feet to artificially shorten toe lengths when horses are chronically overreaching and pulling off front shoes.

Heel Modifications

Farriers also modify the heel of a shoe to address soundness or conformation issues. In general, the types of changes mentioned below are only used on hind shoes. Each leaves a portion of the shoe branch sticking out beyond the actual heel of the hoof, so these extensions could be easily stepped off if applied to front shoes.

Extended Heels

Extended heels are short, straight shoe additions that reach out beyond the hoof. This helps the horse engage his hindquarters more efficiently. These are common in dressage, reining, cow-horse work, or other performance disciplines where the hind end needs support. Longer heels are also used to support the hind limb when a horse has "standing-under" conformation (fig. 2.19).

Trailers

A *trailer* is a farrier-produced modification that is used on the back feet to counteract interference in horses with base-wide, "cow-hocked" conformation. Trailers are only added to the lateral branch of the hind shoes and extend approximately ¾ inch beyond the hoof. The extra steel is turned outward at a 45-degree angle beyond the lateral heel termination of the hoof (fig. 2.20). Horses wearing trailers may need separate turnout because the design increases the chances of injury to others from a kick. Separate turnout also eliminates the possibility of another horse stepping on and pulling off the shoe.

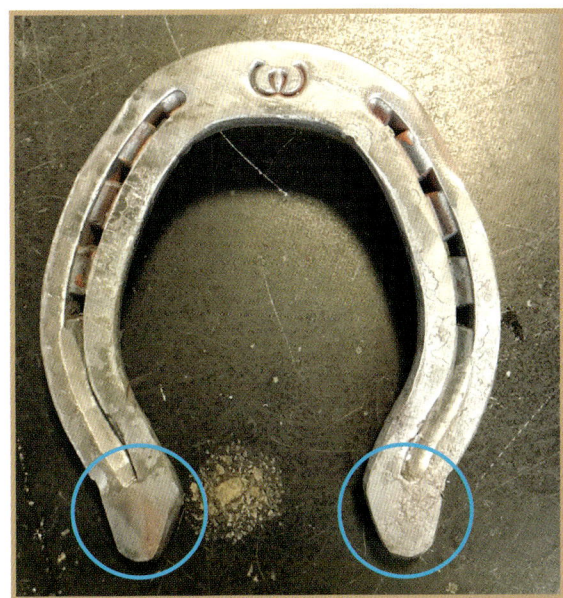

2.19 Hind horseshoes with "extended" heel modifications are used to help a horse that has a standing-under, hind end conformation.

2.20 On this shoe, both heels are extended longer than on a typical horseshoe in order to add support in situations where the horse's leg is forward of the hips.

Closed-Heel Shoes

Riders are familiar with the general shape of a horseshoe, also referred to as an *open-heeled* shoe. But there are times farriers use a *closed-heel* shoe known as a *bar shoe*. The bar shoe has several variations, including the *straight bar, egg bar, heart bar, W-bar, G-bar,* and *Z-bar*. All have specific uses, mostly for therapeutic purposes. The *straight bar* shoe is the most common version used for providing heel protection and hoof stability. It is helpful for excessively upright feet that become heel sore, and for stabilizing hoof cracks (fig. 2.21).

Farriers can buy pre-made styles though a farrier may choose to make his own using one of several methods. For example, he may buy a shoe with a longer heel length, then bend the extra steel to form a bridge across the heels. Another approach is welding an insert to the shoe. Many farriers find forging a bar shoe from a straight piece of steel to the exact needs of the horse is satisfying work, so choose to make the alterations rather than buy a ready-made shoe.

Egg bar shoes are another variation. The name comes from the egg shape that results from continuing the curve of the heels to support the heel bulbs of the foot. The egg bar shoe is typically used when the hoof/leg conformation needs more caudal support, such as in horses with low underrun heels. Farriers can either buy ready-made egg bar shoes or hand forge them. Both straight and egg bar shoes also aid in providing more weight distribution.

The *heart bar* is used to support the frog—a key factor for horses with laminitis. Low or negative coffin-bone angles are also helped with these shoes. Heart bar, egg bar, and *W-bar* shoes are all variations that are used to provide additional support to the bony column in the hoof by using the shoe to provide frog pressure. Like the options just described, these are all available as manufactured shoes, or farriers can choose to hand-shape the modifications.

Unlike other bar shoes, the *G-bar* and *Z-bar* can only be fabricated or forged by farriers with specialized skills. These shoes are strictly used for hoof injuries to provide an unloading of the injured area.

Generally, different types of bar shoes are needed when conformation is less than ideal or when injury or a disease process needs support.

2.21 "Closed-heel" shoes are used for a variety of therapeutic purposes to provide stabilization to the hoof. The example here is a "straight bar" shoe to protect the heel area and also prevent the rear of the shoe from sinking in soft footing.

Horseshoe Accessories

Accessories enhance the fundamental benefits horseshoes offer. Add-ons aren't as plentiful as human fashion accessories, but there are several that serve specific purposes.

Pads

Flat pieces of leather or polyurethane plastic can add a protective layer to the bottom of the hoof. *Hoof pads* create a barrier between the sole and the ground to protect against bruising from stepping on sharp objects like gravel and frozen ground.

Horses with good feet but being ridden in rough terrain may also benefit from hoof pads. Thin-soled and sore-footed horses also appreciate the relief on any surface (fig. 2.22).

Wedge Pads

Used for correcting conformation problems, or when treating the cause of injury or disease, these pads are thinner in the front and are thicker toward the back of the hoof. The change in thickness creates an angle to artificially raise the hoof angle. These pads are available in several different degree elevations. Wedge pads are commonly used for gaited horses to increase animation of their gaits.

Horses with collapsed, crushed, or underrun heels may be candidates for wedge pads. Raising hoof angles must be done carefully, with a thorough understanding of biomechanics in the front leg and hoof. Hoof angles trimmed to a higher-than-normal angle can be as problematic as angles that are too low. A common mistake when applying a wedge pad is not increasing shoe length at the heels to provide enough support.

2.22 This leather hoof pad offers a protective barrier between the foot and the ground; leather pads have natural shock-absorbing properties.

Snowball Pads

Snow packs into shod hooves, making it look as though a horse is walking on high heels. *Snowball pads* prevent this build up. The pads come in two styles: either a heavy piece of plastic or rubber with a convex bubble that pushes snow out with each step, or as a raised rubber tube that follows the perimeter of the shoe but does not cover the sole or frog. An advantage to using a shoe with a raised rubber tube is that it keeps snow from building up while also leaving the frog and sole exposed. This allows the foot to remain open to the ground as full can pads fill up with the muddy slush in paddocks (figs. 2.23 A & B).

Therapeutic Pads

Frog-support pads (aka *therapeutic pads*) provide extra support to laminitic horses. These pads are a two-part mix made with polyurethane. After the shoe is nailed into place, the mixture is poured into the exposed area of the hoof and hardens (fig. 2.24).

All pads, excluding snow pads, need packaging material between the hoof and the barrier. This keeps debris from working its way in between the surfaces, which can lead to thrush and bacterial infections.

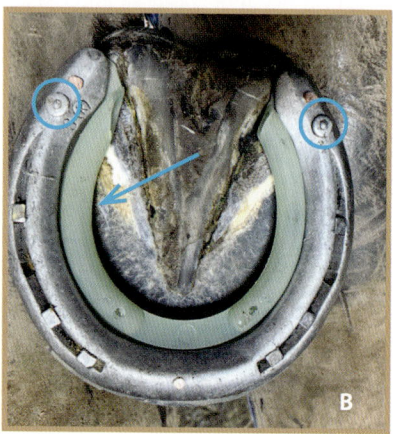

2.23 A & B A snowball that packs into the hoof can give the appearance (and function) of high heels and is a danger to horse and rider (A). The typical winter horseshoe setup includes carbide tipped drive-in studs and an anti-snowball pad made of rubber (B).

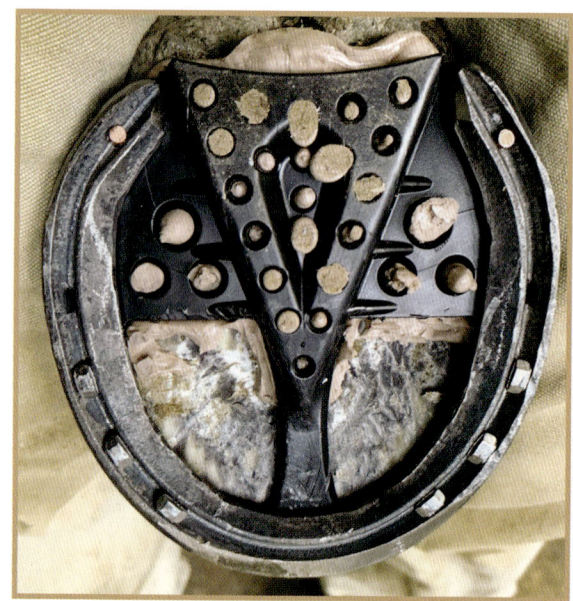

2.24 Pads can be tailored to each individual hoof when created using a 3D printer. The design of this pad, in combination with the brown putty-like filler made from dental impression material, provides optimum caudal support for horses with low heels.

Traction Control

For safety and competitive reasons, horses may need more traction than standard shoes can provide. Traction devices come in many forms: some are manufactured in special types of shoes; some are forged into the shoe as a farrier-produced modification; and others are applied to the horseshoe after the shoe is fitted.

Heel Calks

Heel calks are extra material added to the end of the shoe. Manufactured heel calks are often used on polo horses playing on grass and trail horses traveling in mountainous terrain. "Turned-heel calks" add a bit of height and are regularly used on draft horses, especially for those participating in logging and pulling competitions (fig. 2.25).

Drive-In Studs

Carbide *drive-in studs* or *pins* are popular because the material is easy to install and available in a range of sizes. Farriers drill holes into the horseshoe after fitting the shoe and hammering the pins into place. These studs provide traction on slippery surfaces like wet concrete, blacktop, ice, or hard ground.

This style of traction device is smaller than other types and jars the leg less than calks when it comes in contact with the ground. Drive-in studs are a good all-around choice for any horses that need occasional traction for safety (fig. 2.26).

Removable Screw Calks or Studs

Screw-in style studs give riders the flexibility of changing the amount of traction a shoe offers by swapping sizes

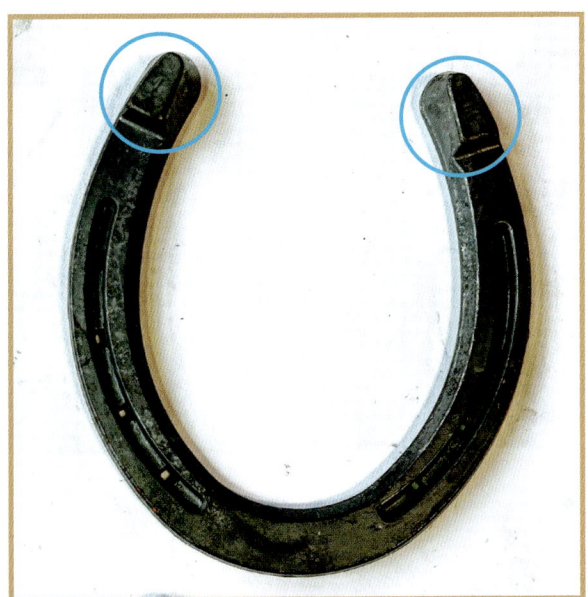

2.25 Heel calks provide added traction.

2.26 This hind shoe has carbide drive-in studs in the heels for slight traction on ice or wet pavement.

or leaving them out altogether. Farriers drill a hole in the locations needed, cut threads into the holes, and install a plug to keep the area clean for when the rider adds the studs. It is the rider's responsibility to have her own screw calks and the tools to change studs and maintain the holes. Experienced riders should be knowledgeable about proper usage—applying studs that are overly aggressive can cause fractures and ligament tears.

An event rider prefers removable screw-in studs because she can make traction adjustments based on footing conditions, especially on cross-country courses. These riders opt for taller calks on muddy, slippery terrain, swap those out for shorter studs in the stadium-jumping phase, and remove the device for dressage.

High-level polo players also opt for removable calks. Aggressive calks can be screwed in for safe playing at speed and taken out for pasture turnout.

An advantage of removable calks is the horse only has them on when needed. Tall, aggressive calks that provide safety during slippery riding conditions can also self-injure a horse in turnout or hurt another horse during play.

Largely Unchanged

In many cases, the modern horseshoe still looks like a simplistic invention developed thousands of years ago. Yet, as I've described, there is more than meets the eye. Advances through research and farrier experimentation have transformed the universal symbol of good luck into a sophisticated device to support horse soundness and performance.

Welded/Brazed-On Traction

Welded or *brazed-on* hard products add grip specifically for use on paved roads and grass. These are typically added to a shoe after it has been fit to the hoof, and they increase the cost of shoeing. The original product of this type was "Borium." Similar to "Kleenex," it is a trademarked name people use to refer to brandname products. *Borium* is welded onto a shoe with an oxyacetylene torch and is popular for trail riders crossing paved roads and Standardbreds training during the winter or on stone dust tracks.

Tungsten carbide is another material that adds traction. The particles become bonded to horseshoes with a tough bronze/copper matrix that holds up well on paved surfaces. Brazed-on tungsten carbide is popular in use on Amish road horses and draft horses because it outperforms Borium for wear on pavement.

FROM THE FORGE
Can Glue-On Shoes Replace Nails?

In 1976, the Mustad Hoofcare Group hired me as a consultant. By the mid-1980s, increasing numbers of farriers were using Mustad nails, and the company began exploring other opportunities for developing new products.

A few years into my role with the company, a German-made glue-on horseshoe emerged. The big question was, "Will glue-on shoes eliminate the need for nails?"

This was a significant concern for a nail-manufacturing company. The original glue-on design was complicated, and assembly was required to use the shoe. It was impractical for everyday use, but I saw a potential purpose for it to help horses with damaged and diseased hooves, and I encouraged Mustad to improve on the design and release a new shoe.

With help from Burney Chapman and Myron McLane, we developed a glue-on model that Mustad called the "Glu Strider." These first glue-on shoes were applied to the hoof wall with an industrial strength "super glue." This application required clean, dry hoof walls and a steady horse. The acceptance of these shoes in the market grew but as often is the case with new methods, there were misapplications and failures. There is still a pervasive misconception that a glue-on shoe is easier to apply.

The work began with a therapeutic shoe for laminitis treatments and developed into a model called the "Baby Glu" for the purpose of correcting angular-limb deformities in foals. Eventually, simpler versions called the "EasyGlue" and "RaceGlue" were developed. Farriers and veterinarians embraced the concept of nail-less horseshoes for horses that had hoof walls too weak or too damaged for nails. The Glu Strider model has since been discontinued, but practitioners still embrace the concept of glue-on shoes.

During this first decade of commercially available glue-on shoes, other innovators began experimenting with different adhesives and shoe styles. For example, farrier Rob Sigafoos at the University of Pennsylvania New Bolton Center developed a fabric cuff-style shoe using methacrylate adhesive. Eventually, this became commercially produced by Sound Horse Solutions. This began the next generation of glue-on shoes, as farrier and horse owner demand steadily increased. By the year 2000 and beyond, the modern horse has many different manufacturers offering glue-on shoes and adhesives.

Glue-on shoes now encompass a wide and growing variety of shoes, and the design of these shoes is far more sophisticated than simply substituting glue for nails (see figs. 2.4 A & B, p. 26). Many of the glue-on shoes available are developed for specific uses of horses. Some are all plastic, others are aluminum with a glue-on interface, and others include nail-on counterparts (see fig. 2.5, p. 26). One misconception is that glue-on shoes stay on the hoof better. In reality, it makes no difference—a horse that overreaches and steps a metal shoe off will do the same with plastic shoes, as the material alone does not alter the horse's gait.

Some glue-on versions use a rim pad to absorb shock. If you were nailing through that same shoe, the "give" of the rim pad would loosen the nails quickly, giving the glue-on option an advantage in this scenario.

3

CHAPTER 3

Modern Horseshoe Styles

Since most horses wear traditional metal horseshoes, it's easy to assume that there are fewer options for horses than the thousands of styles you can choose among at the store. But that's far from the truth. A decades-old display case in the Cornell University Farrier Collection features approximately 400 different types of therapeutic horseshoes (figs. 3.1 A–C). This collection is likely the only place you can see examples of so many types of horseshoes all in one

place. There are bar shoes, shoes with frog support, plastic models for cracks, acrylics for hoof reconstruction, pads, metal plates, and even regular steel shoes.

When the basic rim shoe is simply not enough for a horse, farriers turn to some of these therapeutic shoes to keep the horse comfortable and, in some cases, heal the hoof. Only a handful of specialty shoes are pre-manufactured, so many are custom-made based on a specific lameness or disease problem identified in an individual horse.

3.1 A The upper three rows from this part of the Cornell University Collection features "Scotch" style draft horseshoes by Eugene Layton, Cornell Farrier from 1939–1965. The shoes below from Henry Asmus are those used on driving horses.

3.1 B This panel features horseshoes from Michael Wildenstein, Cornell Farrier, 1991–2010, and some made by me, Cornell Farrier since 2010.

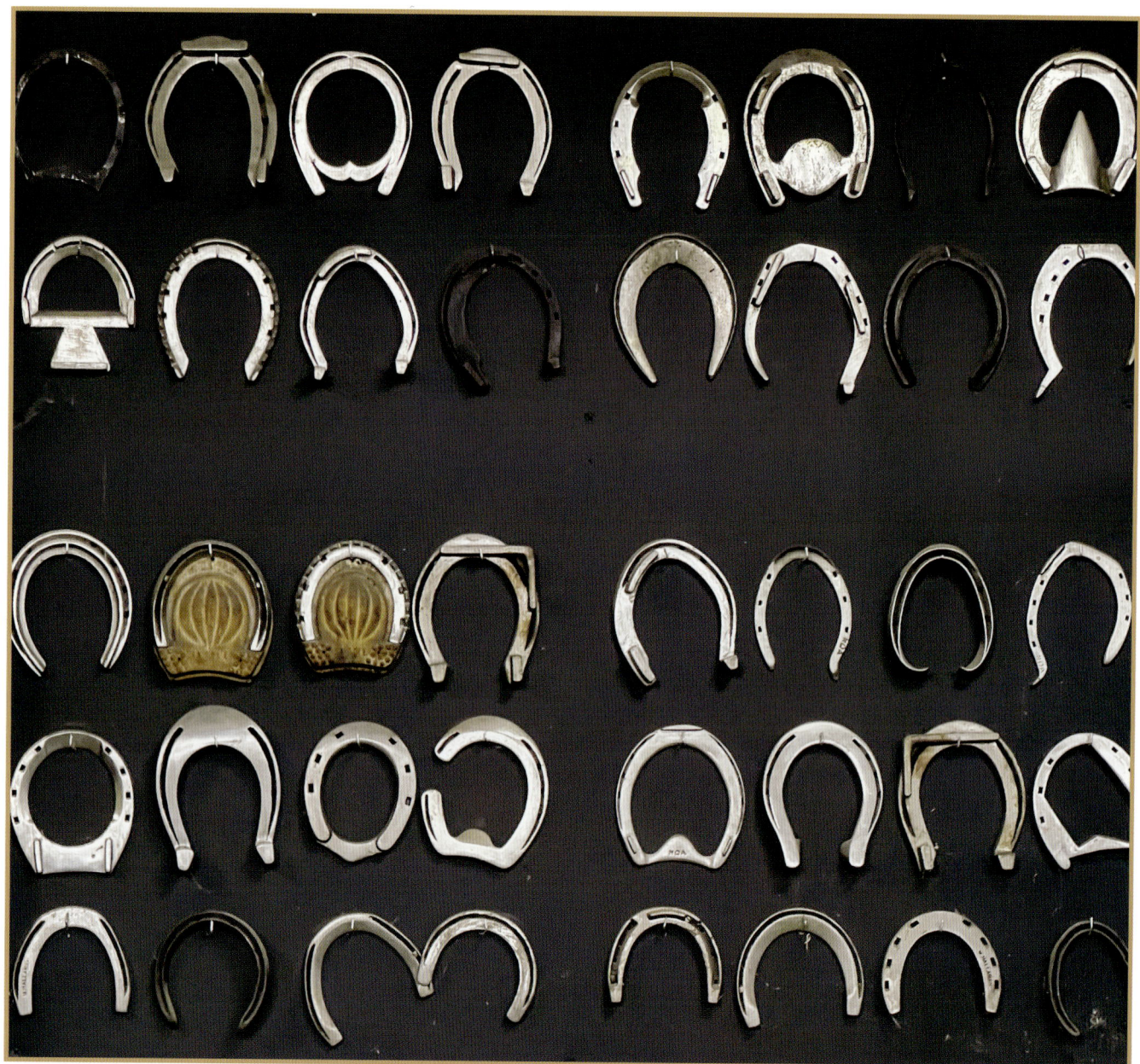

3.1 C Hand-forged shoes like these by Henry Asmus show how farriers can customize horseshoes to treat a myriad of hoof problems. These were specifically for driving horses.

For instance, the Cornell display includes:

- Diverse types of older-style Standardbred shoes with varying modifications to correct gait problems.
- Specialized heavy horseshoes for "street horses" where traction is important.
- Hand-forged horseshoes made by all six Cornell Farrier instructors during their 100 years combined work.
- Aluminum shoes for a fatiguing jumper.
- Plastic shoes once applied to an endurance horse.
- Rubber shoes for a carriage horse.
- Glue-on shoes for thin-hoof-walled horses.
- Titanium shoes where strength and less weight is needed.

When a horse has a hoof issue, these are some of the options a farrier might choose to use.

Modern Shoe Modifications

I have touched on a number of the different shoe style options and modifications in previous chapters. Here, I will review some of that information as well as explore some of the shoeing alternatives in more detail.

Straight Bar Shoe

The basic rim horseshoe has an opening between the branches of the horseshoes where it fits onto the heels. As I explained on p. 40, a *bar shoe* has extra metal that

3.2 A classic bar shoe uses metal to close the gap between the heel branches on traditional shoes.

closes that gap. The additional material is like putting an orthotic in your own shoe—it provides greater heel support, and it can help hold an injured hoof together (fig. 3.2). This style of shoe is useful when a horse has severe cracks, such as sheared heels or a quarter crack, or lameness that can be improved by reducing movement in the hoof capsule.

Egg Bar

The *egg bar* type of shoe is similar to the straight bar shoe, except that there is even more metal connecting the shoe branches. The additional metal gives the shoe an egg-like appearance, hence the name. These shoes offer increased support to the back part of the hoof, leg, tendons, and suspensory ligaments. This style shoe

3.3 Egg-bar shoes provide additional support, though the shoe design can be prone to being "stepped off" by a hind hoof.

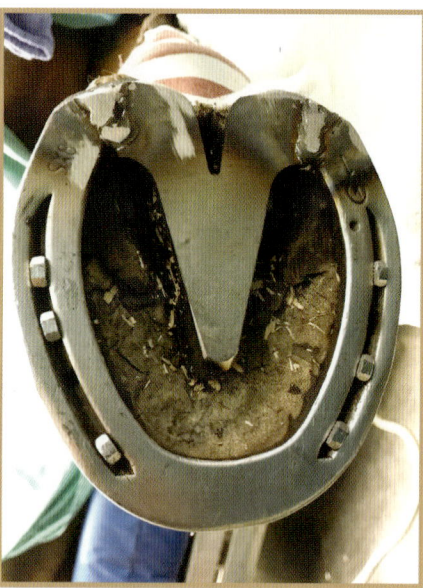

3.4 Another variation of a bar shoe forms a heart shape over the frog.

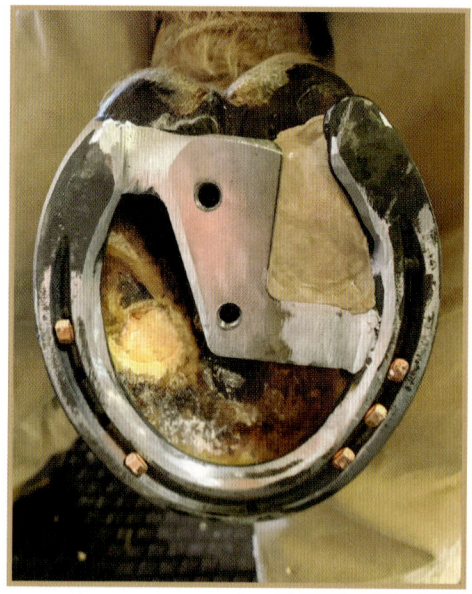

3.5 The Z-bar is another form of a bar shoe. The upper right quadrant pictured here includes an antibiotic packing material.

may be more prone to being "stepped off" during leg interference—being pulled off by a back hoof mid-stride—but the egg-bar shoe can be effective in some situations (fig. 3.3).

Heart Bar

One look at a *heart bar* shoe and you'll understand how it earned its name. A V-shaped piece of metal is forged into the shape of a heart to cover and protect the frog. Pads or packing material can be placed between the space for added support (fig. 3.4).

Most often, these shoes are used on laminitic horses and for horses with hoof and coffin bone injuries that require additional frog support. The wedge-shaped material relieves pressure on the frog and spreads the weight across the area more evenly. This also prevents rotation of the coffin bone (see I.2, p. 3) within the hoof. Before the shoe is applied, X-rays are needed to understand the current position of the bone to avoid putting pressure in the wrong areas, so farriers and veterinarians work closely when these shoes are used.

Z-Bar

When one side of the hoof is damaged or infected, a Z-bar shoe might be what your farrier chooses. Instead of the horseshoe following the traditional curve, a section of the metal is forged into the shape of the letter Z (fig. 3.5). It's often used on horses with heel bruising ("corns"), hoof-wall separations, quarter/heel cracks, and bar fractures. Like the other shoes I've described, this design protects a damaged hoof and shifts the pressure points on the hoof to alleviate pain and encourage regrowth.

Hospital Plate

Sometimes called a "peek-a-boo" plate, a hospital plate is a thin piece of metal with two screws. Unlike shoe pads, the hospital plate is fitted between the hoof and the ground and easily opens. This allows for the treatment of an abscess or application of medications and to keep bacteria out of the hoof to prevent further infection (figs. 3.6 A–C). One of the biggest benefits of this setup is that the therapeutic shoes can stay in place on the hoof while topical treatments are given. It's often suggested to keep horses with hospital plates on stall rest because the smooth surface reduces traction.

Wedges

The wedge shoes in your closet are all about fashion over form, but the angled heels change the way your foot absorbs impact during walking. In horses, *wedges* are more functional than trendy, and the change in weight distribution can be therapeutic. The angle of the wedge and its location on the shoe depends on the individual horse and

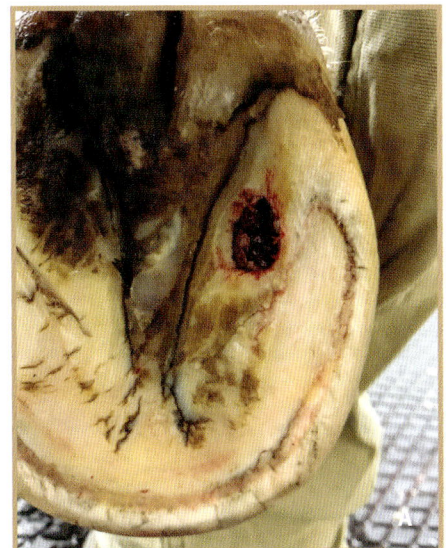
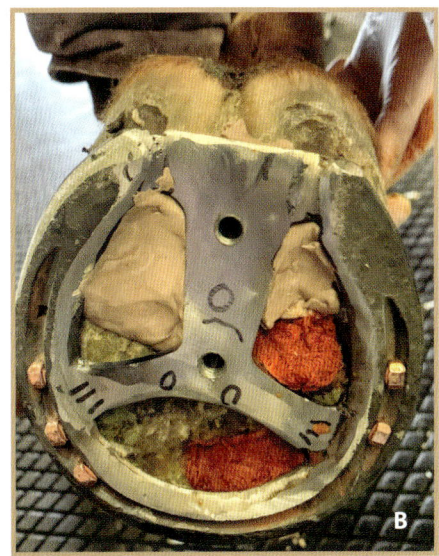
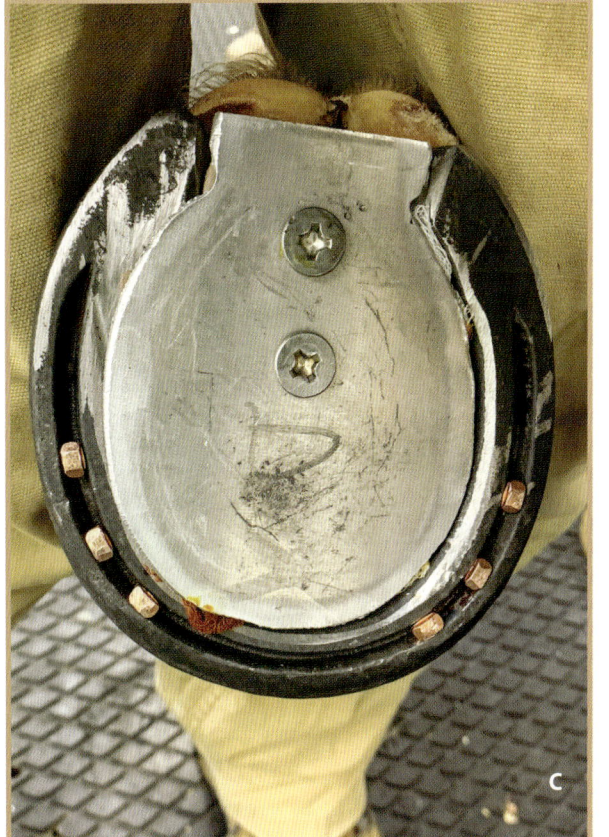

3.6 A–C Serious puncture wounds like the one seen in Photo A need to be protected and treated daily, making a hoof like this an ideal candidate for a hospital plate. Photo B shows the base for the hospital plate, which works well for wounds to the front and side of the sole. The pink impression material keeps debris from entering the rear of the shoe. The finished hospital plate (Photo C) protects and treats injuries or surgeries on the sole. This type of inset plate does not cover the nails and does not change the height of the shoe. The two bolts make it easy to remove for treatment until the hoof has healed.

the issue. Regardless of where it is, you'll be able to spot it as a thicker section on the shoe's heel branch (fig. 3.7).

Your farrier might use a wedge:

∪ To extend the coffin joints.

∪ To shift the load-bearing spot on the hoof onto the thicker portion of the shoe.

∪ To raise the heels and decrease strain on the deep digital flexor tendon.

Wedges must be used carefully. Incorrect angles can have the opposite effect by increasing pressure rather than alleviating it and that interferes with hoof-wall growth.

Pharoah Plate

Despite the number of common horseshoes that are more readily available than ever before, fitting the right shoe still boils down to the individual horse. Triple Crown winner American Pharoah is the perfect example. Before his Kentucky Derby debut, he missed an important race for young horses because of a deep bruise in the hoof.

Farrier Wes Champagne custom-built the racehorse a shoe from a sheet of thin aluminum alloy and shaped it

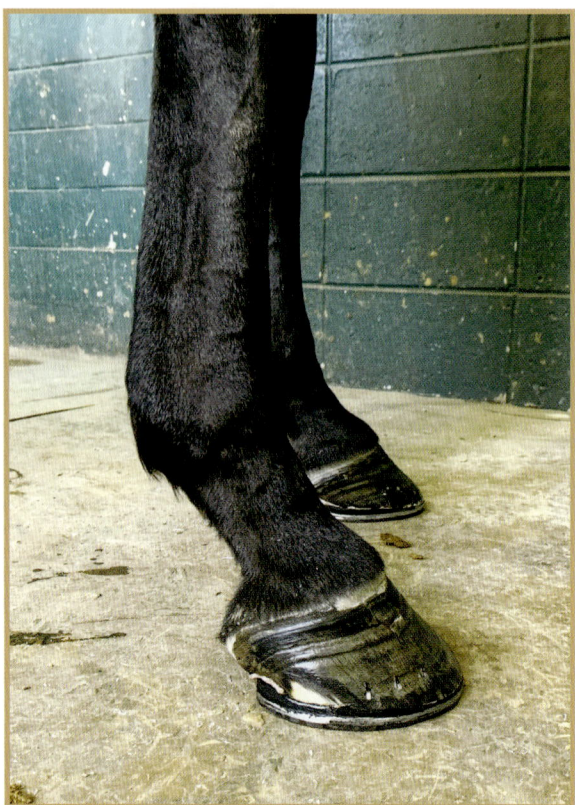

3.7 Wedges, similar to lifts or orthotics in human shoes, can be used with horseshoes to create proper hoof angles.

3.8 The Pharoah plate is an example of how skilled farriers can customize any shoe to fit a horse's individual needs.

to his specifications. Wes used a plate to cover the back portion of the hoof but open on the sole (fig. 3.8). The plate absorbed the impact, a function normally done by the frog. Like traditional shoe pads, this plate, made from aluminum, was put between the hoof and the shoe.

3D-Printed Horseshoes

Henry Burden forever changed the farrier industry when he built a machine that could mass-produce horseshoes. Since then, much of the innovation in shoe design has evolved for therapeutic purposes to include plastic and glue-on shoes. Technology—specifically 3D printers—may one day have an impact similar to Burden's industrial invention (fig. 3.9).

The Netherland's farrier Harold Brommer, DVM, PhD, Dipl. ECVS, a professor of Equine Surgery and Orthopaedics at Utrecht University, is working with two master farriers to "print" shoes, and other farriers are working in this area too. The theory of 3D printing is taken from human medicine, which uses imaging to study a person's movement and measure pressure points. This information is used to create customized shoe inserts. Similar tools are used to capture this same information in the horse.

It takes about 90 seconds to scan each hoof and send the specifications to the printer. At the time of Brommer's 2020 study, it took between six and eight hours to produce each of the four shoes, which were a precise custom fit. More research is needed to better understand how 3D printing technology fits into the farrier trade, but it is an example of how shoeing solutions for the modern horse continue to evolve over time.

Glue-On Shoes

I've already shared some information about *glue-on shoes* on pp. 26 and 45, but they bear mentioning again here. Nailed-on metal horseshoes have served horses well for centuries and are likely to continue to play a valuable role in keeping a horse performing at his best. Nailing on horseshoes does not injure healthy hooves when a farrier has the proper training. Like every industry, access to modern technology and new materials offers opportunities to enhance traditional horseshoes, and one of these advancements includes glue-ons (fig. 3.10).

The phrase "glue-on" horseshoe is a bit deceiving. Don't be fooled into thinking that makes application easier than nailing on shoes. Properly selected and shaped, nailed-on horseshoes can be easier to

3.9 3D printed race horseshoes. CSIRO printed these from titanium.

apply than glue-on options. While the most important part of any horseshoe application is the trimming and preparation of the horse's feet, this is critical with glue-on shoes.

The term is a categorical classification rather than a description of one particular shoe. Farriers have many options—almost too many choices—that can lead to confusion, even amongst farriers. Most farrier schools offer little hands-on adhesive horseshoe training, so farriers interested in these techniques attend clinics or pay for training from other experienced farriers.

Some glue-on shoe varieties do not require blacksmithing skills for shaping, while other types do need specialized equipment and refined fitting skills.

Myths About Glue-On Horseshoes

"Once in glue-on shoes, forever in glue-on shoes." This is not always the case. Often a glue-on shoe is used as a transition—to help improve a hoof in preparation for a nailed-on horseshoe. Horses with "shelly" feet or weak hoof walls simply cannot produce a quality, sound hoof. A glue-on shoe extends that horse's career and may even save his life.

"Glue-on horseshoes stay on better than nailed on horseshoes." Maybe. There are multiple reasons horses lose shoes. Horses that "step off" traditional shoes or are in certain environmental conditions can pop off a glue-on shoe as easily one that is nailed on.

"Glue-on horseshoes are better for the horse because nails cause harm to the hoof." This is only true when a nail is improperly driven into the sensitive tissue of the foot. Trained, skilled farriers rarely hurt the hoof with nails.

"Glue-on shoes are all plastic or synthetic materials." A standard nailed-on aluminum horseshoe can also be direct-glued to the bottom of the hoof with proper technique and preparation. The downside is that the

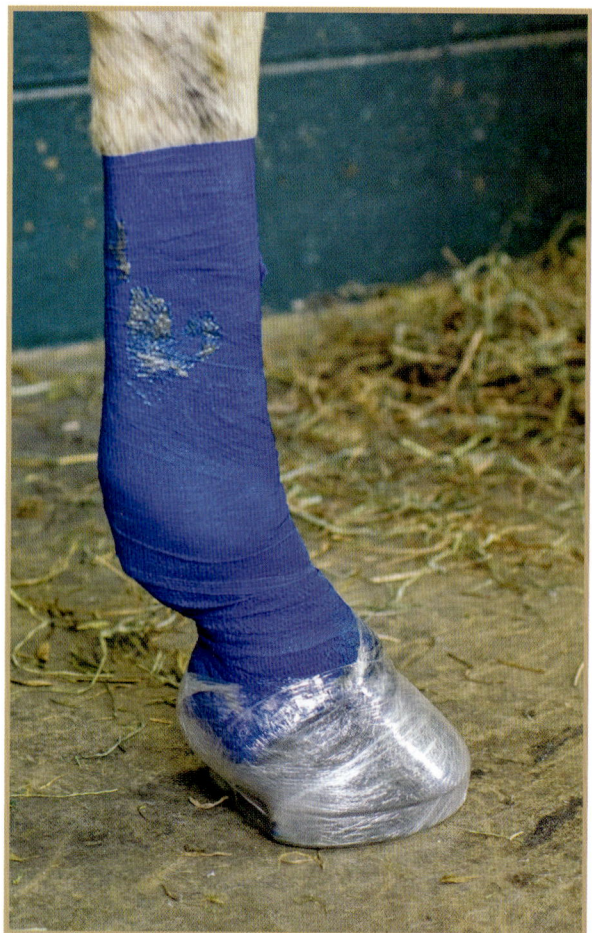

3.10 The leg has been wrapped to prevent getting glue on the hair. The shoe was wrapped with stretch wrap to hold it in place while the adhesive cured.

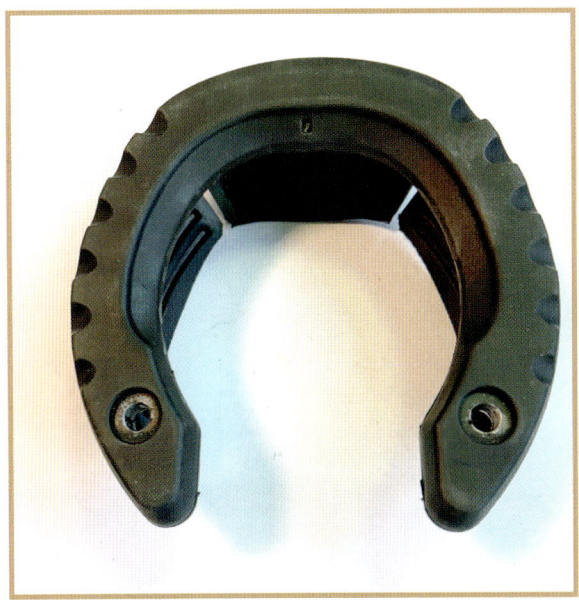

3.11 The GluShu front direct glue horseshoe has an aluminum core that can be tapped for studs.

3.12 The PolyFlex® direct glue-on shoe includes a wire spine to hold the desired shoe shape.

metal shoe is rigid and is bonded to the heel around the hoof. This locks up the entire hoof, prohibiting the natural expansion that occurs in the hoof during the weight-bearing phase of a gait. Over time, this forces the hoof to contract, which is why using aluminum shoes for this method is not recommended for long-term use. Shoes made from flexible materials that are direct-glued are a good option for long-term use (fig. 3.11).

Types of Glue-On Horseshoes

Glue-on shoes put another tool in the farrier's toolbox for finding solutions that keep a horse comfortable, performing his best, and as needed, healing from an injury. Not all glue-on horseshoes are the same (figs. 3.12 and 3.13 A & B). Just like traditional nail-on shoes, there are multiple models and choosing the correct one for the job depends on the individual horse.

Glue-on horseshoes fall into three categories with each having advantages and disadvantages. The horse, his activity, and the situation are used to determine which is best suited for the job. How the adhesive and shoe are applied to the hoof is what sets the options apart.

Direct glue: With a direct glue application, the shoe is affixed directly to the bottom of the horse's foot with an adhesive to replace nails. Some shoes within this group include options for combining glue and nails on the same hoof.

Indirect glue: These shoes are made with a "cuff" or "tab" that is glued to the side of the hoof wall rather than adhering to the bottom of the foot. The "cuff" style shoes have a poly Vectran fabric bonded to an aluminum shoe

3.13 A & B The Easy Shoe glue-on model (A) offers added frog support. Another option is the GluShu (B), which also offers frog support in cases of chronic laminitis.

3.14 Example of a cuff-style glue-on shoe with a therapeutic rim pad.

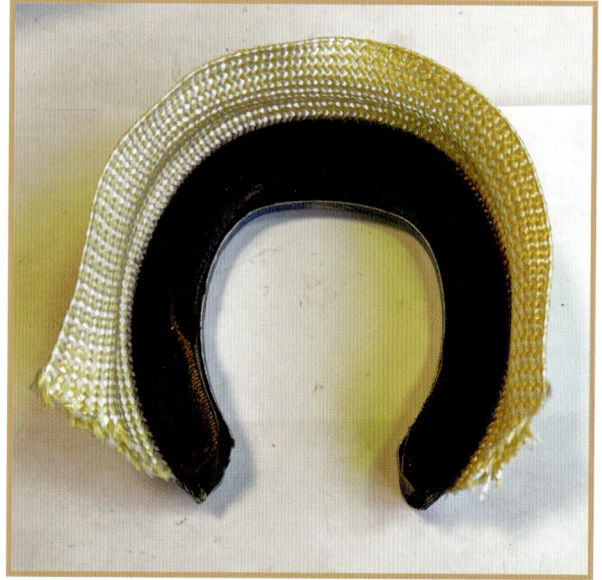

or a molded extension (fig. 3.14). The "tab" style includes either a wide metal flap welded onto a standard metal shoe or has multiple plastic tabs that adhere to the perimeter of the hoof wall. A benefit to this method is that it allows for natural expansion in the hoof and is safe for long-term use.

Side wings: A third type is a hybrid—a combination of a direct glue-on shoe with the addition of side "wings" for easier application and stability. These styles also allow proper hoof expansion and the benefits of both styles.

Adhesives play a critical role in the success of glue-on horseshoes. Applying it isn't as easy as using Elmer's® glue on an art project—timing is essential. If the glue sets up too fast, without the shoe in place, it will not bond. If the glue takes too long to set, a horse can pull his foot away and shift the shoe position.

Farriers use either *methyl methacrylate* or *polyurethane* adhesives. Both are a two-part mixture, but that is where the similarities end. Methyl methacrylate forms its bond at the end of the mixing cycle, whereas polyurethane forms its bond as soon as it comes out of the mixing tip. Polyurethane glues need an applicator gun and mixing tips. Methyl methacrylate adhesives either can be applied with a special gun and mixing tips or dispensed from single-use mixing cups. Glues and applications vary with shoe types.

Proper hoof preparation is essential for successful bonding and shoe adherence. Any glue surface of the hoof and shoe must be clean, dry, and free of oily substances. Horses that are going to have glue-on shoes applied need to be kept out of wet, muddy areas before shoeing. Farriers will usually use a small hand torch to further dry the hoof wall. A painter's moisture meter may be used to check hoof-wall moisture, which needs to be less than 10 percent.

Farriers use either a fast- or a slow-setting glue. The selection is determined by the shoe style and ambient temperature. If the glue begins to set before the shoe is applied to the foot, the shoe will not bond properly. Any adhesive that is not "wet" as it is mating the glue surface of the shoe to the foot will not cement well.

Additional Modern Shoe Alternatives

It's easy to see that farriers have more than the standard horseshoe to find a solution best for each individual horse. These are a few additional options available.

Glue Storage Tips for Farriers

Glue-on shoes have more variables to consider during application as compared to traditional horseshoes. How the adhesives are stored also plays a critical role in a successful application. First, store glue at consistent temperatures. Fluctuating temperatures or freeze/thaw cycles over time degrade unused materials.

Second, glue-on shoes are more costly than nailed-on shoes both in the cost of the shoe and in the adhesive. This means it's important to use glue-on shoes in specific situations rather than as a one-size-fits-all approach to maximize the value.

Thin or damaged hoof walls are well-served by glue-on shoes. Laminitis cases and hoof injuries that would make nailing on a shoe painful are optimal candidates for a glue-on model. For some of the glue-on shoe varieties, the glue is applied while the horse is standing in the shoes. This makes application easy to do for a horse that cannot stand on the opposite foot for long periods of time.

Fast-setting adhesives have also been used directly on the bottom of the horse's feet to provide temporary protection. A hoof pad or a "horseshoe" made entirely from adhesive can provide temporary comfort and protection.

3.15 A–C DE HoofTaps are used in situations where horses need support for a variety of reasons. The HoofTap can be inserted into a crack in the toe, for example (A & B), or used on quarters that need extra support (C).

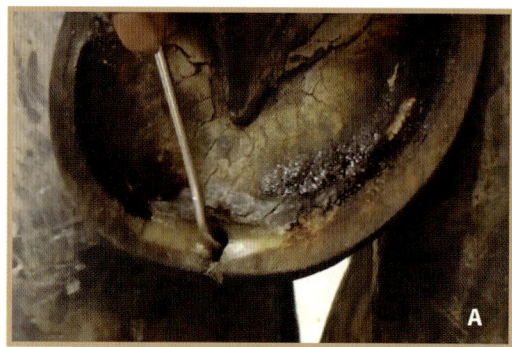

Hoof Taps

A farrier may recommend another shoeing alternative known as *DE HoofTaps* for horses with white line disease, wall separation, excessive wear, uneven growth, and cracks. These metal inserts are driven into the white line in the location(s) where hooves are experiencing excessive wear or breakage (figs. 3.15 A–C).

The HoofTaps are hammered into place after a proper trimming to extend the durability of a barefoot horse. The Taps can also be used to bridge across hoof cracks on barefoot hooves. New York farrier Doug Ehrmann patented the design and experimented with an anti-bacterial zinc-coated insert to help grow out hoof defects from within. Placed under a shoe, the taps help encourage healthy hoof growth. For some horses, taps can also be used instead of shoes on hind feet, and when transitioning to barefoot.

Hoof Boots

The concept of *hoof boots* predates the use of metal horseshoes and was driven by necessity. As horses became the mode of transportation and they traveled on varied terrain, hooves needed protection from excessive wear. There is evidence that leather or woven fibers called "hipposandals" protected hooves centuries ago.

Modern hoof boots follow the same principles and might be a substitution for normal horseshoes (fig. 3.16). Styles and materials vary among manufacturers, and not all styles will fit every horse. To get the right fit, trace your horse's hoof immediately after a trim to get an idea of the hoof size and shape. Sketching out the shape of the hoof this way makes it easy to see if the hoof is wider or longer, which will help you choose between the shapes available.

Your horse's feet will change over time, especially if the horse is transitioning from shod to barefoot. Frequently check the fit to make sure it is not causing pinching or chafing. If your horse is hard to fit, custom boots are an option.

Regardless of the style or reason for using a hoof boot, it should never be left on indefinitely. Hoof boots left on for long periods retain moisture and can cause damage to the coronary band and heel bulbs. Hoof boots also do not provide lateral or caudal support that is necessary for managing conformational defects. Some horses do very well when wearing hoof boots for trail riding. The extra thickness in the soles of boots that provide protection and cushioning, may inhibit sure-footedness at speed.

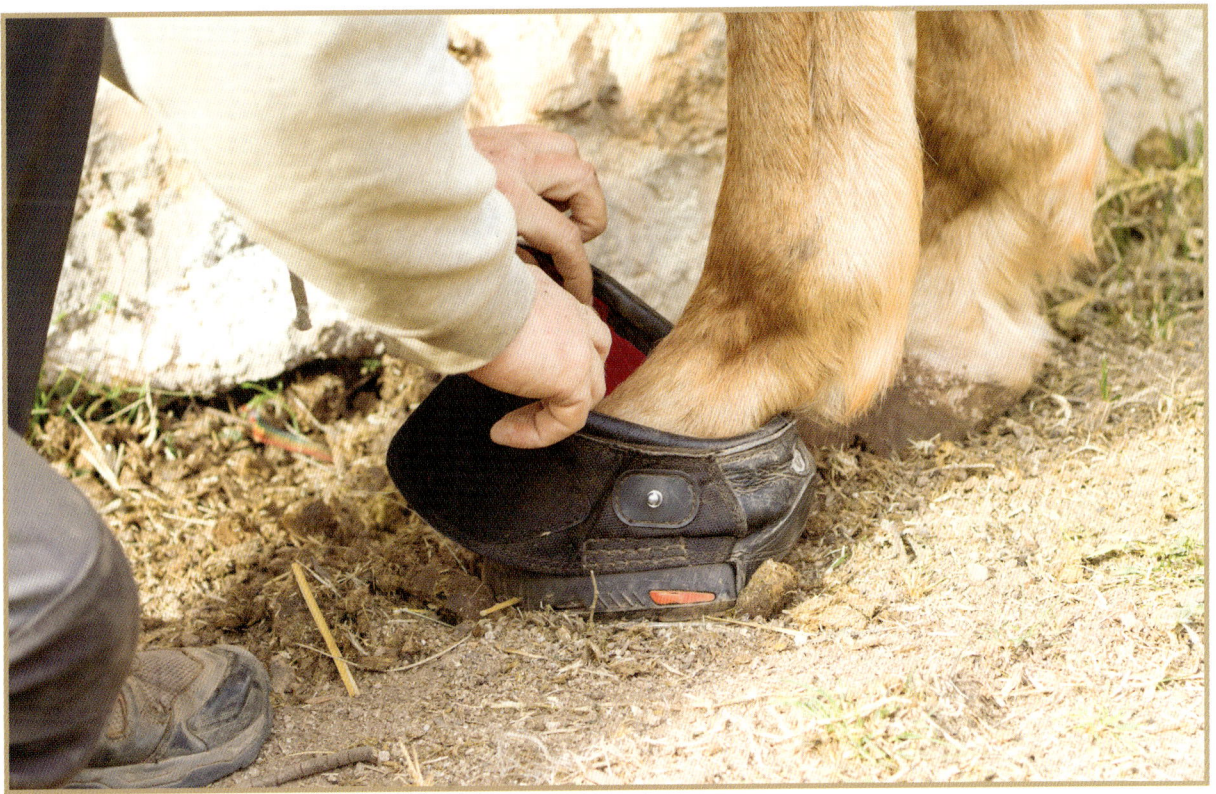

3.16 Removeable hoof boots can also protect a hoof on rough terrain.

FROM THE FORGE
A Modern Approach for Hard-to-Shoe Horses

Featuring Farrier Curtis Burns

In early 2002, Curtis Burns, an Accredited Professional Farrier™ (APF-I), struggled to find a solution to a hoof injury for a client's three-year-old filly. The foot was not responding to traditional shoeing approaches, and she was only completely comfortable barefoot. He wondered if he could create a shoe to imitate being barefoot while offering therapeutic support to encourage healing.

Looking for an alternative to metal, Curtis reached out to friend Joe Schrage who had experience using polyurethane, and he agreed. Curtis' home garage became the workshop for experimenting and building a set of plastic shoes, now known as Polyflex® Horseshoes. Through trial and error, he built a direct glue-on that enabled the filly to move out sound. The design allows the hoof capsule to function naturally, so the shoe mimics the functions of the foot, including expansion, contraction, and absorption of concussion. It is believed that these properties simulate the positive effects of being barefoot while providing the foot with protection and mechanical modifications. When properly applied, this combination of benefits encourages positive growth, increases overall hoof health, and mediates a myriad of hoof concerns.

Plastic shoes are more costly than metal shoes and are not a fit for every horse. High-value performance horses and specialty therapeutic cases make the best candidates. Horses that have had great success with these shoes include (but are not limited to) cases of white line disease, contracted or under-wrapped heels, quarter cracks, severe toe stretching and wall separations, thin/sensitive walls intolerant of nailing, club feet, challenging medial/lateral balance, navicular syndrome, and foals with limb deformities. Often applied as an interim shoe, the goal is to maintain or improve the horse's competitive performance to return him to a traditional shoeing option over time. For many horses, this offers the opportunity to remain competitive while simultaneously addressing hoof challenges.

Most horses in polyurethane shoes do not need the shoes long-term. However, many horses have spent an entire career in the shoes, and competed at the highest levels of competitive disciplines, including racing, hunter-jumper, dressage, polo, and Western performance (see fig. 3.12).

When considering what to apply, it is important to know that Polyflex shoes are available in a wide variety of styles for foals and adult horses. Each style is designed with the horse's natural hoof capsule shape and associated challenges in mind. These offer tailored fits for a wide variety of hoof shapes and needs, including narrow and wide toe patterns, hind patterns, two-degree wedge options, and a wide selection of sizes to choose from.

All direct glue-on shoes require a specific application process that requires attention to detail. The hoof preparation, application, and finishing must be completed in a specific order, within a particular time frame, and with quality.

The knowledge, time, and skill required of the farrier to properly apply these shoes is both an investment and a commitment for everyone involved. In the right hands and with proper application, the shoe offers different ways to address shoeing challenges in the modern horse.

CHAPTER 4

Horseshoes for Specific Uses and Sports

You wouldn't ride in a pair of high heels, and you wouldn't run a marathon in boots. Although there are fewer options for horses, when wearing shoes, they must be right for the job. Horses work on varied surfaces, from perfectly groomed artificial footing to abrasive desert sand, from slick pavement to natural grass. The "right" shoe is matched to the conditions (fig. 4.1).

Many farriers start with a pre-manufactured shoe and make modifications to fit the job. Specialized horseshoes provide a competitive advantage: increased performance and safety (figs. 4.2 A & B). Horseshoes may make the difference between winning or finishing lower in the placings. A properly selected and fitted shoe allows an individual horse to reach his performance potential.

A shoe alone is not the answer; proper hoof trimming and correct application are essential. Also, the best shoes in the world are not substitutes for training and fitness. Shoes do, however, provide substantial benefits when used correctly. As a refresher from earlier chapters, these are the advantages of using shoes:

4.1 Polo ponies wear shoes with added traction to avoid slipping on grassy fields.

4.2 Lite rim (top) and lite heeled, generic pattern (bottom). This combination—using the lite rim on the front and the lite heeled on the hind—is popular for polo ponies.

Protection: When hoof wear exceeds growth, shoes provide a durable interface between the bottom of the foot and the ground. A smooth leather, plastic, or metal hoof pad is sometimes used between the hoof and the shoe for shielding the sole from bruises caused by rocks and hard surfaces.

Limb support: When conformation faults reduce the hoof's surface area in a particular spot, metal shoes fill in where the hoof is lacking. Wider branches give medial or lateral support. Extended heels and egg bar shoes provide caudal support.

Traction: Traction is a necessity for the safety of horse and rider. Traction control options can range from adding a crease, known as "fullering," to a plain flat shoe, to screw-in calks. Horses need appropriate traction to propel themselves forward and execute turns at speed or make hard stops. Too much traction can cause injury, so it is essential to understand the discipline and riding surface.

Traction reduction: Reiners want shoes that glide across the ground so the horse can perform a sliding stop. Wider, light shoes known as *slide plates* allow the hind feet of these horses to glide on top of the footing. Dressage riders also strive for reducing traction so that the horse "floats" on top of working surfaces with a freer movement. Less traction is needed when working on synthetic surfaces.

Leverage reduction: Conformation or injury can compromise lower limb joints, and, in these cases, horses benefit from shoes that enhance breakover by adding rolled, rockered, or square toe modifications. Leverage reduction is often misunderstood and over requested simply because a winning horse was shod this way. Reducing leverage on a horse that doesn't need it can hinder performance.

Gait correction: A horse with abnormal conformation can simply be a sloppy mover, or he might hurt himself when one leg strikes another. Asymmetrical shoes can correct this by adding weight or length on one side of the shoe to straighten out a wobbly foot flight. In these situations, farriers use either side weight shoes or shoes with the extensions we've already discussed called *trailers* (see p. 39).

Horseshoes by Discipline

The proper footwear can transform an average performer into an excellent mover. That's why show hunters and stadium jumpers who are both ridden in English tack wear significantly different shoes. Similarly, reining and Western pleasure horses might both wear Western gear, but each discipline requires specialized shoes.

Disciplines fall into several broad categories. Shoeing for each requires an intimate knowledge of the sport, so many farriers specialize. Concentrating on one of these main groups of performance horses allows a farrier to develop an intimate knowledge of the event and the horses within the sport. Here's a broad look at how farriers group horses based on work type and breed.

4.3 Gaited horses entered in shows typically wear weighted shoes that exaggerate their natural gaits.

Endurance: Competitive long-distance horses are often Arabians, though many breeds are well represented. The varied terrain requires horseshoes that are durable and allow free movement.

Gaited: Known for a natural four-beat gait, gaited horses move each leg separately from the others. Examples include Tennessee Walking Horses, American Saddlebreds, Icelandic Horses, and Paso Finos (fig. 4.3).

Racing: Thoroughbreds, Standardbreds, and some American Quarter Horses share a common goal—speed—but the shoes each wear are not the same. Even within harness racing, pacers and trotters are shod

4.4 Working horses wear wider-webbed shoes to support the larger hoof structure, but shoe style is customized based on the job.

differently. On most racetracks, the term "blacksmith" is still used to refer to anyone who shoes horses there as a carryover from when all racing shoes were handmade. Today, manufactured shoes are standard, and farriers on the track may also be called "platers."

Sport horse: This group includes horses entered in stadium jumping, dressage, and eventing competitions. Warmbloods, Thoroughbreds, and related crosses are the most common mounts in these events. Even within the same sport, horses wear different shoes—heavier-boned horses need wider shoes than finer-boned Thoroughbred types.

Western performance: Stock breeds like the Quarter Horse, Paint, and Appaloosa are most common in Western performance disciplines. Competitions range from cattle work to pleasure, jumping, and driving, which

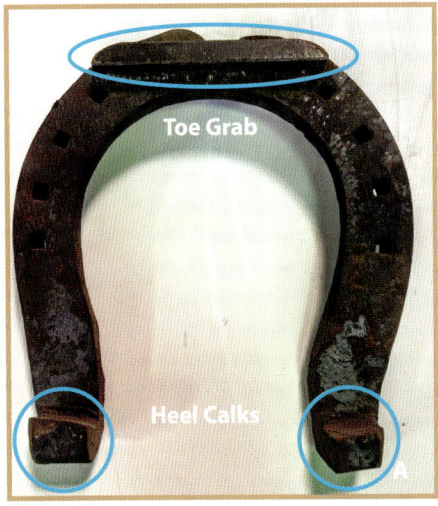 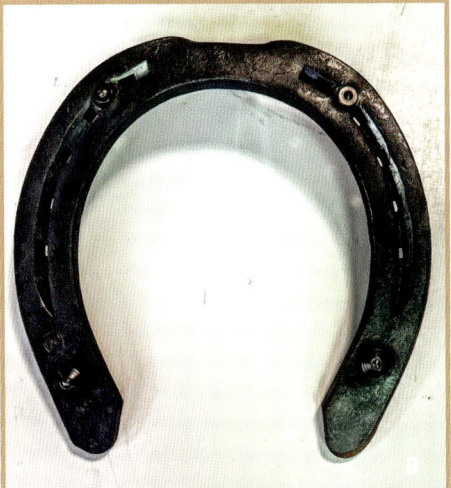 

means shoe selection is based on the event as much as the breed.

Working horses: Draft horses like Percherons, Shires, Clydesdales, and Belgians require larger, wider-webbed shoes to support a denser bone structure (fig. 4.4). While each of these breeds is similar in having a larger stature than other horse breeds, the work can be dramatically different. A horse used in the fields has different needs from those used in the show ring, on paved roads, or in pulling competitions (figs. 4.5 A–C).

Rules and Regulations

Farriers have much to consider beyond the technicalities of shoeing, breed, and discipline. Some organizations and associations have specific rules on the horseshoe type, weight, and toe length. The rules specify what is allowed or forbidden from the competition. For example, the United States Equestrian Federation (USEF) has developed extensive guidelines

4.5 A–C Draft horses may be similarly built but the type of work the horse performs decides which shoes he will wear. Work horses wear a heavy front shoe with a toe grab and heel calks (A). Carriage-style draft horses wear a light horseshoe with drive-in studs to provide traction (B). An older style known as a "giant grip" horseshoe was manufactured in the late 1880s and early 1900s (C). These high-quality, factory-made shoes were mostly used for street-driven horses and had removable calks.

for shoes. Members participating in any approved USEF event must follow these rules. Because rules can change over time, the precise measurements and weights are not included here, and it is recommended to review the most current rulebook.

Here are some examples of breeds and disciplines that follow USEF policies:

American Saddlebreds: Known for having a high-stepping, animated gait, these horses wear heavier, toe-weighted horseshoes and "pad stacks" to support and encourage this movement. While these shoes are

4.6 Shoes support the floating look that dressage judges score in a competition.

4.7 An example of a wide-web shoe used for Warmblood-type horses, which often compete in dressage. On the left is a right-hind pattern, and on the right is a left-front pattern.

necessary to achieve the flowing gait, USEF rules specify weight and size to limit the chance of strain on the horse's legs and joints.

Arabians: A breed show competitor can also show her horse with toe-weighted shoes to enhance the horse's gait if the guidelines are followed for size and weight. Generally, Arabians wear basic shoes that are appropriate for the situation and follow similar shoeing protocols for the discipline of choice—for example, a reiner wears slide plates.

Morgans: Another breed judged on leg action. Farriers use toe-weighted horseshoes and pad combinations that fall within the USEF rules to enhance the horse's movement. The width of the shoe and toe length must meet these guidelines. Outside the show arena, many Morgan horses wear basic horseshoes.

Dressage: While many breeds of horses are used for dressage, riders in the discipline share a common goal—to prioritize collection and movement. On any horse, wider shoes provide more support to help a horse stay on top of the footing to achieve the desired "floating" look (fig. 4.6). However, shoes must meet specific measurements, according to USEF rules (fig. 4.7).

Eventing: Again, a wide range of breeds are used in this sport. The horses compete on changing surfaces across the three different phases of competition—dressage, stadium jumping, and cross-country jumping. As a result, a horse needs variable traction levels, and there isn't time to pull and reset shoes in between each phase (fig. 4.8). For example, more traction is needed on the cross-country course, while less is required in jumping, and no traction in dressage. Wide-web rim shoes, or flat shoes and clips, are commonly used on these horses. Farriers drill threaded holes into the shoes for screw-in calks so the shoe can serve multiple purposes. Temporary plugs keep debris from clogging the holes. Before each phase, the studs are added or removed in a matter of minutes. But the size and weight of the shoe and any modifications must still fall within USEF guidelines.

Outside USEF Jurisdiction

Not all breeds and disciplines follow USEF rules. Here is a look at the common shoes a farrier uses in these disciplines.

Barrel racers have no restrictions on shoe choice. Lightweight aluminum or steel rim shoes are most used on the front hooves, while the hind feet have basic shoes (fig. 4.9).

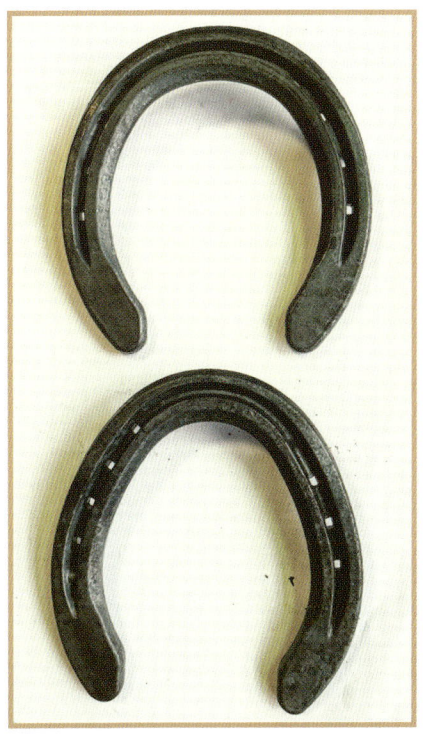

4.8 This set of eventer front and hind are an example of wide-rim shoes that feature solid heels, which provide the option for drilling holes and tapping for threaded studs.

4.9 Know the shoeing rules for the discipline you are showing in. Some organizations have detailed specifications where others do not.

Cutting horse competitions do not have rules for shoes. These horses wear light rim shoes that make it possible to perform the quick, cat-like movements needed to work a cow.

Draft horses include several breeds and engage in multiple activities. Shoe selection is based on the type of work. For example, those used for logging and agricultural work need traction, so the shoes have calks. In the show ring, drafts wear wider, heavier, fuller-fitting shoes to enhance hoof appearance and gait in the hitch and halter classes. Pulling contest draft horses wear shoes with large toe grabs and heel calks for maximum gripping needed to move heavy loads.

Endurance and competitive trail horses work on a wide range of terrain that can change from hard roads to sand, mud, or mountainous footing. In these events,

4.10 Reining horses need hind shoes that reduce traction and resistance to perform the iconic sliding stop.

4.11 Sliding plates for reining horses. Here are two different versions. The shoe on the right is the more common version; the left shoe has a "rudder" to keep the foot straight during the slide.

shoe selection is also based on farrier and owner preference. Wide-web rim shoes are a popular option because the style offers traction, support, and protection. Rockered or rolled toes are also common because the change encourages a smooth gait over many miles. Polyurethane, glue-on, and removable hoof boots are also used.

Fox hunters prioritize safety, so traction is crucial to shoe selection. Concave, wide-rim shoes that are durable are most popular among working field hunters. Screw-in calks or Borium are used to avoid slipping.

Polo has its own rules set by the United States Polo Association (USPA). Professional players run at racehorse speeds and need traction to make immediate direction changes. The USPA has some of the most specific guidelines to keep the high-speed game safe for horses and riders. USPA Rule 6a specifies that "shoes with an outer rim, toe grip, screws, or frost nails are not allowed. Dull heel calks are allowed on hind shoes only. The calks can either be fixed or removable (screw-in) and should be dull, without sharp edges, and no greater than one inch from the sole surface of the shoe to the ground surface."

The polo plate has a high inner rim specifically developed for the game and is used on the front feet. The hind feet are often shod with dull factory-made heel calks for traction on slippery grass.

Reining horses, similar to dressage horses, need less traction (fig. 4.10). Many of these horses are shod with plain shoes in the front and wear slide plates on the hind necessary for performing the signature sliding stop. These shoes are typically one-quarter inch thick and at least one inch wide (fig. 4.11).

Standardbred racehorses wear different shoes depending on how they are used. A combination of aluminum and steel horseshoes is the go-to choice based on the horse's leg action. Both trotters and pacers have an

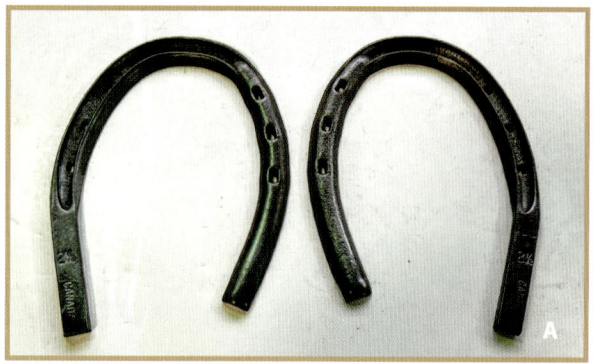

4.12 A & B A pair of hind half-round, half-swedge Standardbred shoes used commonly by a pacer are shown in Photo A. This shoe design is used to prevent "cross-firing" interference when racing at high speeds. A full-swedge horseshoe, as shown in Photo B, may be used on the front hooves of a Standardbred racehorse.

increased possibility for limb interference. Modifications like trailers and square toes can help reduce this problem (figs. 4.12 A & B).

Thoroughbred racehorses wear the lightest of all horseshoes. Every ounce matters in horse racing. Shoes are paired to the track conditions and the horse's needs. Some include small toe grabs to provide extra traction (fig. 4.13).

Tennessee Walking Horses are strong and durable with a smooth gait. These horses typically have solid feet with thick hoof walls and do not experience as many hoof conditions as other breeds with thinner-walled hooves.

4.13 A front (top) and hind (bottom) pattern of typical aluminum Thoroughbred racing plates. Note the small steel toe grabs in the front of these shoes that provide grip. Race plates come in several styles and toe grab heights, which are regulated by state racing commissions.

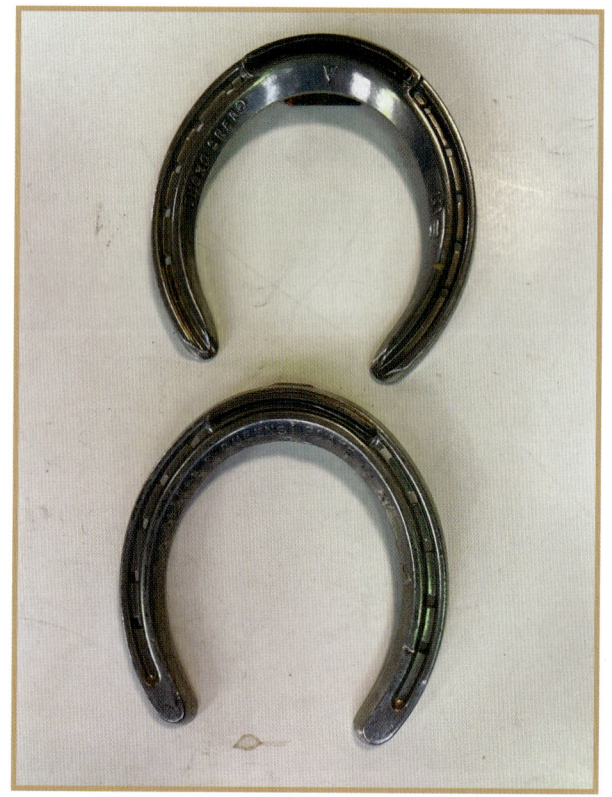

This breed falls into two categories: trail/pleasure horses and show horses. Originally bred to provide smooth transportation for plantation owners crossing vast lands, the sturdy horses are well suited to trail riding. In these scenarios, farriers use shoes with a wider web to accommodate these sturdy feet and provide an appropriate traction for trail conditions. In the show ring, Tennessee Walking horses wear heavy shoe/pad packages to accentuate the horse's gait. The extreme action is known as the "Big Lick," a gait that is artificially created. In extreme cases, the shoeing and trimming practices are abusive. For example, a hoof is trimmed nearly to the quick, and a tight shoe is nailed to the hoof. The pressure the horse experiences encourages the accentuated leg movement. In other situations, caustic chemicals are rubbed onto the legs and a wrap is applied so it penetrates the skin. The resulting pain forces the horse to lift his leg in a high-stepping motion. Collectively known as "soring," these practices have been outlawed by Congress since the 1970s, but the practice continues today and often evades inspectors.

Shoeing for Performance

You know from personal experience that you can hike farther, dance longer, or ride more comfortably with the right shoes. And just as in human shoes, horseshoes designed with specific features are customized to the discipline. Bottom line: remember that each horse is an individual and that just because a style of shoeing works for one champion does not mean every horse in similar work should be shod the same way (fig. 4.14).

4.14 Jumpers tend to wear shoes with clips on them to counteract the shear forces of taking off and landing a fence.

FROM THE FORGE
What Hoofprints Tell Us

Featuring Farrier Dave Farley

Ohio farrier Dave Farley specializes in shoeing A-circuit show jumpers and hunters. The International Horseshoeing Hall of Fame member has honed his craft to keep his clients' horses sounder and competing longer. Here he shares the method behind his shoeing decisions based on observations about different footing.

"I love to watch the horses that I shoe work in their environment. Through simple observations I've made studying horses in motion, I have seen how they move at speed with confidence and ability after a shoeing. It is quite an amazing comparison," he says.

Humans are bipeds, walking and balancing on two limbs. When in motion, people usually have one foot on the ground and can quickly sense if they are on an icy surface. When that happens, people adjust by wearing footwear with a deep tread that provides traction to keep them upright. More grip isn't always better—too much makes the feet grab the ground and can lead to stumbling.

Different footings are developed to provide a more consistent, safe surface that is easier to maintain and retain moisture longer to compensate for weather impacts on dirt and grass. The mix of materials used is important to shoe selection. Most horses competing at high-level English-style competitions work on synthetic footing, whereas Western horses compete on a sand/clay/loam mix. Synthetic surfaces are dramatically different from dirt or grass. In a properly constructed arena with synthetic footing, the space drains quickly after a hard rain. If the weather is dry, the arena requires less water, hence, less maintenance and consistent conditions, especially for traction.

Observe your horse's hoofprints in various footings to visualize the impact of varied surfaces. Compare the hoofprints left in the dirt, grass, and a synthetic footing. The hoof impressions will not look the same, even when moisture conditions are similar.

Dirt and grass footing materials are hard on bones and joints, which may cause injury to these tissues during the stride's impact (landing) phase. The loading phase is the point in time when the soft tendon and ligament tissues of the horse's leg are more prone to injury.

When the foot strikes the ground at speed (landing), a certain amount of slide occurs in dirt or grass. As the hoof transitions into a weight-bearing (loading) mode, an imprint of the back portion of the foot, but not the front, can be seen. Normal slippage is the cause. Horses working in a synthetic footing ring leave a perfect imprint of the foot without any sliding at the toe.

How does synthetic footing add to a horse's traction? Think of it as a pencil eraser. Erasing pencil marks from paper creates friction. Synthetic footing is like an oversized eraser. It is sticky—as the horse's foot strikes the ground it stops quickly and smoothly. Synthetic footing combined with too much traction may cause a horse to stumble or injure the stay apparatus of the equine limb. I have seen a huge increase in suspensory injuries since synthetic footing has been developed and used. Using shoes with less traction and easier breakover through rolled toes on synthetic footing benefits the horse's ability to function better and stay sounder.

So, study the hoofprints your horse leaves behind on different surfaces. Think about how the horse's stride felt on a flat surface compared to when your horse stumbles or slips. Changing the amount of traction on a shoe can help, but sometimes less is more. Most importantly, the shoe and traction choices must be compatible with the footing that the horse is working on.

CHAPTER 5

Hot Shoeing vs. Cold Shoeing

You've likely heard (or used) the terms "blacksmith" and "farrier" interchangeably, depending upon locations around the country, but there are distinct differences between the two professions. Both tradesmen need an anvil and tools to shape an item—be it a horseshoe, a gate latch, or a nail (fig. 5.1). However, each demands specialized skills related to the individual's purpose for metalworking.

A *blacksmith* is a tradesperson who uses tools and heat to bend, cut, and shape metal. Often, he uses iron and steel to make hinges, railings, tools, sculptures, equipment, and more. (You might be familiar with the popular television show *Forged in Fire*, which spotlights skilled craftsmen who forge weapons from raw pieces of steel.) The word "blacksmith" came into use because iron is called "black metal," hence, working with this material became known as "blacksmithing."

In the horse industry, people use the terms "farriers" and "blacksmiths" (platers for racehorses) and even "horseshoers" to describe hoof-care professionals. The Merriam-Webster dictionary defines farriers as "blacksmiths who specialize in shoeing horses, a skill that requires not only the ability to shape and fit horseshoes, but also the

5.1 Blacksmiths also work in the forge to bend and shape metal but may or may not have the expertise to shoe horses.

5.2 Horseshoers (farriers) use blacksmithing skills, but have a deep understanding of horse conformation, anatomy, care, and more.

Around this time, iron replaced leather and bronze as horseshoe materials. Modern horseshoe steel is made of iron and mixed with a small amount of carbon, which makes the metal more durable.

The word "farrier" first appeared in English (as *ferrour*) and was used to describe a person who shod horses and provided veterinary care. The dictionary entry explains that middle English *ferrour* is derived from Anglo-French *ferrour* (a blacksmith who shoes horses), a noun derived from the verb *ferrer* (to shoe horses). These Anglo-French words can be traced back to Latin *ferrum*, meaning "iron."

ability to clean, trim, and shape a horse's hooves." Farriers need blacksmithing skills to care for horses, while blacksmiths may never need to learn about or be around horses (figs. 5.2 & 5.3).

The first known reference to the word "farrier" dates back to the fifteenth century, according to the dictionary.

5.3 A glimpse into a blacksmith shop in the 1800s.

Hot-Fit Basics

A forge was once a necessity. Before the Industrial Revolution, every single horseshoe (and nail) was made by hand. The process began with a piece of raw steel placed into a coal-burning furnace to soften the material. Once it was malleable, the farrier hammered straight bar steel into the proper shape atop an anvil.

The temperature inside a forge reaches between 2,150 and 2,375 degrees Fahrenheit. At high temperatures, the metal becomes more pliable, requiring less exertion to make changes to it (fig. 5.4). Too much heat burns the metal, forcing the farrier to start over.

Since the heat was a necessity for making horseshoes in the early days, farriers "hot fit" every shoe. That means that before nailing on a shoe, a farrier first placed a heated shoe on each hoof. This seared the shoe path into the hoof and helped him confirm the shoe was an accurate shape and size. While fewer farriers today start from scratch with bar stock, those who hot shoe follow the same process to manipulate pre-manufactured shoes to shape and fit the shoe to the horse's foot.

Before portable gas forges were available, a horse owner took her horse to a blacksmith shop for "service," much like you take your car to a mechanic for an oil change or tire rotation. Some farriers still embrace the "haul-in, haul-out" model and operate a forge and shop at home where owners travel for a trim and shoeing. However, most farriers today are mobile, and those who hot fit shoes have small gas forges in the back of the truck (figs. 5.5 A & B).

5.4 There is a fine line between heating the metal enough to make it malleable and overheating it to the point it melts.

5.5 A Most farriers have a shop set up in the back of the truck and travel from barn to barn to see clients.

5: HOT SHOEING VS. COLD SHOEING | 75

5.5 B Some farriers prefer to have a facility where clients haul horses in just like in years gone by. This is an inside look at the Cornell University Farrier Shop.

Cold-Fit Basics

Modern manufactured horseshoes can be shaped to fit a horse's hoof without heat in a process called "cold-fitting" or "cold-shaping" (fig. 5.6). The farrier makes any adjustments to an "off-the-shelf" shoe with the force of hammering it on an anvil.

Even though shoes can be cold-fit, as the shoe increases in width, weight, and thickness, it becomes difficult, even impossible, for farriers to get it precise. For this reason, larger breeds like Warmbloods, drafts, and draft crosses are usually always hot-shod.

Aluminum is a softer material than steel, making it malleable without heat unless a heavier shoe style is needed. This metal is easier to melt, does not glow when heated for shaping, so it is easy to ruin an aluminum shoe by overheating it.

Glue-on shoes are applied without heat; however, farriers use a small propane torch to remove moisture from the hoof before applying the adhesive.

The quality of manufactured shoes has given farriers a choice between fitting shoes with or without the help of fire. Both hot and cold shoeing are effective, safe methods for providing regular hoof care. It is the farrier's preference and training that determines which approach he will use. Here's a closer look at the hot-fitting process and the reasons a farrier chooses one over the other.

Why Hot-Fit Shoes?

What exactly does it mean to "hot fit" a shoe?

A hot fit occurs when the farrier removes a shoe from the forge and briefly places it directly onto the

5.6 Today's manufactured shoes make it possible for a farrier to shape and bend a shoe without heat.

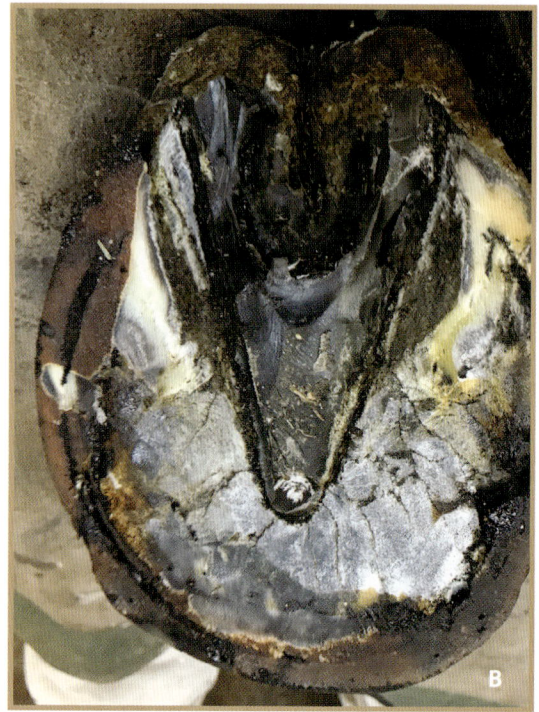

5.7 Hot-shoeing is easy to identify by the billowing of smoke that is created when the heated metal makes contact with a hoof.

5.8 A & B Farriers hot fit shoes to confirm that the trim is correct and that the surface area of the hoof is level (A). The hot shoe leaves a dark imprint on the hoof to create a visual guide for any last-minute alterations before nailing the shoe in to place (B).

horse's hoof. It's often also called "hot-fitting," "hot-shoeing," or "hot-setting." If you've ever seen a "hot-shoeing," you'll likely remember the smell and smoke as the heated metal makes contact with the hoof (fig. 5.7). Earn bonus points with your farrier by providing a well-ventilated area and fan to diffuse the smoke while he is working.

It may seem like it would be painful to place a hot piece of metal against a horse's foot. Scientific studies have shown that the amount of heat transfer to sensitive hoof structures shows no negative side effects when done properly. Experienced farriers leave a bit of extra hoof wall to accept the "burn" as a precaution.

Precision is the biggest benefit of hot shoeing. The heated metal is more flexible, allowing farriers to make the slightest changes (figs. 5.8 A & B). By placing a hot shoe on the hoof, the farrier can easily see any high spots in the hoof wall and identify adjustments that may be needed before nailing on the shoe. Rocker toe shoes must be hot fit so that the modified toe seamlessly meets the hoof wall, reducing the potential for gaps between the shoe and the horse's hoof. The heat from a hot shoe also seals the horn tubules of the hoof wall, preventing excessive moisture loss (fig. 5.9). The high temperature kills any fungi and bacteria present, limiting the chances for organisms to invade the hoof and create an infection.

Clips are another reason farriers hot fit shoes. Burning the base of the clip into the hoof ensures a tight, secure fit. Essentially, clips "lock" the shoe to the hoof.

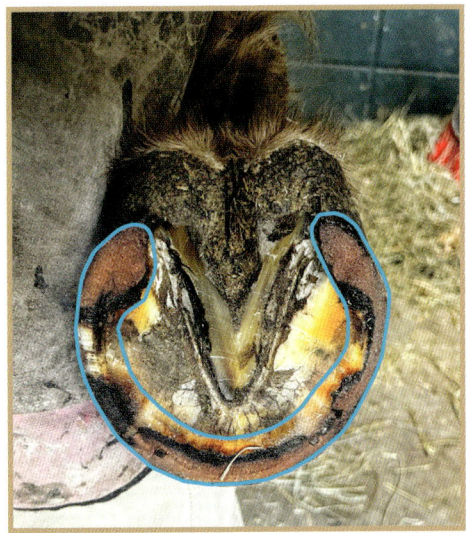

5.9 The heat from a hot fit shoe seals off any openings in the hoof to prevent environmental bacteria from migrating into the foot, thus reducing the risk of an infection. The slightly orange/brown shoe-shaped pattern is the imprint left by the hot shoe touching the hoof material.

Using a "Hot Plate"

Skilled farriers use the fundamentals of shoe fitting to create innovative solutions to client situations. For example, show horses that transition between northern climates and humid South Florida weather are prone to moisture imbalances in the hoof. A sudden and extreme increase in moisture weakens hooves.

Many horses showing on the Florida hunter-jumper circuit wear aluminum shoes. The metal is one-third the weight of steel and encourages freer movement desired in these horses. However, aluminum cannot be heated to high temperatures like steel can be for the benefits of hot-fitting.

Farriers working on these horses designed a "hot plate" made of steel for hot-fitting when using aluminum shoes. Aluminum cannot be heated to an adequate temperature to properly hot fit without melting it. Horses in this wetter climate benefit from hot-fitting steel shoes to kill fungi and bacteria and seal off horn tubules. The "hot plate" is heated to the proper temperature in the gas forge, then briefly applied to the bottom of the hoof after trimming, similarly to hot-fitting a steel horseshoe. That provides a method of hot-fitting to dry and tighten the hoof wall when using aluminum shoes.

5.10 Some horses need time to adjust to the noise and smell of hot shoeing.

Horseshoeing is hard work. Joint pain is common after a lifetime of work bending beneath horses and hammering metal into shape. Hot shoeing actually reduces wear and tear on the farrier's body, specifically on the wrist and elbow, since a more flexible metal requires less human energy and less bone-jarring shock to properly shape a shoe.

Disadvantages of Hot-Fitting

To inexperienced handlers (and horses), the pungent smell associated with hot-shoeing can be unpleasant. If you think it's bad, consider that the farrier is the closest to those acrid fumes; as already mentioned, a fan can be useful to reduce this exposure. (Unless the farrier has underlying lung problems, the hoof smoke, although unpleasant, has no long-term health impacts.)

Some horses can be downright afraid of the sizzle of hot metal meeting the hoof and the resulting billowing smoke (fig. 5.10). A horse that continues to be fearful, even after additional handling is better off with cold-fit shoes—it is not worth risking injury to the horse, handler, or farrier.

Another drawback is that an improperly handled hot shoe can create a dangerous situation. If a horse moves suddenly, he could knock the shoe out of the fitting tongs, resulting in painful burns to the farrier's arms or legs.

Horses with thin walls and soles, such as young horses, horses trimmed too short, or those with some hoof conditions, can be injured when the hot-shoeing process is used. The hoof wall acts as an insulator to easily tolerate heat. Generally, the thicker the sole and hoof wall, the less likely any injury will occur. Typically, shoes are around 1,000 degrees Fahrenheit and glow at a red-hot, incandescent color. Farriers know how much heat a horse's feet can take and address each horse based on his individual needs (fig. 5.11).

Another drawback to consider is the barn's fire risk when combustible items are too close to the farrier's forge. Be aware of fire hazards and store gas cans or flammable chemicals out of the shoeing area. Have a fire extinguisher accessible inside the barn. The good news is that fires resulting from farrier work are rare. If the work area increases any of these risks, it is not wise to proceed.

Although hydraulic shaping machines have been developed to shape horseshoes, the forge and anvil remain the predominant tools of the trade. As technology continues to evolve, portable magnetic induction heating devices may one day replace the propane forge, which replaced the original coal-fired forge. And as we've already talked about, it is even possible to use a 3D printer to create a carbon/nylon fiber shoe, which cannot be done with steel or aluminum.

Training Horses for Hot-Fitting

Over time most horses come to accept the sights, sounds, and smells of a hot-fitting. You can help a young or new horse become comfortable with the process. Often, simply having a buddy horse nearby, so the horse quickly sees that there is no reason to be alarmed, is enough. Choosing a handler the horse knows and trusts also builds confidence (fig. 5.12).

Some farriers shorten the amount of time a hot shoe touches the hoof, which cuts down on the noise and smell. He may place a hot shoe on the hoof momentarily for fit, remove it and try again, instead of creating a

5.11 Farriers are trained to recognize a healthy hoof that can tolerate a hot fitting from a hoof as opposed to one with hoof walls that are too thin.

5.12 The handler's skills and comfort level around horses play an important role in a successful shoeing visit.

lot of smoke. A fan that blows the smoke away from the horse's front end can also be helpful.

Historically, horses have been desensitized for battle and other work, far more intense than hot-fitting horseshoes, so introducing a horse to hot-shoeing is a part of a larger training program. Spending time developing ground manners in all aspects of handling contributes to a horse that is more willing and cooperative for the farrier.

Going without Heat

Thousands of horseshoes are fit properly without heat. It takes more skill with a rasp to level the bottom of the hoof without hot-fitting, which makes imperfections more easily visible. But for some farriers and horses, cold-shoeing is the best choice.

Some horses simply will not tolerate the heat of placing a hot shoe on the hoof. The smell and smoke

The Influence of WWII

World War II marked a significant turning point in the horse industry—one that had lasting effects on the farrier industry. The United States Cavalry traded in four-legged horsepower for mechanized transportation, and gas-powered vehicles replaced buggies and carts, significantly reducing the size of the horse-owning population. During this time, metal was precious to the war effort. Train cars brimming with anvils,

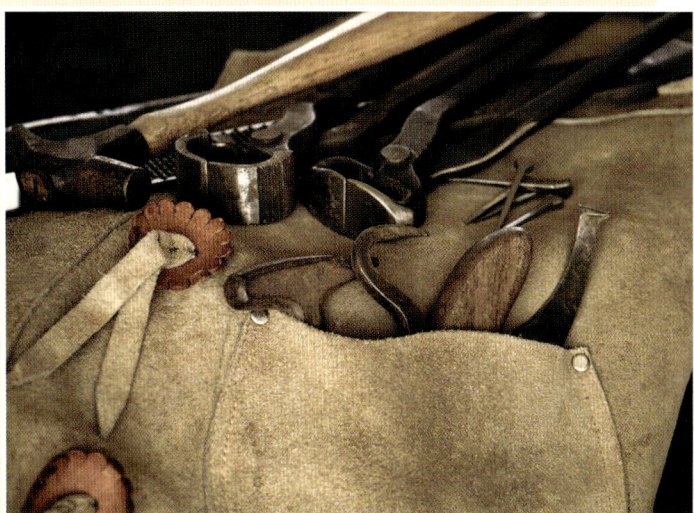

5.13 The basic tools of the trade have remained similar for decades with manufacturers making improvements over time based on farrier feedback. The most common items include a hoof pick, hoof knife, shoe pull offs, creased nail pullers, and a hammer to nail shoes into place.

5.14 Common farriery tools were in short supply after WWII until manufacturers could catch up with the increasing demand among baby boomers for recreational horses.

tools, and horseshoes were shipped, melted, and reused as war supplies (fig. 5.13).

After the war, baby boomers gave rise to a new type of horse industry—one that was focused on owning recreational and competitive partners rather than working animals. The sudden resurgence in horse ownership was met with a shortage of farriers and quality horseshoes.

The few experienced farriers still working after the war carried portable coal forges in their truck and continued hot-fitting shoes, a skill they used to differentiate themselves from other horseshoers. Modern farriers have access to abundant supplies and tools though the number of farriers available to shoe is still in short supply (fig. 5.14).

5.15 Just because horseshoes are premanufactured doesn't mean all models are the same. This rack of horseshoes at the Cornell Farrier School includes models used for draft horses, racehorses and everything in between.

unsettle them to the point it becomes unsafe for all involved. Horses with certain hoof conditions may also be unable to be hot shod. For example, open hoof wounds are sensitive to heat while checking the fit.

Cold-fitting is harder on the farrier's body—it takes effort and energy to shape the unyielding metal, but it can be faster for shoes that do not need significant adjustments. Some farriers choose to cold shoe despite the extra effort required because pre-made shoes are such high quality (fig. 5.15). But you might also see a farrier heat a pre-made shoe to make the metal more malleable. Horses with solid, healthy feet may not need extensive shaping. Another reason is that it can be cumbersome to travel and use a portable forge, which requires time to get up to temperature before use.

Regardless of which method or combination of approaches is used to shoe a horse, the end result is what matters. The horse is always the final judge of a farrier's work. One hundred years ago, hot-shoeing was a necessity. When shoeing the modern horse, new methods and shoes are being developed that do not require heat to produce a satisfactory result.

CHAPTER 6

How Conformation Determines Soundness and Performance

When it comes to buying property, all you hear is "location, location, location." When horse shopping all you should *listen to* is "conformation, conformation, conformation." Eye appeal, bloodlines, and color dominate the conversation, but how a horse is put together is more important to predict his future performance than any other criteria.

A horse's build is often discussed in terms of how it enables him to succeed in a given discipline. For example, does the horse have a shoulder tying in too low so that he cannot elevate his front end in quick turns? Can he gather his hindquarters to perform a piaffe?

Just as a house needs a sturdy foundation, a working horse needs a correct base. That starts at the bottom of the horse at his hooves and legs. Deciding which horse to buy or how he must be trimmed or shod always starts with conformation (fig. 6.1).

Now, let us get to the actual details.

Where Do Conformation Defects Start?

Conformation starts in the breeding shed. Focusing on single traits like coat color, competition accomplishments, or show-ring fads emphasizes a

6.1 This symmetrical front foot shod with a racing plate shows perfect medio-lateral and anterior-posterior balance.

"desired look" over functionality. Line-breeding limits genetic diversity, which can bring out hidden conformation defects in subsequent generations. An unsound horse often becomes breeding stock because he can't perform. Unfortunately, he is likely to produce unsound offspring with the same conformation that predisposed him to lameness or underperformance.

Think of having a basic understanding of equine conformation as being similar to having a crystal ball—it offers a chance at predicting the future. For example, a large horse with small hooves is predisposed to lameness issues more than a horse with appropriate-sized hooves.

The good news is that many conformation abnormalities are manageable through hoof care. Regardless of the discipline or work a horse does, his body structures follow the basic laws of physics: force always equals mass times acceleration. Without reasonably correct conformation, the abnormal forces produced during performance work will cause lameness in predictable ways.

Farriers and veterinarians are in the business of managing the results of unsuitable conformation to enable horses to keep working. When this skilled assistance contributes to a successful career there is a tendency to worry less about conformational defects, especially when the horse does well competitively.

The real trouble begins when a talented performer, with undesirable conformation, is selected as a breeding prospect. By selecting horses for breeding based solely on performance, the resulting cross usually reproduces the same defects.

In the upcoming chapter about foals (see p. 122), there is an explanation of conformation defects of these young horses. This is the only time defects can be corrected, either with trimming, shoeing, or surgery. Flaws in the mature horse can only be managed, not reversed, with detailed trimming and horseshoe modifications.

The visible features in a horse's body characteristics, like size, color, and conformation, are *phenotypes*, whereas the *genotype* is a horse's genetic constitution. When the phenotype is altered with interventions like corrective shoeing or surgery, the genotype does not change. So, when foals with crooked legs have been corrected in these ways, they still have the predisposition to reproduce future offspring with the same defects.

In worst-case scenarios, a horse is only pasture-sound. In less severe cases, the horse may not be performing to his fullest potential. As the horse ages, naturally weaker areas are susceptible to tendon and ligament injuries, and arthritis. Specialized shoeing and additional veterinary treatments may be necessary, both of which can significantly increase the cost of ownership—all as a result of not considering conformation in the breeding or selection process.

The tricky part is that there is no "perfect" horse. If you waited for a horse with ideal conformation, you will have an empty stable. It's unrealistic to think you will find a horse without some conformational aspect that could be improved. That being said, learning the basics of equine conformation remains a guide to good buying and breeding decisions.

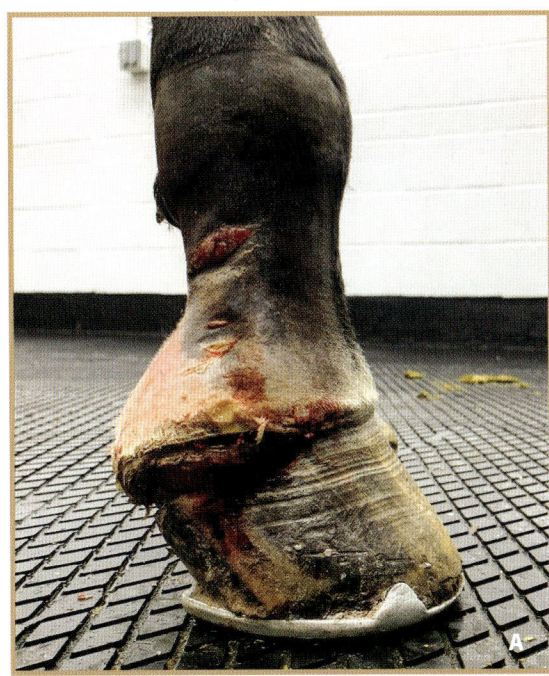
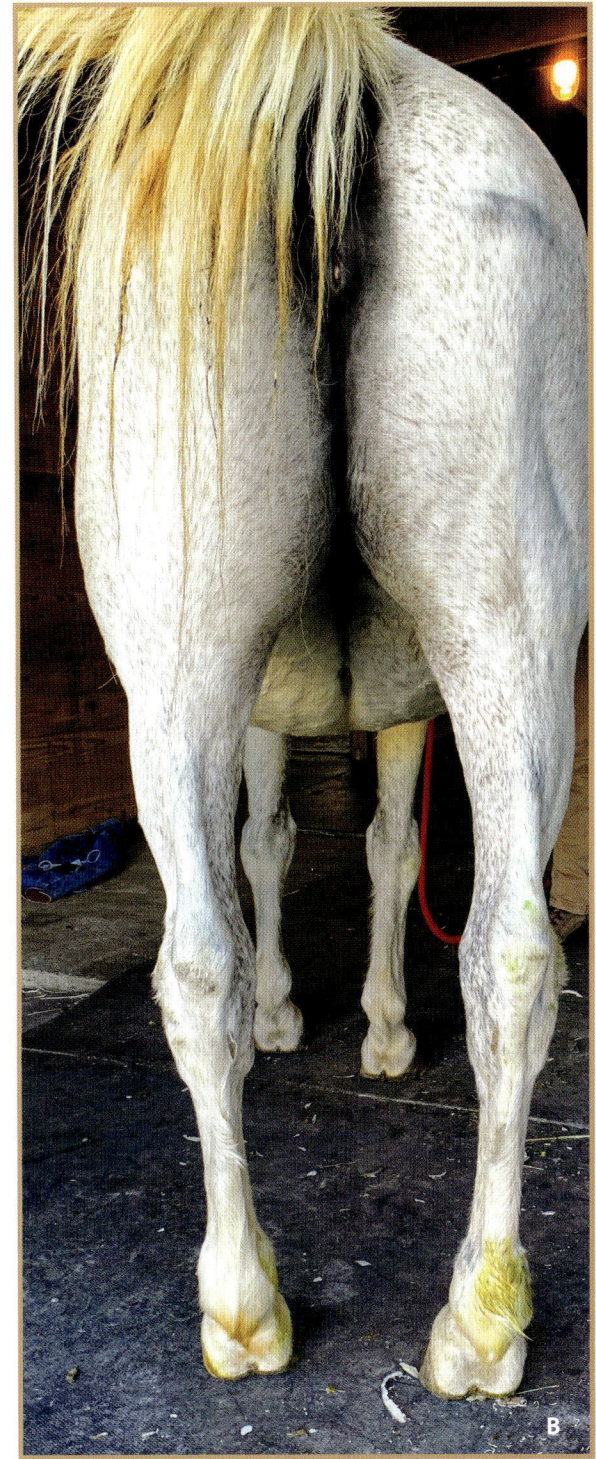

6.2 A & B In Photo A we see how a severely toed-in stance created an excess of pressure on the coronary band that split the coronary band away from the hoof. This separation is painful and at risk for infection. The bow-legged hind end in Photo B also has a right hock pointing straight backward. This conformation is impossible to keep sound.

Defining the Level of Conformational Issues

Understanding the severity of the defect and management options can be used to support a decision to buy or walk away from a horse (figs. 6.2 A & B). For this reason, it's helpful to classify conformational defects as *mild, moderate,* or *severe.*

Mild defects are quite common and are not easily recognized. Some can even be considered "normal" when they fall within certain limits. For example, horses

6.3 Shoes with a lateral extension on the heel help to support a horse with base-narrow conformation.

can tolerate a slightly crooked leg or pastern angle. A slight misalignment of the fetlocks or knees can also be tolerable. Regular trimming that makes slight adjustments to align the foot with any minor imbalances serves these horses well. A horseshoe that is appropriate for the horse's work is shaped and further modified to adapt it to any misalignments that the trim could not achieve.

Moderate defects require extra attention, often through shoes specially designed to add support in specific areas of the horse's foot.

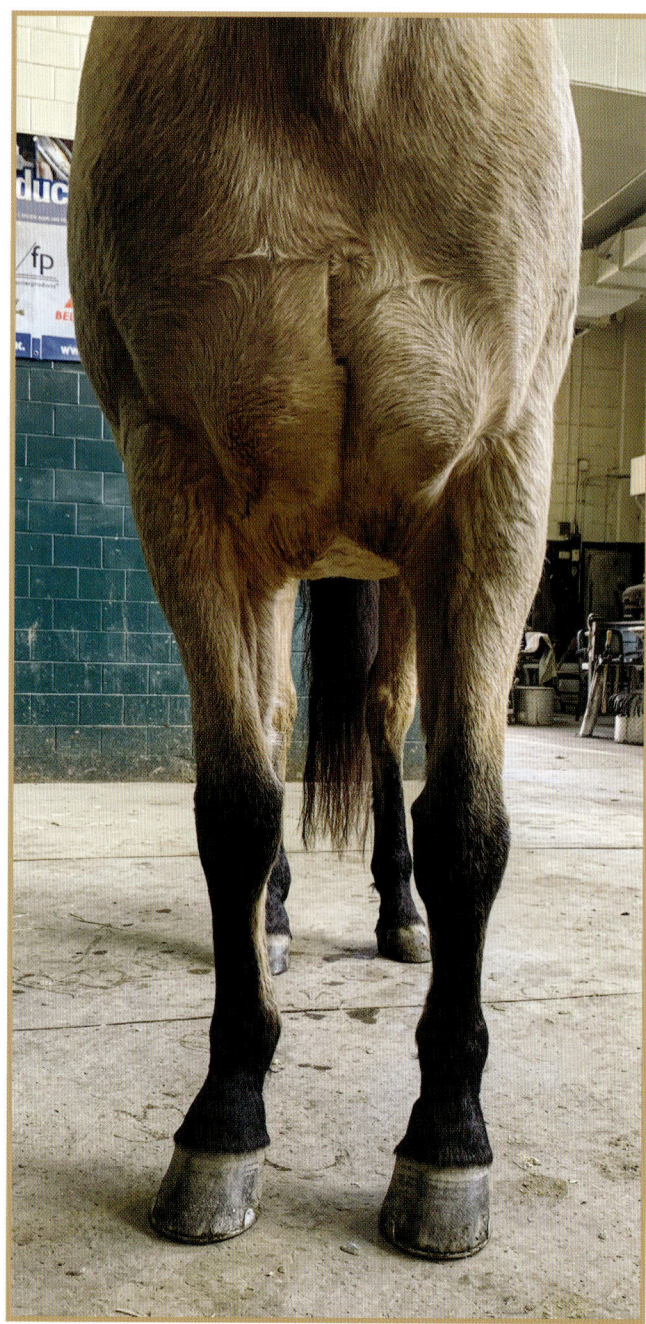

6.4 A severely toed-in, base-narrow stance has led to osteoarthritis in this horse's knee.

For example, a shoe that is shaped to reduce leverage and correct gait faults can keep the horse sound and comfortable. Here is where attention to detail matters. Generic horseshoes without specific modifications will not help a horse with moderate conformation defects (fig. 6.3).

Severe defects require critical management decisions. These abnormalities are obvious—there is a noticeable crookedness to the leg or a twist at the joints. Often there are multiple severe defects on the same leg.

A high-maintenance individual may not hold up under hard work regardless of the care he receives (fig. 6.4). Surgery and specialty shoes may be the only options. Caring for a horse with severe defects requires teamwork between a farrier, a veterinarian, and the horse owner to provide the level of trimming and shoeing to compensate for the issue (fig. 6.5).

Another thing to consider is that the taller and heavier a horse, the more likely he is to have soundness issues from conformational abnormalities. Taller horses produce more leverage on crooked legs or joints that can have negative consequences for bones, joints, and soft tissue.

An Objective Evaluation Method

A "pretty" horse has wildly different meanings from one horseman to the next. Even within the same discipline, what one person finds attractive about a horse doesn't always resonate with another. When buying or breeding your next horse, it's okay to look for color, desired head size, or spots. But also take the

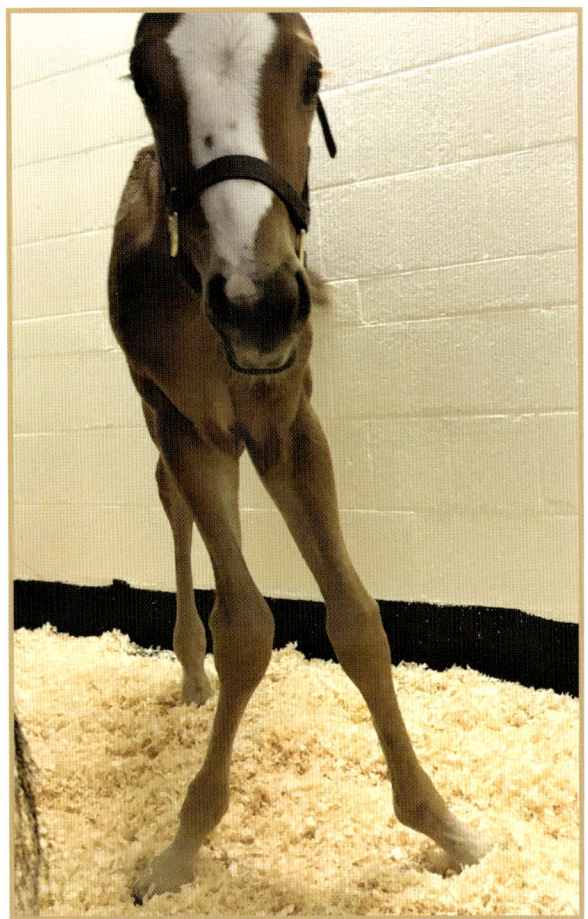

6.5 A horse with severe defects needs a team that includes his farrier, veterinarian, and owner working together.

time to consider any conformation weaknesses that can become problematic.

An objective method to evaluating conformation removes the emotion and considers the facts. One way to do this is by using what farrier Doug Butler, PhD, defined as the "X, Y, and Z axes" in his book, *Shoeing in Your Right Mind*.

This method divides the horse into three sections and is based on visualizing vertical reference lines, or

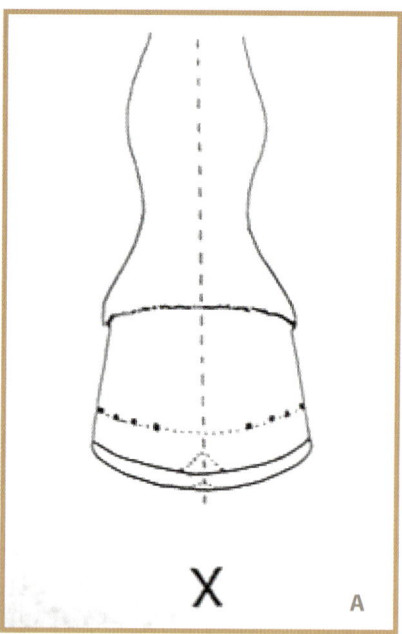

plumb lines, dropped from key points on the horse. Using these plumb lines as the "X," "Y," and "Z" axes of the horse highlights any deviations.

Before starting, make sure the horse is standing in a square, relaxed position. If the horse is not standing in a neutral position, the posture can play tricks on your eyes.

The "X axis" is the view seen when standing directly in front of or behind a horse. This vantage point determines if he has a base-wide or base-narrow stance in relation to shoulders or hips (figs. 6.6 A & B). The "X axis" affects whether the hoof lands flat or not.

6.6 A & B Stand in front of the horse and picture an imaginary line dropping straight down in front of the leg to the ground to find the "X-axis" (A). This horse shows nearly perfect hind-end conformation from the rear "X-axis" view (B). She engages her hind end well and has very smooth gaits.

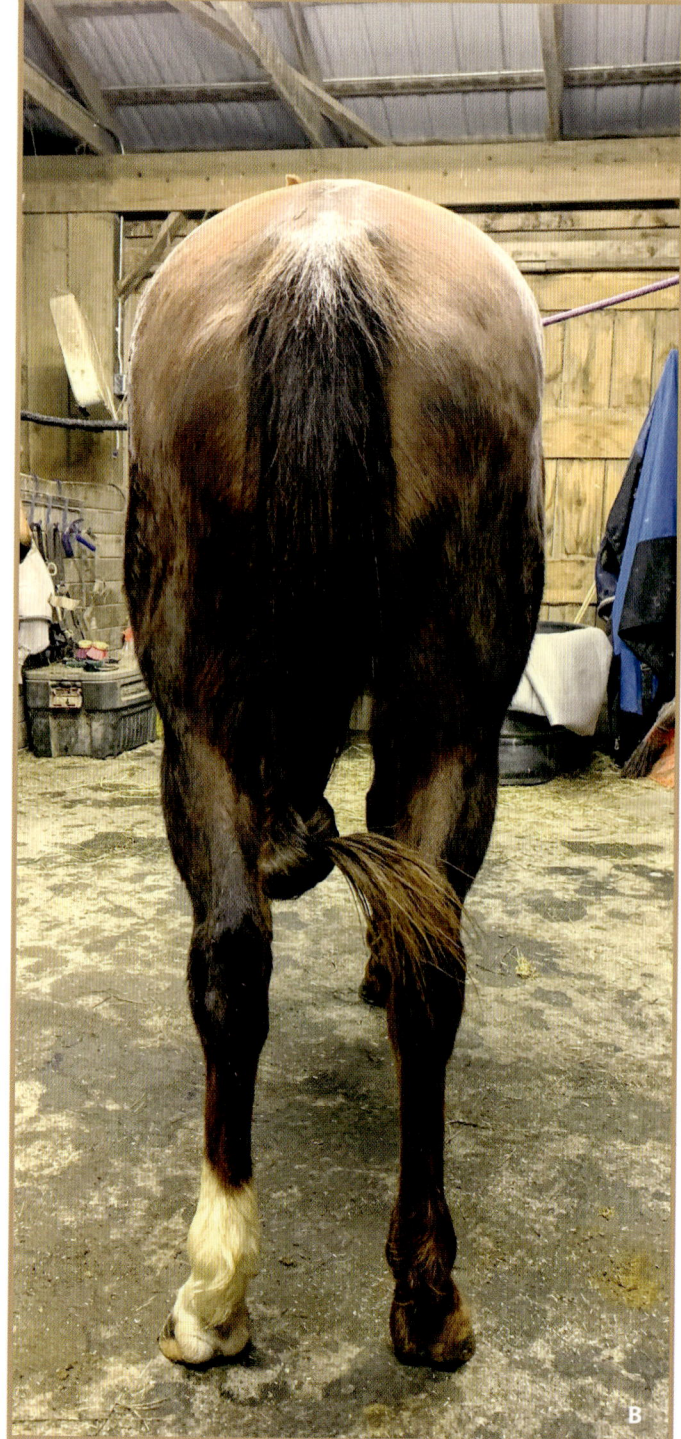

The "Y axis" considers what a horse's leg looks like if you were to lie on the ground and look upward at his belly. It is as if the horse is standing on a glass table above you. The same view is also offered if you stood above your horse and looked straight down his legs. This assesses whether a horse "toes in" or "toes out." (Both are considered rotational deviations.) The "Y axis" also reveals bone and joint alignment and evaluates how the leg swings when the hoof comes off the ground (fig. 6.7).

The "Z axis" is viewed from the horse's side. It concentrates on the foot position under the body, and the angles or stance of the hoof and leg. In this view, the plumb lines descend from the center of the shoulder or center of the hip (figs. 6.8 A & B). The "Z axis" is used to observe stance, anterior/posterior hoof balance, and position of the hoof under the leg.

The most common conformational flaws are a combination of those seen in the "X" and "Y" axes. These are called *base-narrow, toed-in,* and *base-wide, toed out* (see more on p. 94). In a normal stance, the front hooves line up directly under the center of the horse's shoulder, are parallel to the cannon bones, and directly align with the radius (figs. 6.9 A & B).

Any misalignment of the limb's joints ("Y" axis) leads to arthritis. Deviations from the plumb line ("X" axis) produce bone remodeling known as *Wolf's Law.* This name is used to describe the process that happens when the bone adapts to the force exerted on it (fig. 6.10).

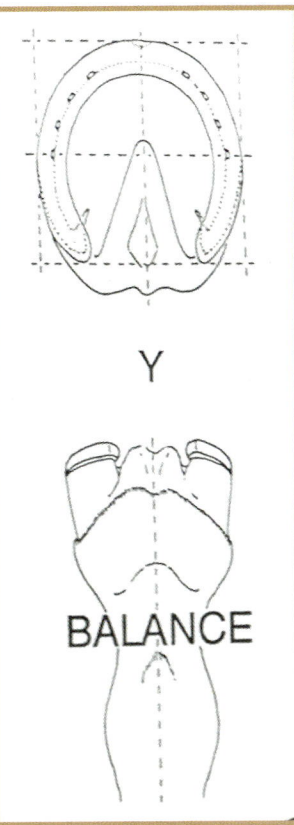

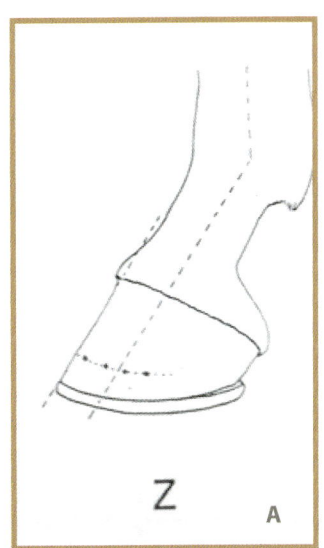

6.8 A & B An illustration of an ideal "Z-axis" angle (A), and a horse that shows near perfect conformation of the hind end from the side "Z-axis" view (B).

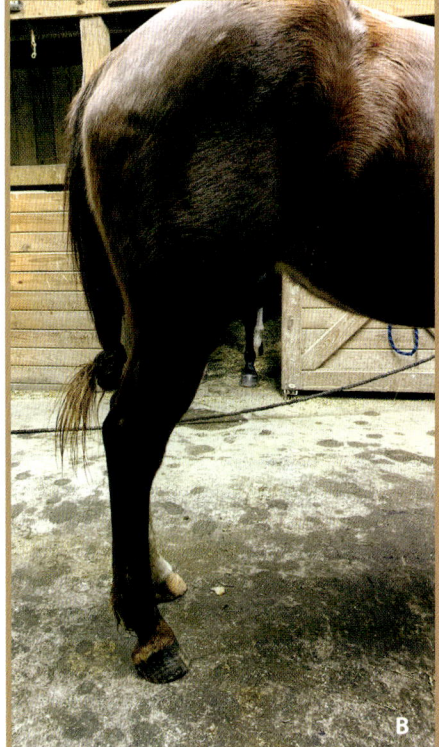

6.7 The "Y-axis" projects a line straight upward from the center bottom of the hoof drawing on the left. The "Y-axis" accounts for rotational deviations from the leg's center line, which can be seen from the rear of the hoof. Rotational deviations can be internal (toward the spine of the horse) or external (away from the spine of the horse). The "Y-axis" also accounts for misalignment of joints.

6: HOW CONFORMATION DETERMINES SOUNDNESS AND PERFORMANCE

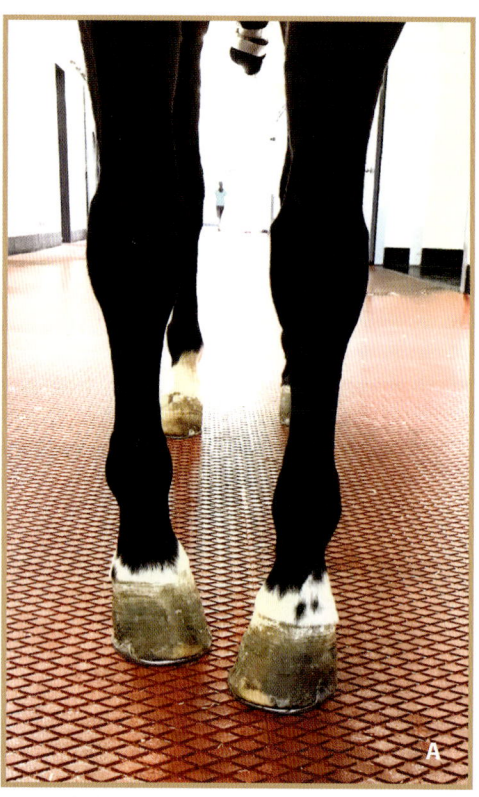

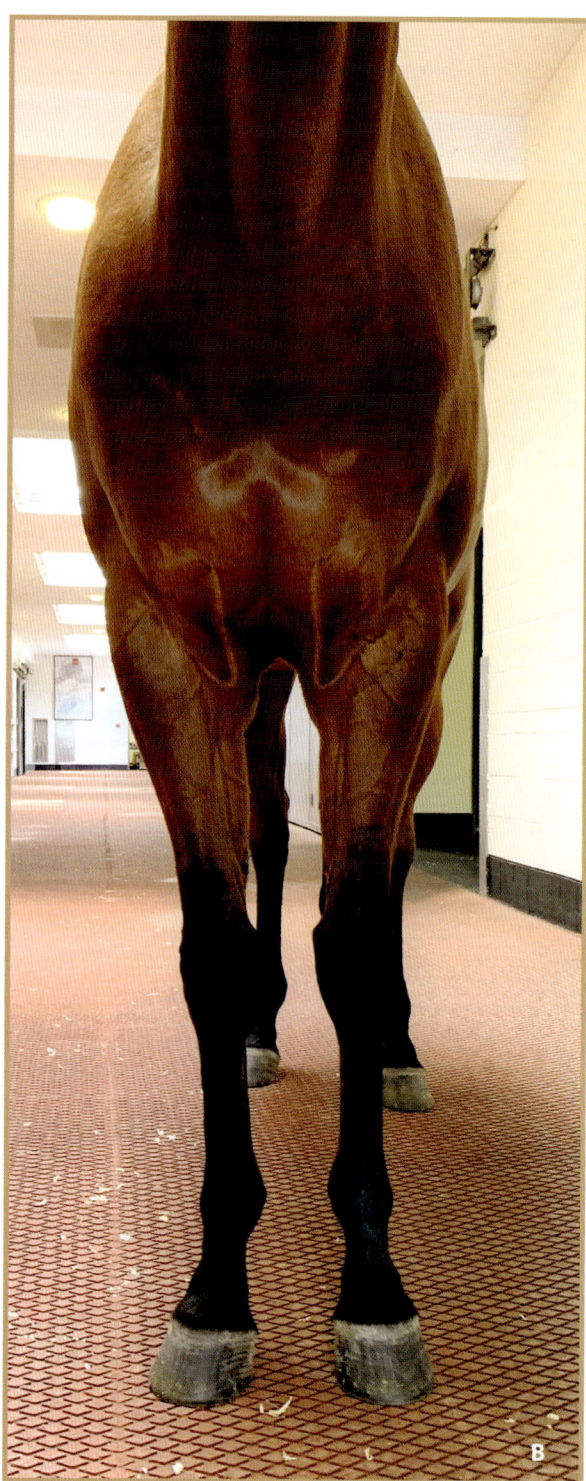

6.9 A & B An extreme example of base-narrow and toed-in conformation, a blend of "X-" and "Y-axis" defects, thus predisposed to high and low ringbone, and collateral ligament strains (A), and a front base-narrow toed-out stance cannot be corrected in the mature horse. It can only be managed with proper trimming and shoe fit (B).

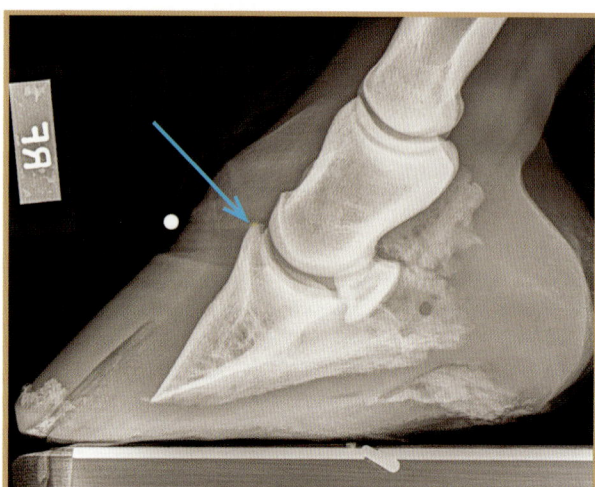

6.10 Osteoarthritis occurs where joints receive excessive wear and tear from unbalanced conformation or inaccurate trimming. This radiograph shows the formation of osteophytes (bony lumps) at the coffin joint.

Defining Key Terms

To understand how conformational defects impact the horse, it is important to define the terminology farriers use to explain these imperfections.

Lateral: The lateral portion of the hoof is on the outside of the foot structure.

Medial: The medial side of the hoof is the portion on the inside of the horse's leg—the side closest to the opposing leg.

Palmar Angle (PA): Used to describe the front hoof, the palmar angle is the distal (center) surface, or bottom of the coffin bone. In a radiograph the lateral view of the coffin bone is essentially a 3D object in a 2D format.

Plantar Angle: Specific to the hind hoof, the plantar angle refers to the spot where the bottom of the hind hoof (sole) meets the hock and takes into consideration the positioning of the coffin bone in the back feet.

Negative palmar or negative plantar angles: A negative coffin bone angle in the front (palmar) or hind (plantar) is a reverse angle from "normal." Typically, the palmar coffin bone angle falls within a range of 3 and 6 degrees as it extends toward the ground. When a horse is said to have a "low PA," the angle of his coffin bone is between 3 and 0 degrees, and a negative angle occurs when it is less than zero (fig. 6.11).

Quarter cracks: These splits in the hoof often start at the top of the foot and work down to the toe. Some cracks are narrow and shallow, others are wide and deep into the hoof.

Radius: The bone in the horse's forearm. The top end of the radius is called the *ulna*, or elbow of the horse.

Sheared heels: These occur when the length of the inside (medial) and outside (lateral) heels are different lengths.

Sidebone: This is a condition where the cartilage in the hoof transforms into hard, inflexible tissue.

6.11 The coronary band of the hind foot points to the horse's stomach rather than at a 45-degree angle toward the horse's chest. This is evidence of a negative plantar angle of the hind foot's coffin bone.

The implications of these conformational defects will vary based on severity. To review:

Mild defects are common and may be considered "normal." These slight deviations are usually not easily recognized. Regular trimming and shoeing practices can help control these issues.

Moderate defects are where farriery makes a positive difference. Detailed trimming combined with constructive horseshoe configuration will keep a compromised horse sound and useful.

Severe defects need the highest level of farriery combined with veterinary teamwork. These high-maintenance horses usually do not stay sound long term.

As each axis deviates away from "normal," strain is exerted on the legs and feet. Appropriate trimming and shoeing can compensate for one axis that is lightly deviated from normal, especially when the deviation is below a moderate level. A horse with deviations on all three axes is the most difficult to help, even with trimming and shoeing. A farrier's only choice in these cases is to work on the most prominent defect. These high maintenance horses typically require joint supplements and injections in addition to good hoof care in order to remain comfortable.

Consequences of Conformational defects—Front End

There are six common defects that can be observed in the horse's front end.

X-Axis Front-End Defects

Base-wide: The hoof flares out toward the edges. Quarter cracks and sheared heels signal a horse is base-wide. These horses likely experience front limb interference where one leg strikes another (fig. 6.12).

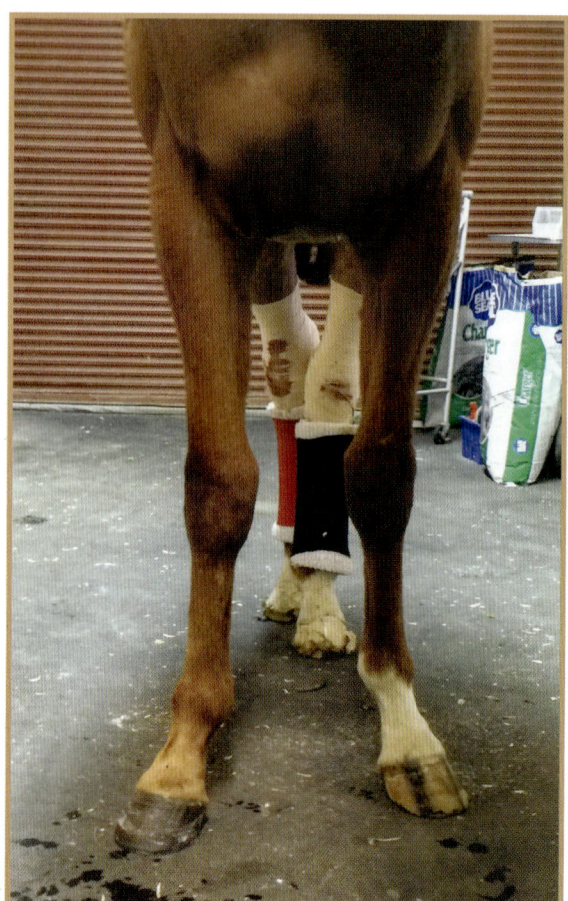

6.12 A base-wide front end is often a blend of X- and Y-Axis deviations, as seen here in this horse.

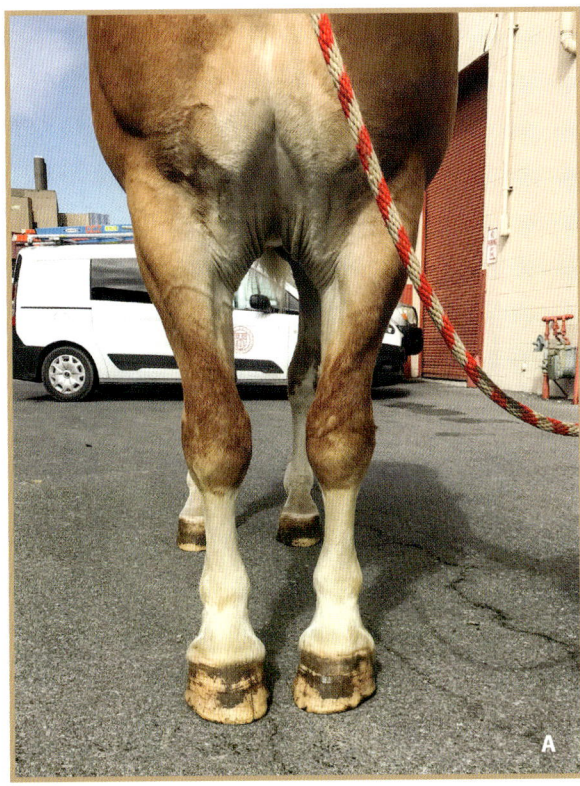

Base-narrow: These horses also have a medial flare, lateral side cracks, and can develop lateral sidebone. A base-narrow stance is often noticeable by a "paddling" movement where the lower part of the front leg rolls or swings out instead of forward or backward in a straight line (figs. 6.13 A & B).

Y-Axis Front-End Defects

Toed-out: When the horse's toes point outward, this is called *toed-out*. It occurs because the cannon bone is improperly aligned with the radius. This can cause interference of the front legs. *Splay-footed* is another term to describe this defect.

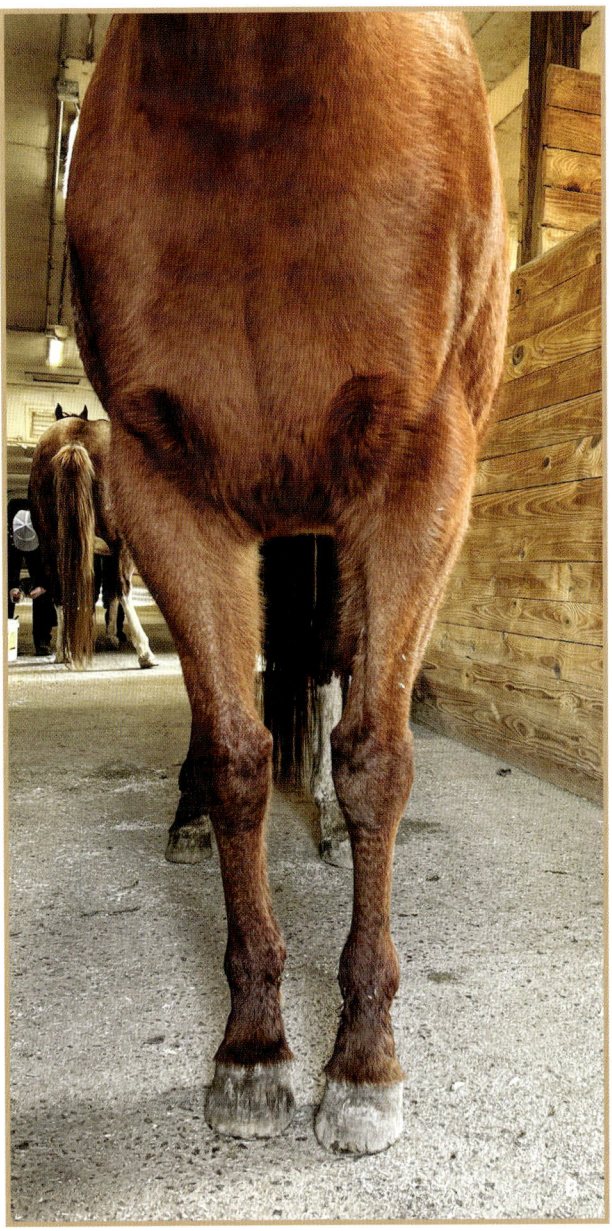

6.13 A & B Two base-narrow, toed-in horses with deviations of the X-axis.

Toed-in: It's easy to identify a *toed-in* horse because he has a sloppy paddling movement. There is an obvious misalignment between the cannon bone and the radius. This defect often leads to arthritis in the knee, and lateral heel cracks.

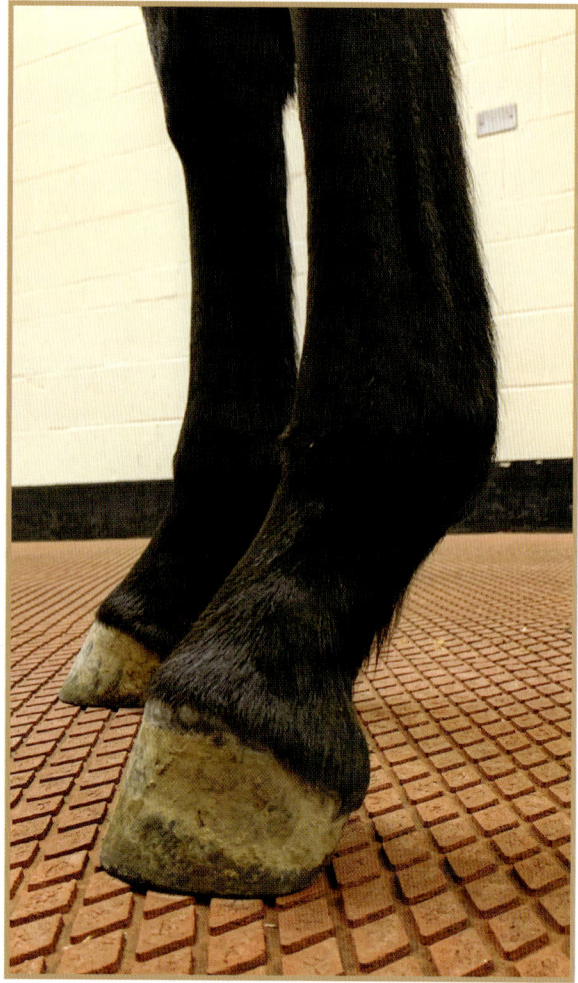

6.14 Club feet are a highly inheritable trait. Early intervention and ongoing trimming can allow these horses to be ridden. This one is classified as a Grade 3 club foot.

Z-Axis Front-End Defects

Long toe, low heel: An abnormally low hoof angle makes these horses heavy on the forehand, and more prone to tripping. Over time *long-toe, low-heel* conformation contributes to the development of navicular disease, bowed tendons, and negative palmer angles.

Upright or clubfoot: An abnormally steep hoof angle forces the horse to strike the ground toe first. A horse with an upright angle looks like he is stabbing the ground at each step. This predisposes horses to navicular disease, sidebones, and hoof cracks (fig. 6.14).

Consequences of Conformational Defects—Hind End

The hind end provides the energy in a horse's gait. One or more conformational defects in the back hooves and legs can interfere with a horse's ability to develop propulsion. Here's a look at hind-end defects.

X-Axis Hind-End Defects

Base-narrow: Hind legs that are too close to one another are called *base-narrow*. The hoof tends to have a medial flare and a rolled-under lateral heel. This can lead to medial hock arthritis.

Base-wide: Often called *cow-hocked*, these lateral flared hooves can lead to hind limb interference and arthritis in the hock.

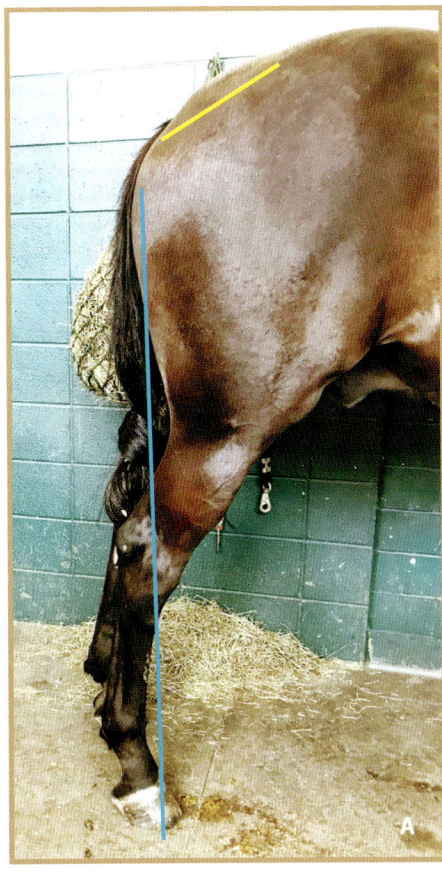 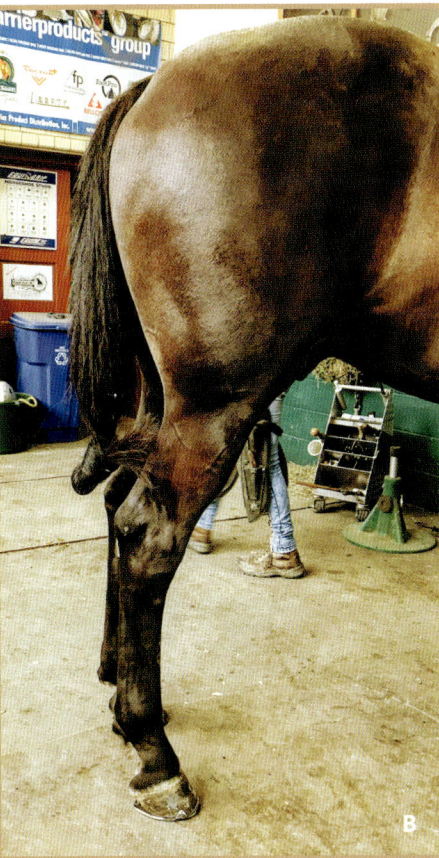

6.15 A & B A horse that is standing with his legs behind the imaginary line of his buttocks is described as "camped-out" (A). After trimming and shoeing with extended heels and a wedge pad, there is a noticeable improvement in the horse's posture and stance. His hocks are in line with rear of his buttocks (B).

X- and Y-Axis Hind-End Defects

The Y-axis specifically describes misalignments of bones to joints and rotational defects but often there is a blend of X-axis (plumb line) and Y-axis (rotational) defects. For instance, a cow-hocked horse is *base-wide* ("X") and *toed-out* ("Y"). This creates osteoarthritis on the outside of the hock joint.

Another common blend of X- and Y-axis hind-end defects is the *base-narrow, toed-in* stance. Aside from osteoarthritis on the inside of the hock joint, this incorrect stance diminishes hind-end engagement. The rider may feel her horse's hind end sway sideways, or back and forth while riding.

Z-Axis Hind-End Defects

Standing under/sickle-hocked: Hocks and hooves that fall in front of the hip plumb line are considered "standing under." This creates a negative plantar angle, which increases the risk of hock and stifle injury and arthritis. Dressage horses and jumping horses that are sickle-hocked lack thrust needed for key movements.

Camped out: Hocks and hooves that line up behind the buttocks are considered *camped out,* creating a strung-out movement. This makes horses susceptible to gluteal and back injuries and limits the impulsion needed for jumping and dressage (fig. 6.15 A & B).

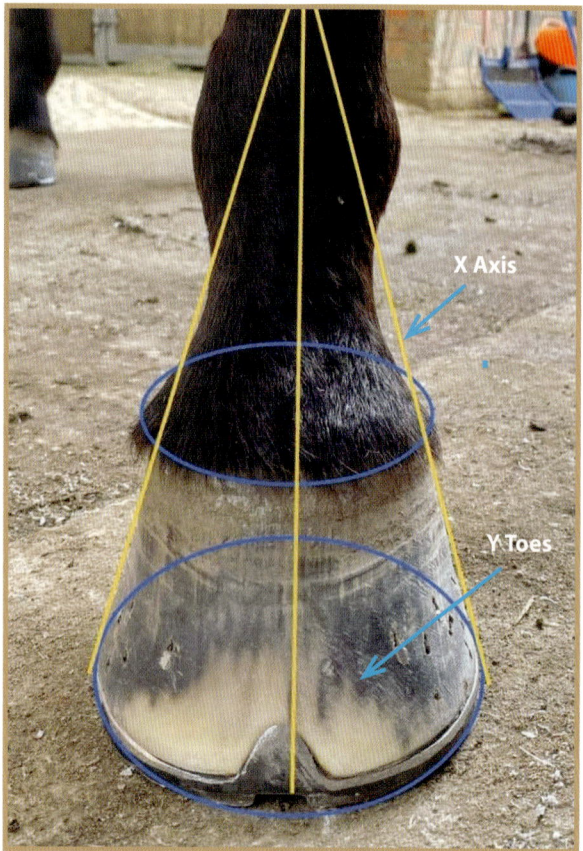

6.16 A balanced hoof has the same amount of hoof wall on each side of the "axis" in the legs.

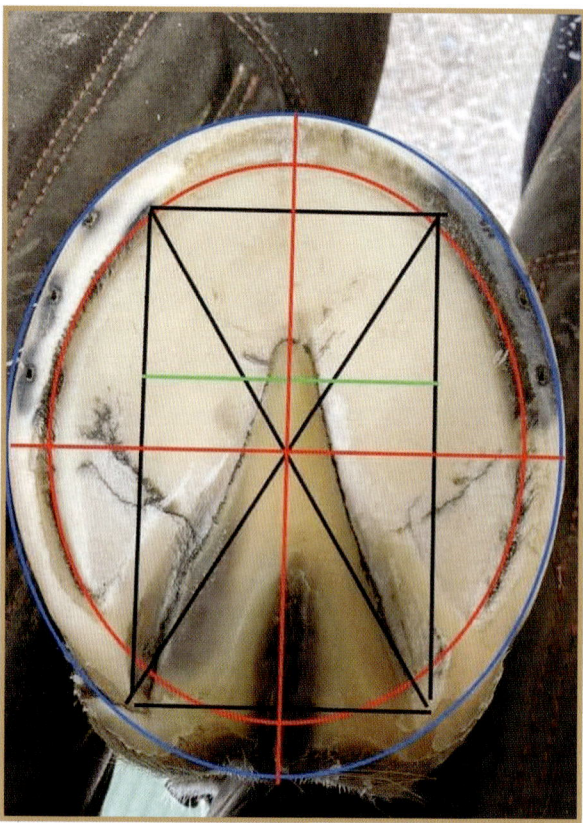

6.17 In a perfect world, the ideal hoof has matching angles in all directions and is flat on the bottom so it lands evenly on the ground.

Management of Conformation Defects with Farriery

When a farrier uses "corrective shoeing" on mature horses he is using a combination of trimming and shoeing principles to manage a problem. The term "corrective horseshoeing" can be misleading. A horse's legs and feet can only be fixed within the first six months of life. Specialty trimming, shoes, and sometimes surgery, can correct some conformational defects while a foal's bones develop.

Developing the proper hoof alignment to the leg can't be an instant change. It takes several cycles of gradual adjustments to achieve the desired outcome. Trimming concepts take into consideration all three axes as they relate to each foot and leg.

Trimming

The X and Y axes take into account the medial/lateral aspect of hoof alignment. Imagine drawing a line down the middle of a horse's pastern and a line perpendicular

98 | SHOEING THE MODERN HORSE

to that underneath the hoof. Ideally, there should be the same amount of hoof on the right and left side of the midline (fig. 6.16). The angles on the hoof wall should also match (fig. 6.17). Farriers trim the hoof so it is square with the leg when that doesn't happen. The goal is also to trim the hoof so that it is flat as it makes contact with the ground.

The Z axis looks at the anterior/posterior aspect of hoof alignment, meaning this view looks at the hoof from front to back. A perfect alignment would have a plumb line from the center of the shoulder or hip down to the widest part of the hoof. A goal to achieve this is using the Golden Ratio (p. 36) from toe to heels.

The objective is to support a heel-first landing, with the loaded hoof under the leg. In a perfect scenario, a heel-first contact provides a shock-absorbing system. When the reverse of this happens, as in a toe-first landing, the coffin bone, and the joints above it are compressed.

The key to proper trimming is to remove what the horse does not need and leave what the horse needs. That may sound simple; however, the difficult part is knowing exactly what that is for each foot on each horse. Trimming is a blend of artistry, physics, and horsemanship.

The Whole Picture

When three-dimensional thinking is used to evaluate and trim/shoe a horse the results are instantly noticeable. Horses will have a better attitude and improved movement. A rider who knows her horses can feel the differences under saddle. Earning higher dressage scores, running faster barrel times, or scoring higher on a sliding stop are visible proof making shoeing and trimming changes guided by conformational analysis is effective.

Horses Do Not Lie

The handlers warned me about a grouchy demo horse that I would be working while explaining the three-dimensional approach at a three-day farrier clinic at the University of the Horse in Sorcocaba, Brazil.

The roan stallion stood with his ears pinned and a pinched look on his face. Visualizing plumb lines on his body, I noticed he was base-narrow. All four feet had lateral heel cracks and the plumb lines fell outside the hooves, exactly where the cracks were.

First, I trimmed the hooves to improve the horse's medial/lateral balance and alignment. Then, I shaped shoes with rolled edges on the medial branches with a generous fit on the lateral side. All went well, without any problems and the horse moved off much better to the amazement of the group.

The following week, the host called to check in and thank me for the clinic. She reported the stallion's owner called her ecstatic because the horse no longer wrung his tail in work, nor did he pin his ears.

Horses may not be able to speak to us, but horses do not lie. Both behaviors were clues to discomfort and the correction in trimming provided relief. Using an objective three-dimensional approach to hoof care can transform unhappy horses into willing partners.

FROM THE FORGE
Having Courage

In the early nineties, I received a phone call from a client I'll call "Mr. Smith." He owned two high-level Quarter Horses. Neither could show because both were lame. This was keeping him from earning enough qualifying points for the world championship show.

The call for help came in June and the world show was in November. Mr. Smith regularly flew farriers in to work on his horses and had a full shop on-site, including a forge, anvil, drill press, and shoeing supplies.

It sounded like an adventure, so I agreed to go. I booked a flight, and loaded up my hand tools and some aluminum bar stock. Mr. Smith met me at the airport and invited me to lunch so we could get to know one another. The house was full of trophies, saddles, awards, family pictures, and framed magazine covers.

When Mr. Smith left the room his wife whispered to me, "Can you shoe these horses without being intimidated by my husband?"

She explained these horses were in trouble because her husband dictated how to shoe them, and other farriers were afraid to disagree with him.

The first horse was a tall, national hunter champion. Mr. Smith reported the bay gelding was striking his left front leg around left corners at the trot. He offered to use a white polo wrap on that leg and apply blue chalk to the right foot to illustrate where the right foot hit the left leg. I didn't need the visual aid because it was clear the horse had a crooked leg. Mr. Smith bristled at the observation and said no veterinarian, judge, or farrier had ever said so. I reminded him he'd paid me a lot of money for a visit and asked if he wanted to listen.

When I picked up the horse's left leg he shifted all his weight onto his right leg, the knee pointed away from the body while the foot pointed toward the opposite leg. Standing in front of the horse, it was obvious the cannon bone was misaligned with the radius at the knee. Mr. Smith had insisted previous farriers trim the hoof low on the lateral toe, which would be correct if the horse's leg was straight. Since it was not, this trimming approach only compounded the problem.

The trim that had been done previous to my visit left the hoof with too much hoof on the inside and not enough on the outside. First, I trimmed the excessive flare on the medial side of the foot. There was not much hoof wall to work with. I used aluminum bar stock to forge a shoe that was thinner on the medial side and thicker on the lateral side and fit it wider laterally to support the rolled-under heel.

After re-shoeing all four feet we saddled the horse and he walked away straight and never hit himself again. Turns out that horse was just a test.

The next horse was the previous year's AQHA Superhorse, which is decided by the horse that wins the most points at the World Show. The horse was moving so poorly he couldn't show and that threatened his opportunity to qualify. The horse's hind feet brushed against one another and then struck the heels of his front feet.

His conformation was good, an indication that something was off in his trimming and shoeing. At Mr. Smith's direction, farriers had been trimming this horse so that his hind legs looked like an upside-down triangle when viewed from the rear. The hind shoes were set so far back to stop the overreaching that the hoof wall was rasped to the laminae. The horse was nearly crippled.

Redoing the front was as easy as a good trim, which brought his feet back under his legs. For the hinds, a longer shoe was used and placed in the appropriate spot on the toe to provide more support. A quick jog down the aisle confirmed the horse was moving cleanly and properly. I continued shoeing for Mr. Smith, and after that year's World Show he called to tell me his horse had repeated the Superhorse title.

CHAPTER 7

Hoof Conditions and Diseases

A horse's hooves account for less than 10 percent of his anatomy. Yet, the hoof is one of, if not the most important structures in the horse's body. After all, "no hoof, no horse," right? The hoof is deceiving. On the outside, the horny material looks tough and sturdy. But not far beneath the surface is a dense network of sensitive blood vessels. The tissues pump blood that delivers oxygen and nutrients needed to keep the foot healthy. Typically, the blood-delivery network inside the hoof falls to a veterinarian's care as part of the circulatory system. However, farriers are acutely aware of how trimming and shoeing can impact the blood flow and soft tissues invisible to the eye.

The hoof is susceptible to several injuries and diseases. There is a range of conditions a farrier identifies and addresses on his own. Legally, farriers can't provide a medical diagnosis—only veterinarians can do so. That means farriers and veterinarians often team up on significant issues (fig. 7.1). The location of the issue and the severity determines the diagnosis, treatment, and prognosis.

Acute injuries always cause alarm, and some diseases or conditions can be career-ending. In some cases, an injury can spark the

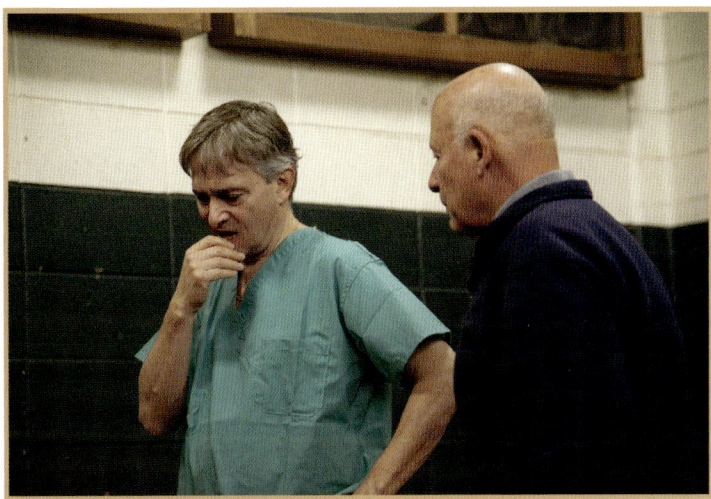

7.1 Severe hoof conditions and diseases require a close partnership between the farrier and veterinarian. I work closely with Dr. Norm Ducharme (left), the professor of surgery and Chief Medical Officer at Cornell University Ruffian Equine Specialists.

development of a disease process. Here's a look at the diseases and conditions farriers look for when working on client horses—those that can be addressed through farriery alone, and those that require a vet-farrier partnership.

Abscess

Chances are you're familiar with hoof abscesses. At some point during your horse-owning lifetime, you have (or will have) at least one surface (figs. 7.2 & 7.3). Essentially, abscesses are like a blood blister that forms under your fingernail. The blood buildup creates painful pressure. When bacteria invade the area, a pustule forms inside the hoof.

Signs

A tender-footed stride and strained, uncomfortable look. The boil-like infection creates pressure. When a farrier sees a horse with a potential abscess, he first uses hoof testers to pinpoint where the infection is by finding the source of pain.

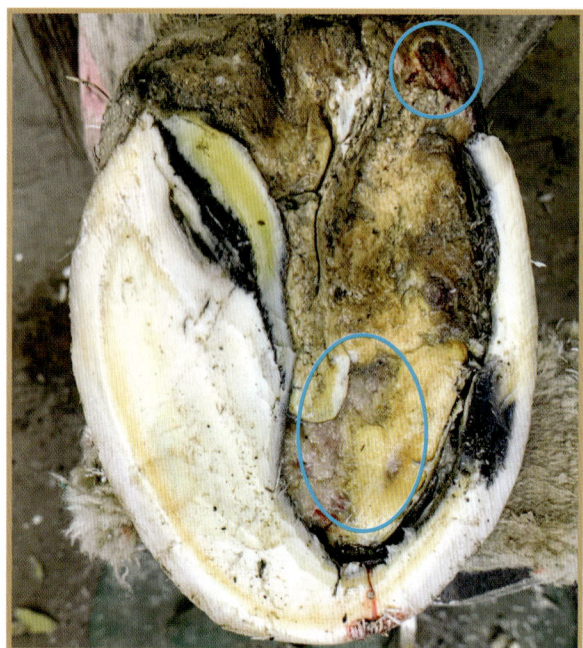

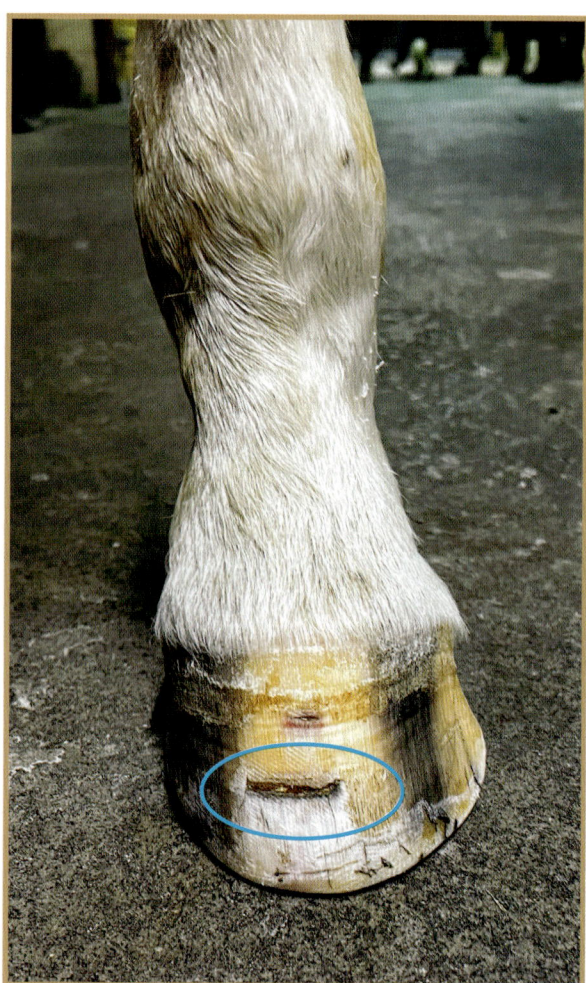

7.2 This hoof illustrates what happens when an abscess is unnoticed. The necrosis undermined the sole (oval) and finally broke out at the heel (circle).

7.3 The horizontal crack in the hoof is evidence of an old abscess that has blown out the hoof wall.

Treatment

Using a hoof knife, the farrier scrapes away at the hoof until the spot bursts and the infection drains. When the boil-like sore pops, the pressure is released, and the horse feels instant relief. The severity of the infection and how deeply it penetrates the hoof guides the farrier's decision for the next steps, which may include soaking in Epsom salts and poultice wraps until the area heals.

Outcome

When caught soon enough, the horse can be feeling better and back to work in three to four days.

Bony Growths

People who have experienced a bone spur can sympathize with how painful bony growths in the foot can be—each step can be excruciating. Horses, too, can have uncomfortable bony growth in the hoof. These fall into one of three categories and are named by the specific location.

Low ringbone occurs at the coffin joint, the area where the short pastern and coffin bone meet (fig. 7.4 A).

High ringbone emerges in the front part of the hoof at the top of the short pastern. A bump above or around the side of the coronary band may be visible (fig. 7.4 A).

Sidebone develops when lateral wings grow off the coffin bone (fig. 7.4 B).

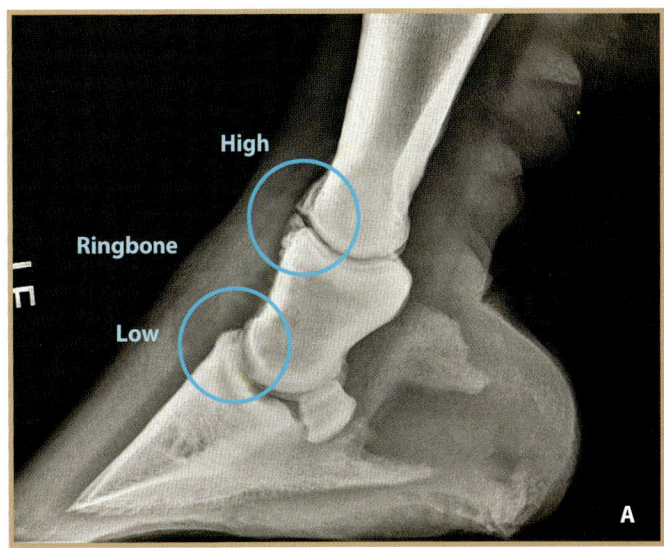

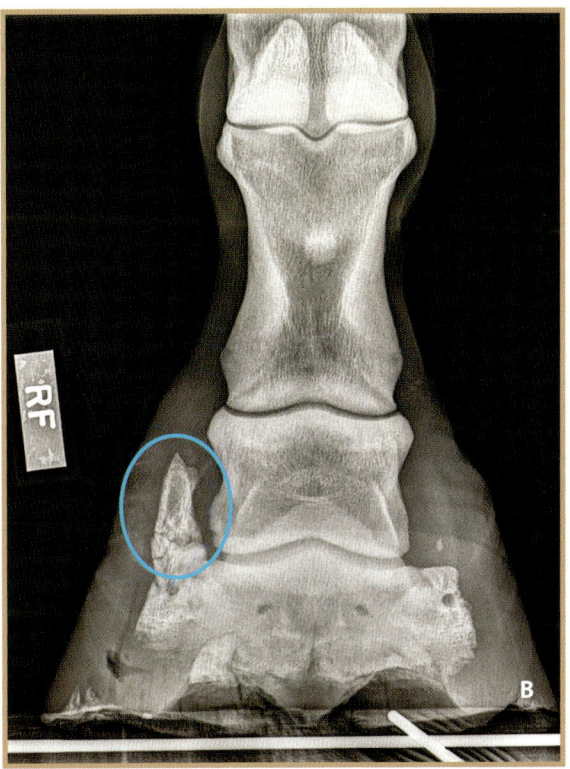

7.4 A & B Low and high ringbone (A) and sidebone (B).

Signs

Lameness, decreased performance, and resistance to work are indicators that a bony growth may be developing. In more advanced cases, visible bumps can be seen with the naked eye, whereas in mild cases, the formations are only visible with radiographs. *Sidebone* is especially difficult to identify. Advanced cases show swelling on either side of the coronary band, but many do not. The ossification on lateral cartilage of the coffin bone usually can't be seen without radiographs.

Treatment

All bony problems in the foot or leg develop because of concussion, which can occur during regular riding, or as a result of trauma to the front of the foot. This can range from getting stepped on by another horse, kicking the wall, pawing, or frequent road work. Poor conformation may also be to blame.

Farriers use trimming and shoeing methods that reduce the impact of ground forces to keep these horses comfortable. For low ringbone, this means reducing the motion in the coffin joint with rolled or rocker-toe shoe modifications. Pour-in gel pads are also often used to add cushioning and absorb concussion.

For side bone problems, farriers use half-round style shoes or bevel the shoe on the affected side to reduce the impact when the hoof strikes the ground. Steroids may also be needed to control pain.

Outcome

The earlier in the process shoeing mechanics can change, the less damage is created, and the better chances a horse will remain sound and continue in work. Long-term bony diseases are progressive and can end a horse's career.

Canker

In old textbooks, *canker* is referred to as "hoof cancer." This skin disease is rare and not widely researched. What is known about canker today is largely based on anecdotal evidence of treating affected horses. Leading veterinary podiatrists believe it to be an autoimmune response that often begins similarly to thrush (see p. 103).

Signs

Canker can look like *scratches*. It may even originate as a case of scratches, which occurs when bacteria first enter the soft tissues in the hoof. In response, the horse's immune system kicks in to fight off the foreign body, creating noticeable soreness. There is still much to be learned about canker, but there is a consensus that living in poor conditions such as dirty stalls and muddy, manure-filled areas can start the process.

However, those factors alone do not mean a horse will develop canker. There are many more horses living in similar conditions that never develop it. And there are cases of high-performing, perfectly cared for horses developing the disease.

Treatment

Treating a horse for canker is not a backyard procedure. The infected tissue must be removed. Given the significant blood supply in the hoof, it can bleed profusely. The horse is treated at a veterinarian hospital while under sedation and receives a nerve block during the procedure. Keeping the hoof clean and dry is essential.

Outcome

It can take a long time for a horse to overcome this immune response. The earlier canker is caught and addressed, the better chances the horse recovers to soundness. However, recurrent flares are possible given the theory that it is connected to an autoimmune response.

Coffin Bone Fractures

Classified by type, coffin bone fractures can only be seen with radiographs. The categories describe where the break is located within the coffin bone and determine the severity (fig. 7.5). A "wing bone" fracture can be stabilized with surgery and therapeutic shoeing. Any fracture up the middle of the coffin bone indicates a serious problem and increases the risk of progressing to ringbone (see p. 103).

Signs

Sudden, moderate-to-severe lameness after a ride can suggest a coffin bone fracture. At the same time, a

Fracture Types	
Type	**Location**
Type I	Fracture of the palmar process (wing) of the distal phalanx.
Type II	Articular wing fractures at the top edge of the coffin bone where it flares out.
Type III	Divides the coffin bone into nearly two equal halves.
Type IV	Break where the coffin bone meets the pastern bone.
Type V	All other types of fractures not described in I through IV or in foals.
Type VI	Chip fracture off the tip of the coffin bone pointing toward the toe.

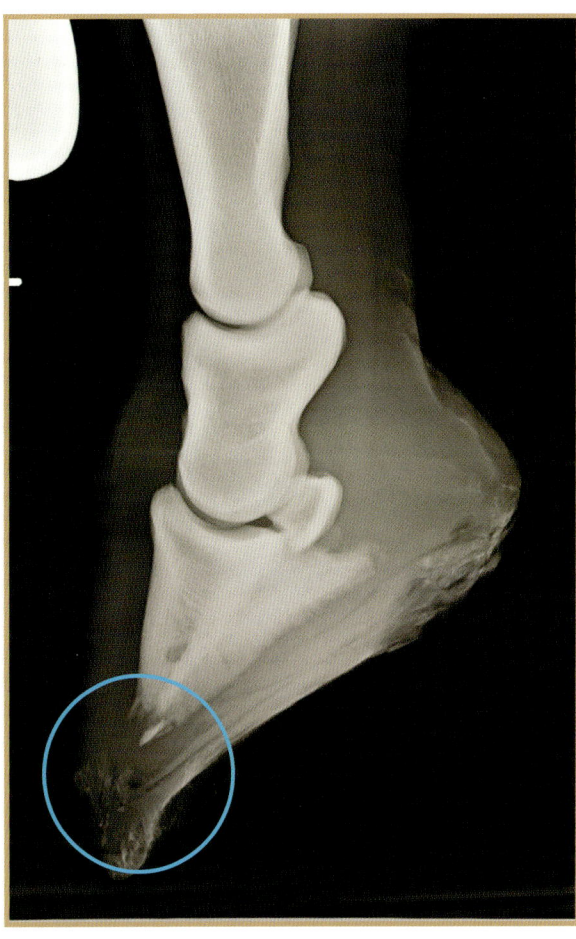

7.5 This radiograph shows the side view of a fractured coffin-bone tip where just the end of the triangular bone has broken.

strong digital pulse can be felt. The breaks are typically the result of an impact like kicking a stall wall, stepping on a rock, or hitting a fence post. Improper shoeing, repeated riding on hard surfaces, infections, and nutritional deficiencies may also contribute to a break. Fractures can also develop from an object penetrating the hoof. For example, if a horse pulls a shoe and steps on the toe clip, the impact can cause the injury.

Treatment
Radiographs are necessary to identify where the fracture is located and its severity. These two factors determine treatment protocols. The farrier will most likely use a bar shoe to stabilize the hoof wall until the bone heals. Pour-in polyurethane pads are also used to alleviate pressure on the bone. In some cases, surgery may be necessary to remove loose fragments, and screws may be used to support the bone as it heals.

Outcome
The fracture category influences the long-term soundness of the horse. A Type I and Type II fracture have the best chances for a return to soundness if the hoof is stabilized and rested, while a Type II fracture means the horse is likely to have future problems with ringbone.

A horse with a Type III or IV may not recover as well and is prone to arthritis. The long-term prognosis for Type V fractures is based on what caused the break, and the outcome varies in how well the horse will recover. Type VI fractures have the best chances of healing well and the horse returning to soundness.

Contracted Heels
Considered more of a condition than a disease, contracted heels are related to conformational defects. Contracted heels are an indication of a malfunction in the hoof and are often a precursor to navicular disease. Horses with upright feet are most susceptible, as are horses with club feet. Improper shoeing can also contribute to contracted heels (fig. 7.6).

7.6 Contracted heels are a condition when the heels are narrower than the toe. This can be a precursor to navicular disease.

Signs

Contracted heels are easily visible because the hooves are noticeably narrower at the heels than the toe. The heels squeeze together, often pinching the frog. Improper trimming and a horse that lands toe first instead of heel first increases the chances of contracted heels.

Treatment

The first step is trimming and shoeing based on the horse's conformation to encourage the horse to land heel first. It starts by removing excess heel and bar growth. Then shoes are fit with room for expansion to help this condition. Often the frog is not contacting the ground, so some type of frog support pad is recommended to alleviate pressure.

Outcome

The condition does not develop overnight, nor can it be corrected in one visit. With good, routine farrier care, a horse can be comfortable and stay in work.

Corns

Ever had calluses develop on your feet? Caused by rubbing, irritation, or pressure on the skin, the small blemishes can be painful. Horses can develop *corns*, a condition that results from improperly short-fitted shoes. Shoes that have not been reset in a timely fashion can also lead to corns as the hoof grows out (fig. 7.7).

A stone or other irritant that gets lodged between the shoe and hoof may also result in bruising. Corns can come on suddenly or be chronic.

Signs

In severe cases, the horse is head-bobbing lame. Other signs become apparent as the farrier begins to trim the hoof. Bruising of the sole is noticeable as he cuts away hoof tissue.

Treatment

Farriers first remove the shoes and trim away the corn itself. In some cases, farriers may recommend using a poultice and dry protective bandaging until the area has healed.

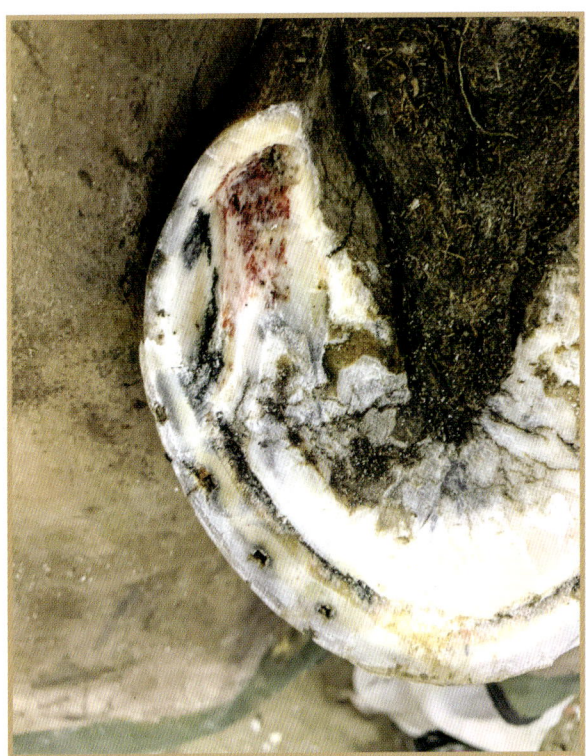

7.7 A hemorrhage in the heel is known as a corn. It's usually caused by the affected heel hitting the ground too hard from an unbalanced trim.

A horse that develops corns typically has high or underrun heels. As the hoof lands toe-first, the impact causes micro-fracturing of the blood vessels, which show up as bruises. Proper trimming and shoeing for the individual horse can help avoid this condition. Specifically, wide-webbed egg-bar shoes are used to support the heels and encourage growth.

Outcome

Some horses will simply be more prone to bruising than others. However, with good, routine farrier work the horse can be sound and perform at his best.

Coronitis

A swelling above the coronary band indicates a case of *coronitis*. Scientifically it is called *hyperplasia*, and there are several reasons it develops. Overuse or poorly fitting hoof boots that regularly rub the coronet band is one cause. Another cause is heavy hair growth at the fetlocks, which attracts mites. Small pests like to get in and live in the fluffy hair, making feathered horses like Clydesdales and Friesians more susceptible than other breeds.

Signs

As a farrier brings a horse's hoof forward to finish trimming and shoeing, he has a clear view of this portion of the hoof. Irritated, flaky skin or oozing pus indicate a problem (fig. 7.8).

Treatment

Cleaning the area with a non-irritating solution is the first step. Then, medications may be used to treat an infection.

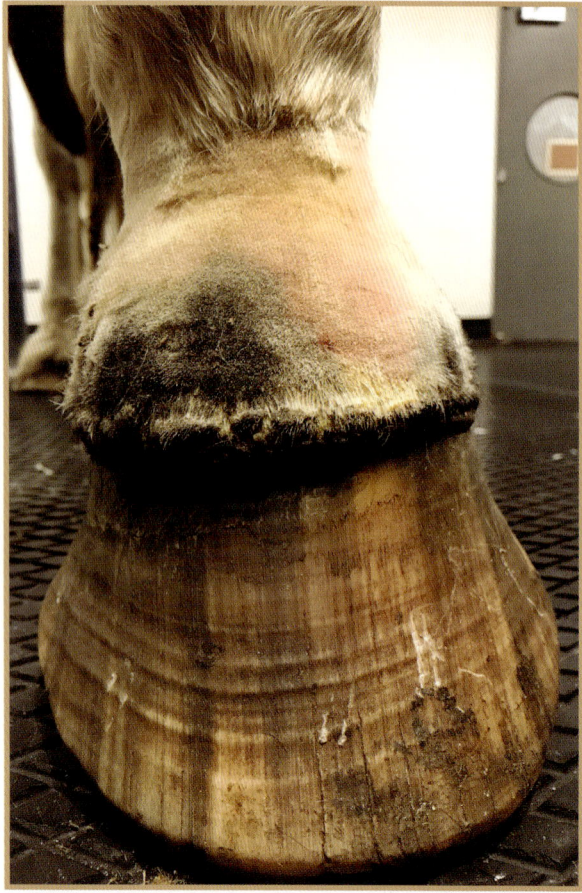

7.8 Coronitis is an inflammation of the coronary band often occurring in breeds with long feathers. The long hair covering the coronary band harbors mites and other pests that irritate the coronary band.

Outcome

When caught and treated early, horses make a full recovery. However, left unchecked, it can lead to more severe problems, such as hoof-wall separations and abscesses (see pp. 102 and 109). This also creates a potential pathway to canker.

Cracks

Split hooves can also be painful and lead to lameness. There are three common hoof cracks to watch for. Each is addressed differently.

Toe cracks appear vertically across the front of the hoof and are a result of dramatic moisture changes, poor nutrition, uneven weight-bearing, and coronary band injuries (figs. 7.9 A & B).

Quarter cracks, as the name suggests, refer to cracks on the "quarters" or sides of the hoof. This is also a vertical split. The most severe quarter cracks extend from the coronary band to the toe (figs. 7.10 A & B).

Horizontal cracks are usually caused by a coronary band injury or the eruption of an abscess (fig. 7.11).

Signs

The crevice is noticeable during basic observation. The openings may invite bacteria that can invade the soft tissues and potentially cause an abscess. Lameness may be another clue.

Treatment

The remedy for each type of crack is slightly different. Farriers often use a standard shoe with quarter clips to stabilize the hoof wall. Severe cracks need debriding, a medical process that removes dead, damaged, or infected tissue. When the crack is infected, the infection must be cleaned up and that space left to allow for drainage.

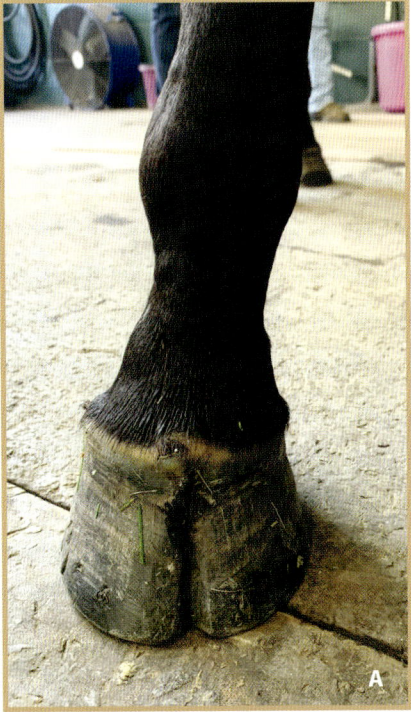 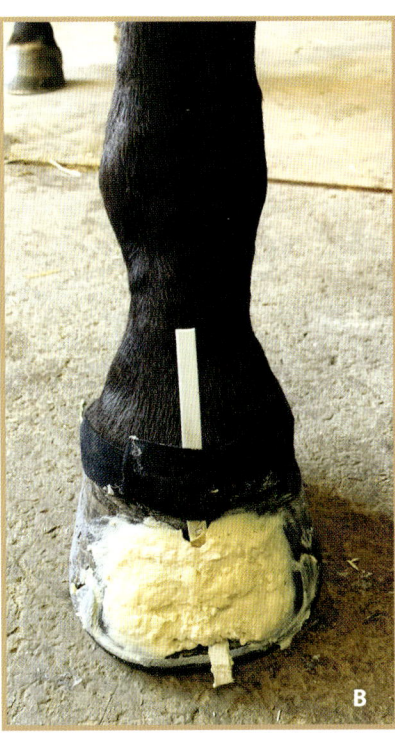

7.9 A & B This chronic toe crack is caused by a coffin bone defect (A). A hoof-wall patch is used on a chronic toe crack like this and includes a drain so it can be flushed regularly (B).

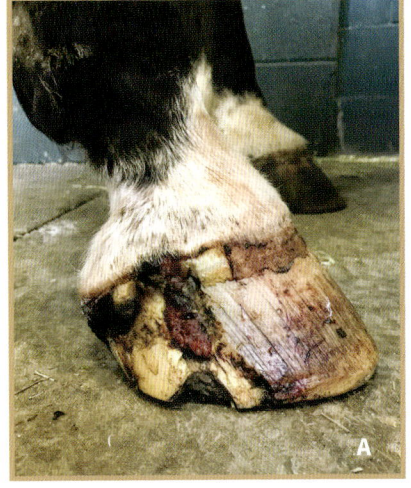 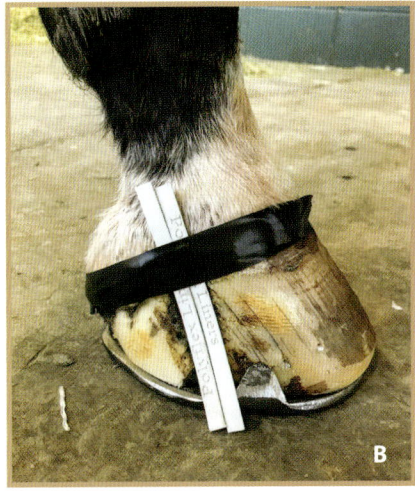

7.10 A & B An example of a quarter crack on the lateral side of a right hind leg (A). The hoof has been cleaned and a temporary drain is affixed to it (B).

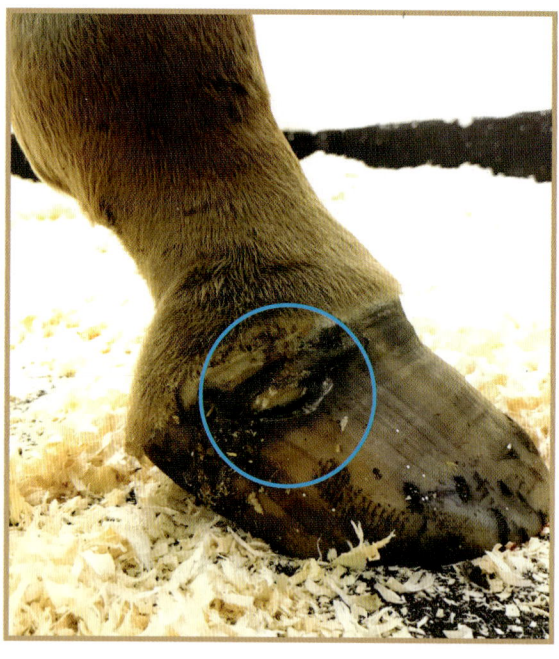

7.11 A horizontal crack is usually evidence of an abscess that started on the bottom of the foot, traveled upward, and finally broke out.

7.12 Interbulbular dermatitis is a deep infection between the heel bulbs, which is dangerously close to the tendon sheath for the deep flexor tendon. Note the gauze being used to medicate the area with furacin ointment.

For toe cracks, farriers use different methods of stabilization, including stainless-steel sutures, glued-on Kevlar fabric, or glued-on aluminum bands. A bar shoe is also used to stabilize the foot (see p. 49). Other times, a pour-in polyurethane pad can be used to provide extra support without extra pressure on the weak spot.

To correct quarter cracks, the hoof must be balanced. When working on a quarter crack, farriers sometimes use a shoe with a Z-shaped bar to help redistribute pressure on the hoof (see p. 50). Since this crack can start at the coronary band it has the potential to bleed as pressure opens and closes the space, making it extremely painful for the horse.

Horizontal cracks are best addressed with hoof-repair materials that create a "patch." It's imperative that no bacteria are trapped inside to avoid the risk of infection.

Outlook

With proper care, a horse can regrow a healthy hoof. It takes about two months for a hoof to grow from the coronary band to the base, so it's a joint effort between the farrier and the owner to provide the horse with the needed care.

Interbulbular Dermatitis

Characterized by a deep heel crack between the heel bulb and wall, a case of *interbulbular dermatitis* can develop because of debris getting into the opening (fig. 7.12). Horse owners can sometimes create this condition by being too aggressive with the hoof pick.

Signs

A flap of skin is visible around the area where the heel meets the leg.

Treatment

Clean the wound and keep it dry and clean. Thrush treatments are popular options but may aggravate the discomfort from this condition, so the cleft may be cleaned out with gauze and furacin ointment.

Outcome

Like many of the hoof conditions and maladies discussed, the prognosis is good for a horse to return to work with mechanically solid trimming or shoeing.

Keratoma

This rare disease is essentially a tumor of the hoof wall. To date, not much research exists on its causes.

Toxic Plant *Hoary Alyssum*

A few years after a student graduated from the Cornell Farriery program, he called to ask about "that weed" I'd lectured on. The individual was working for a high-end show jumping barn in Wellington, Florida, and during a visit, he observed that every horse had swollen legs. The graduate remembered being warned about symptoms associated with a horse eating this toxic plant. He checked the hay and sure enough found it in the bale. Two of the horses developed laminitis. Several other horses had edema in the lower limbs, which could have progressed to laminitis. This former student's alertness contributed to saving these horses.

Hoary alyssum is one of the most common poisonous plants to horses (fig. 7.13). Horses prefer not to eat it but can ingest it when it is in baled hay or when the grass is sparse. It may take 12 to 24 hours to notice a change. Symptoms include a 103-degree Fahrenheit or higher fever, heat in the hooves, pronounced digital pulse, stiff joints, unwillingness to move, and a "camped-out" stance. Death is rare.

Removing the plant from the food supply is critical. The clinical signs may disappear within a few days with supportive care such as oral and intravenous fluids. If eating the plant develops into laminitis, recovery time will be extended.

7.13 Hoary alyssum is one of the most common poisonous plants to horses, and when eaten, signs of toxicity can show up in the hoof.

Signs

Swelling at the coronary band or hoof wall with some growing to the size of a golf ball. As the tumor grows, it forces a painful separation between the laminae and hoof wall. Lameness is also apparent in this situation.

Treatment

Farriers and veterinarians must work together to surgically remove the growth, which may be done under local or general anesthesia. The wound is soaked in antiseptic to prevent bacteria from taking hold. These horses are often outfitted with a hospital plate, a shoe with a pad designed to unscrew for easy treatment and cleaning (see p. 51).

Outcome

Surgery is necessary and is followed by a layup. The long-term prognosis is positive for horses with a keratoma. As with all hoof problems, the sooner it is diagnosed and treated, the better the outcome.

Laminitis

Another poorly understood hoof condition is *laminitis*. The painful inflammation of the hoof laminae can be career-ending for some horses. Inflammation is triggered by overeating and obesity, or a shock to the system, such as a retained placenta, a high fever, Potomac Horse Fever, or toxic plant ingestion. Horses with equine metabolic syndrome are at great risk for developing laminitis. Insulin resistance or malfunction of the pituitary gland from Cushing's disease can also be to blame.

Signs

The hoof is hot to the touch, and there is a bounding digital pulse, as blood flow increases as the circulatory systems begins to malfunction. A horse with laminitis frequently shifts his weight, is short-strided, or leans backward to relieve pressure on the front feet and "walks on eggshells."

Treatment

The underlying issue that triggered the inflammation must first be addressed to develop a treatment plan. That means calling the vet and taking radiographs. In severe cases, the toxins in the blood cause rotation of the coffin bone, which is called *founder*.

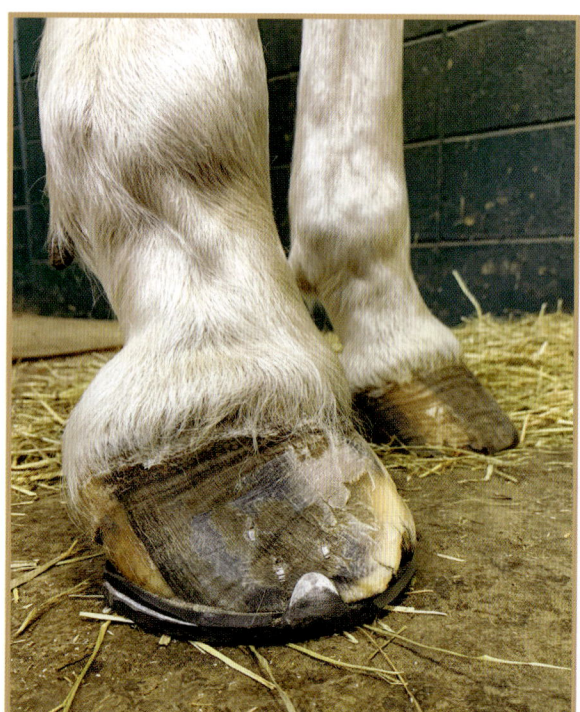

7.14 Therapeutic shoeing is used on horses with chronic laminitis to provide pain relief and support to the internal hoof structures.

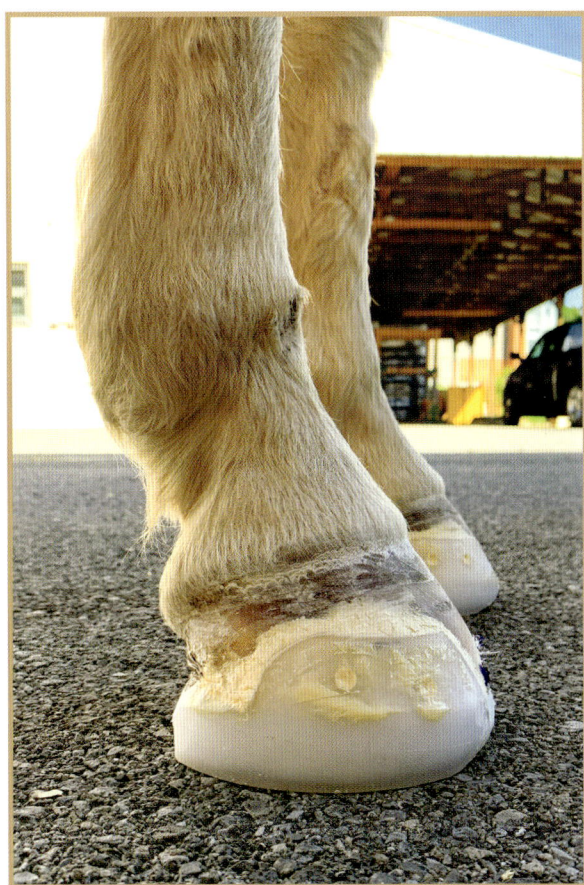

7.15 Glue-on shoes are often used for horses with acute laminitis. The glue-on shoe pictured here is called a Nanric Ultimate. It is rolled at the toe and includes elevation on the heel.

Outcome

There is no cure for laminitis. Mild to moderate cases are managed through trimming and therapeutic shoeing (figs. 7.14 & 7.15). Cold hosing has been proven to help treat flare-ups though ice boots are a more effective method for cooling the feet. In severe cases, the horse can't be saved.

Navicular Disease

Navicular is a syndrome more than a disease that creates soundness problems in the horse. It is typically seen in the front feet and can lead to severe lameness. The navicular bone is at the back of the coffin joint and connects several bones in the joint through the suspensory ligaments (see fig. I.1, pg. 3). Interference with blood supply or trauma to the bone can lead to navicular (fig. 7.16).

Horses with abnormally low or high hoof angles are more susceptible to navicular disease. Low-angled feet create excessive concussion on the heel as it lands on the ground. Conversely, horses with high-angled feet land toe-first, which smashes the heels on the surface with each stride.

Signs

Early clues include subtle lameness, stumbling, and "pointing"—the term used to describe when one side is

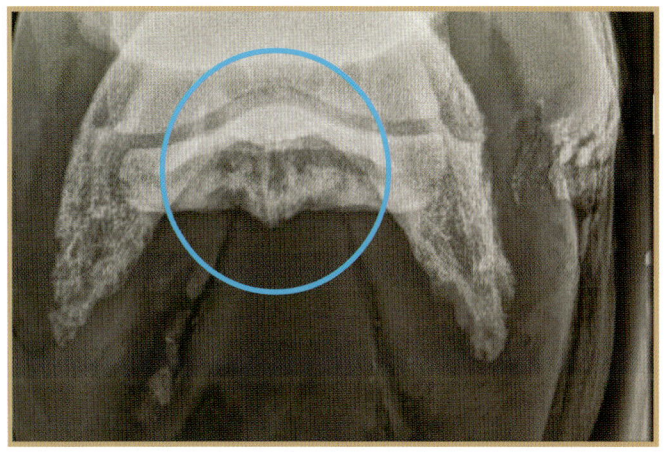

7.16 This radiograph shows degeneration of the navicular bone. Notice the rough edges and irregular shape of the bone (circled), indicating the progression of the hoof pathology.

affected more than another. The horse shifts his weight off the affected leg more than the other because, like us, the horse is a little more dominant on one side. A horse that repeats this motion multiple times during a 15- to 20-minute period is likely experiencing navicular pain. Another indication is frequent, unasked-for lead changes without prompting from the rider.

Treatment

Corrective trimming and shoeing, often with a rolled-toe egg bar shoe (see p. 49), is used to lessen pressure and pain to reduce leverage on this sensitive area. Painkillers like Bute are used to keep a horse comfortable. In some cases, the nerves in the hoof are removed in a process called a "neurectomy" to provide relief.

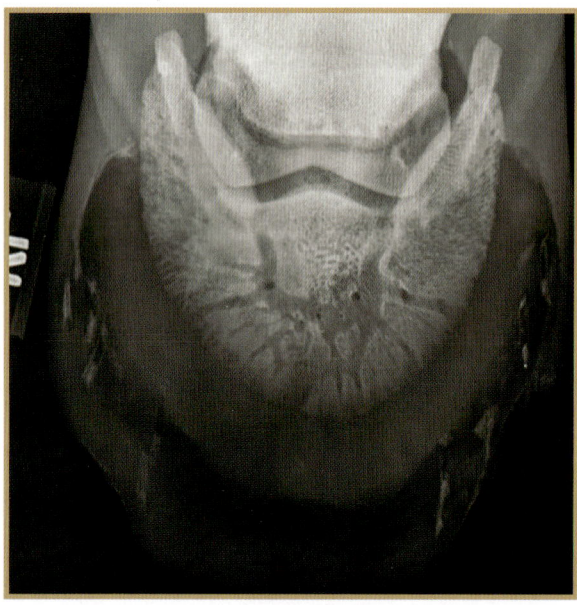

7.17 An advanced case of coffin-bone deterioration is called pedal osteitis. The radiograph shows the poor margins around the coffin bone.

Outcome

Navicular can never be cured, but the horse can be kept comfortable with proper shoeing and trimming. Horses with milder cases return to work.

Pedal Osteitis

In advanced cases, *pedal osteitis* makes the coffin bone look like a piece of Swiss cheese because the disease is a demineralization (breakdown) and inflammation of the coffin bone. The area becomes inflamed, causing severe pain. Chronic flat feet and extremely poor blood circulation in the hoof can contribute to the development of pedal osteitis.

Conformation and breed are significant contributing factors to the development of pedal osteitis rather than intensity or duration of work. For example, one would think Amish buggy horses pounding on the pavement would be at a higher risk for the breakdown of bone, but it is not common in these horses (fig. 7.17).

Signs

Outward signals can suggest this condition is occurring inside the hoof. Visible signs include lameness, a shortened stride, and flat feet. Puncture wounds or abrasions on the sole are also common in these hooves.

Treatment

Wider-web shoes, pads, and unloading frog support are all ways a farrier can help a horse with pedal osteitis.

Outcome

When a farrier catches pedal osteitis early, he can stop the progression of bone loss. Good management can keep the horse comfortable and potentially get back to work in a short timeframe, but the bone damage can never be reversed. In undiagnosed cases, the coffin bone can continue to deteriorate.

Punctures

A *puncture wound* is the result of stepping on a sharp object—a nail, wire, or screw, for example. This injury was called "street nail" when horses served as the main transportation option. At that time, people dropped all kinds of debris in the street. The working horses would step on the waste and wound themselves.

Signs

It is easy to identify a foreign item lodged in the horse's hoof. It may be noticed during routine hoof picking or when the horse won't bear weight on one foot. (Tip: Add gauze or some type of soft material to your first aid kit. This can be used to create a cushion around the area of the horse's hoof that has been punctured to keep him from pushing the object farther into the hoof until it is removed.)

Treatment

Calling the vet is the first step. If possible, leave the object in the hoof while awaiting the vet's arrival. The vet will likely take a radiograph to see how deep the penetration is. A sterile probe and contrast dye can help determine if the wound is superficial or in the danger zone. The coffin bone and the deep digital flexor tendon (DDFT) are not far below the sole and frog of the hoof. Both are right behind the middle of the frog, and these structures can be severely injured by a tiny object.

The depth and other structures involved determines if a horse will have a difficult or simple chance of recovery. A combination of antibiotics, soaking the foot, and using a hospital plate shoe to keep out bacteria and dirt are typically routine treatments for puncture wounds.

Outcome

The prognosis is based on how deep the object pierced the foot and if it affected other structures in the hoof, such as the coffin bone or DDFT. Most often, with proper care, a horse can fully recover. When the object invades tendon sheaths, it is an expensive treatment with poor recovery and when an item hits the coffin bone, *osteomyelitis* may develop (see below).

Osteomyelitis

This is the scientific term used to describe an infection of the bone. In this case, it occurs in the coffin bone. When an abscess is unable to drain properly, the infection can work its way into the coffin bone. The painful infection can also follow a case of laminitis (see p. 111).

Signs

The horse's posture is one indicator of osteomyelitis. The affected horse positions his legs underneath his body and shifts weight downward, so he is standing on his toes. Severe pain might mean the horse lies down for long periods, which can create sores on his elbows and legs.

Treatment

Removing the infected tissue is the only solution. After surgery, the horse is often outfitted with a hospital plate for regular flushing and cleaning until the wound is healed.

Outcome

When caught early enough and when the treatment protocol is closely followed, the horse can heal. However, advanced cases are difficult to turn around, and prognosis is guarded to "fair."

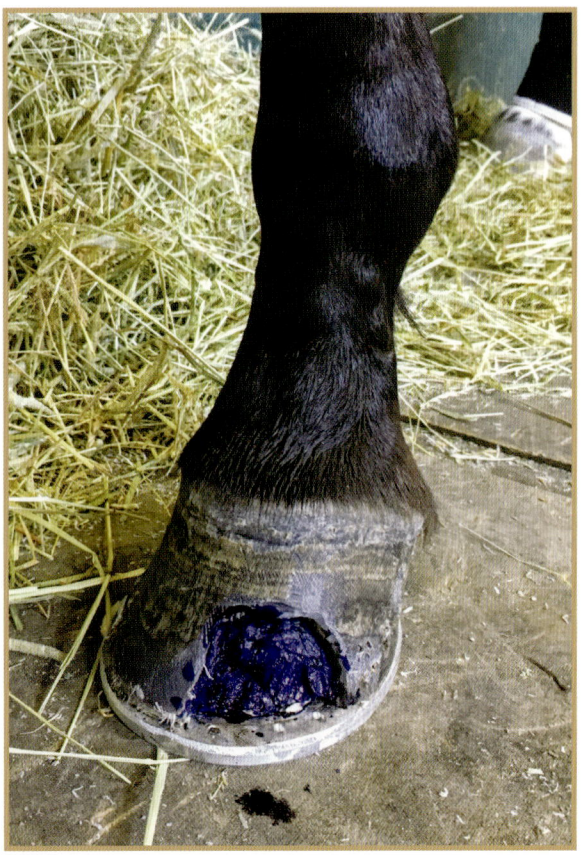

7.18 In cases of white-line disease the affected tissue is cut away or resected, treated with topical medications, and a shoe is used to support the frog while the hoof tissue regrows.

White Line Disease

This fungal infection of the hoof is more difficult to treat than you would think it should be. It should be as easy as killing the offending spores. However, treating *white line disease* is complicated. Bacteria and fungi naturally exist inside the hoof wall in a mutually beneficial relationship. But in some horses, this turns into an infection of the tissues in the hoof wall (fig. 7.18).

It is a difficult disease to predict. You might see multiple horses living in the same barn without this issue, then you end up with one horse prone to developing it. The fungi that are found in white line disease are commonly found in the environment and tend to be opportunists by finding a way into an individual horse with immunocompromised tissues.

Conformation flaws such as club feet or low heels and long toes, which usually have flares in the quarters, potentially predispose a horse to hoof-wall separation. Pathologies such as laminitis can also create opportunities for the development of white line disease.

Signs

The outside of the hoof looks like a piece of wood chewed by termites. The fungi enter the bottom of the foot and eat their way up into the hoof. This is a slow-developing situation and may not be visible until up to three-quarters of the hoof wall is affected.

Treatment

The first step is to remove the infected tissue. There is a fine line between resecting enough and taking too much. Once the affected area is opened, drying and antiseptic products are applied to disinfect the area. Sometimes copper sulfate is used; however, this substance should be used carefully and not applied on sensitive tissue near the coffin bone. The horse typically ends up in a heart-bar shoe (see p. 102). The separated hoof wall is usually removed exposing the laminae. Antifungal products are applied, the hoof must be kept clean and dry, but wrapping is not recommended to avoid moisture retention.

Outcome

Treating white line disease is complicated. It's a delicate balance between prevention and treatment, and once a horse has a case, it is predisposed to recurrences.

Thrush

Similar to an abscess (see p.102), *thrush* is a bacterial infection in the hoof. Thrush is the second-most-common hoof issue horse owners must be aware of, and it is preventable with proper management. Standing in damp, dirty conditions in a stall or muddy lot, and a lack of hoof picking is typically to blame, so changing management practices has the biggest impact on avoiding this malady.

Horses with an upright club foot are more prone to developing thrush because the deeper frog is more likely to hold manure than a flatter hoof. Proper trimming and shoeing, a clean, dry living environment, and regular hoof picking are even more critical for these horses than those with a normal hoof.

Signs

A putrid smell. A rotten scent wafting up as you pick out your horse's feet is an indication thrush is developing. Early in the infection, a black, oily, or greasy coating can be seen on the frog. Another indication of thrush is when the frog looks like a shriveled raisin rather than a plump grape. The infection can become painful, causing the horse to limp.

Treatment

Routine trimming is typically enough to cure minor cases of thrush because the farrier cuts away the areas that look infected. Horses on regular farrier schedules are unlikely to develop a more severe case. Horses trimmed every six months or at longer intervals are at a much higher risk for developing thrush and will take longer to treat.

In addition to trimming, topical treatments can help dry out the hoof and kill the bacteria living in the hoof. There's an old wives' tale recommending the use of bleach to kill the infection—but that is *not recommended*. The caustic solution can kill healthy cells along with infected tissue.

In extreme cases, veterinarians may recommend medical maggots packed into the hoof. These "medical-grade" fly larvae eat away at the infected tissue.

Outcome

How long it takes to heal is case-specific. Some horses clear up and return to work within two to three weeks. Even though the damage to the frog is still there, the sensitivity is gone. New frog growth pushes out over time, and affected tissues are trimmed out over the next few farrier appointments. In drastic cases, it can take a month or more for the sensitivity to go away.

High/Low Syndrome (Mismatched Front Feet)

This condition is considered a conformation problem; however, it leads to several hoof diseases. Unsoundness is common when one hoof has a higher-than-normal angle and the other foot has a lower-than-normal angle. It can be congenital (present at birth) or develop over time and be impacted by how the horse is managed and ridden. Excessive counter-cantering or working in one direction can contribute to high/low syndrome.

Foals born with this condition need immediate intervention for correction. When a young horse begins grazing, he may tend to keep one foot forward more than the other, especially if he has long legs and a small, refined head. Known as "grazing stance," the extended front leg becomes the low-angled, flat, wide hoof, and the leg that is retracted backward becomes the steep-angled narrow foot. Eventually, the horse becomes dominant-sided to the wide flat foot, with an overdeveloped shoulder on that side as the horse matures. The side of the foot with a narrow, steep angle develops an atrophied shoulder.

The consequences of high/low syndrome can be indicated by a reluctance to canter on the lead on the steep-foot side, uncomfortable while posting to a trot on the steep-foot diagonal, and a predisposition for navicular disease on the steep-foot side. Since the low-angled foot is being overloaded, it contributes to navicular disease and pedal osteitis (pp. 113 and 114).

Treatment

How the horse is managed varies based on farrier preference and how far the situation has progressed. Lateral radiographs can be used to determine the coffin bone angles, which are more important to observe than dorsal hoof wall angles. The goal is getting the horse to strengthen the atrophied side of his body to reduce strain on the overused side. Shoeing methods allow for mechanical options; however, it is important to have a well-fitted saddle and to ride in both directions on the correct lead.

Outcome

Young horses are helped the most with early intervention, which can influence how the bones and structures of the hoof and leg develop. Mature horses can only be managed with appropriate shoeing and training. Shoeing protocols can have a mechanical influence on the horse's gait but do not change the underlying bony changes that have occurred.

The Vet-Farrier Partnership

Veterinarians and farriers share a common goal—to provide the best care possible for the individual horse. Often the farrier and veterinarian must work together to find the best solution for supporting horses with chronic or acute hoof diseases and conditions. Both professionals bring specific tools and skills that complement each other.

Usually, the veterinarian is the first to arrive on the scene when lameness or injury is observed. The veterinarian has the equipment and diagnostic skills to identify the problem or provide first aid. In an ideal situation, the veterinarian talks with the farrier to discuss therapeutic horseshoeing options for the problem at hand.

Technology makes communicating with one another on a case or meeting at a client's barn easier than ever. Yet, many professionals on both sides struggle to work well together. In new relationships, the horse owner can invite both parties to schedule a call at the same time to meet one another and the horse. In situations where one professional or the other refuses to communicate or work together, it may be time to find someone new.

The Lameness Exam

When a veterinarian is first called for limping or soreness, he starts with a lameness exam. The typical lameness exam begins with a physical evaluation of the horse as he stands.

The next step is to walk the horse away and toward the person observing the animal. Severe lameness is obvious as the horse limps or bobs his head with every stride. Other cases are more subtle with a change in posture.

He also watches for a normal hoof landing pattern—where the heel contacts the ground just before the toe. The opposite—landing toe first—indicates a problem. The third step is to trot the horse looking for an asymmetrical gait (fig. 7.19).

Jogging the horse in hand on a circle offers further clues to the cause of lameness. When a horse nods his head downward mid-stride, skilled professionals an decide specifically where the source of pain is coming from.

Veterinarians use a 5-point grading scale developed by the American Association of Equine Practitioners (AAEP) to classify lameness severity (see sidebar

AAEP Lameness Severity Scale	
Grade	**Degree of Lameness**
0	Lameness is not perceptible under any circumstances.
1	Lameness is difficult to observe and is not consistently apparent, regardless of circumstances (under saddle, circling, inclines, hard surface, and so on).
2	Lameness is difficult to observe at a walk or when trotting in a straight line but is consistently apparent under certain circumstances (weight-carrying, circling, inclines, hard surface, and so on).
3	Lameness is consistently observable at a trot under all circumstances.
4	Lameness is obvious at a walk.
5	Lameness produces minimal weight-bearing in motion or at rest, or a complete inability to move.

above). Once the veterinarian identifies the affected limb, hoof testers are used to pinpoint soreness in the foot. When no pain is present in the hoof, the vet moves to other parts of the leg to find the source of the problem. Temporary nerve blocks may be part of the evaluation procedure to narrow down the location.

A Lameness Locator is another tool that can be used and offers an objective method for grading and recording lameness. Sensors placed on the horse's croup and lower leg capture precise movements of the horse's head, pelvis, and leg. The device transmits 200 data points per second. When used with Bluetooth

7.19 Veterinarians like to watch a horse moving toward and away from them to help them isolate the source of lameness.

The Bottom Line

For front-end lameness, the role of horseshoes is varied, depending upon the disease or injury. In general, lameness involving the front limbs mostly occurs below the fetlock as a result of the front feet bearing most of the horse's weight. For instance, navicular disease is typically a front-end problem, seldom affecting the hind feet. Horseshoes and pads may be used to protect the sole and frog, improve breakover for arthritic joints, support the bony column, or aid in medication.

technology, it allows for long-range, real-time analysis. Keeping records like this over a horse's lifetime can make it easier for farriers and vets to observe a change early in development.

Radiographs are also part of the lameness diagnostic process. An internal view of the hoof shows if any bony abnormalities or joint misalignments are present. Spaces that look like a pocket of air, signal that there might be an abscess. However, X-rays are limited to skeletal structures. MRI imaging and CT scans are needed to see soft tissue injuries.

Lameness involving the hind limbs mostly occurs from the hock, stifle, and hip joints, which take abuse from muscles used to propel the horse forward. However, direct trauma, hoof conditions, and hoof abscesses can happen on either end. Laminitis can occur on all four feet but tends to be more painful on the front feet due to the higher weight-bearing function. Although hind shoes may offer the same support benefits as front shoes, the function of hind shoes is to alleviate problems farther up the leg. Added lateral or caudal support aids in shifting weight bearing and supporting the muscle mass above the hocks.

Hoof diseases, injuries, and injuries of joints and soft tissues of the leg are best treated with veterinary-farrier teamwork. Both have the unique skills to combine for the horse's benefit. Commonly veterinarians do the diagnostic work and farriers make the application of recommended shoes. Some veterinarians possess both skills, and the specialists are known as "equine podiatrists." Lameness and shoeing can create a gray area defining whether a veterinarian or farrier is "responsible," so teamwork is the best solution for the horse.

FROM THE FORGE
Meeting Burney Chapman and Learning About Laminitis Treatment

Laminitis or "founder" has been a problem for horses as long as they have been around. Laminitis refers to inflammation of the sensitive laminae that surrounds the coffin bone, whereas founder refers to the actual sinking or rotating of the coffin bone. Most commonly, we think about it occurring in obese horses, but other forms of laminitis occur for other reasons. Laminitis can limit a horse's career and may even be a reason to euthanize a horse. Up until the 1980s, farriers and veterinarians were relatively powerless to treat the disease effectively. That all changed when farrier Burney Chapman decided to work on it.

Along with veterinarian Dr. George Platt, Burney started experimenting by using frog-support shoes on feedlot horses that developed laminitis in West Texas. The early results of their work produced repeatable, effective treatment for these horses. The frog support consisted of fabricating a heart bar shoe to produce the right amount of frog pressure after removing the excess heel growth. Then the removal of the diseased laminae in the front of the foot aided in the recovery process. This work appeared in the *American Farriers Journal* and created enough excitement that Burney and George were invited to demonstrate at the American Farriers Association Convention in Houston, Texas, in 1983.

Buster Conklin (Resident Farrier at Cornell University) and I were eager to see the work, so we headed to Texas. At the host hotel, a horse with chronic laminitis arrived at the third floor ballroom in the freight elevator. To protect the carpet, a large blue tarpaulin was spread out. There Burney showed the attendees how to treat this awful disease, and Buster and I put his method to work after seeing it and produced similar results. From that point on, we had a means of helping afflicted horses.

Burney would say that the heart bar shoe is nothing new and was not his invention, but his reimagining of it has helped more horses than any other modern-day procedure. Burney became a worldwide expert at helping afflicted horses and farriers treating laminitis. Along with Myron McLane, Burney gave many clinics throughout the world, teaching farriers how to properly do a toe resection, and fabricate and apply a heart bar shoe. Their work led to other innovative treatments and saved many horses.

CHAPTER 8

Hoof Care for Foals

Few things in life are cuter than a gangly-legged foal chasing after his mother. It's incredible how quickly a newborn colt stands on wobbly legs and takes his first steps. Birth to walking all occurs within the first few hours of life—it takes humans 8 to 18 months to achieve the same milestone. Given how quickly a foal must stand and walk, his hooves are critical to facilitating this process. Examining his hooves and legs within his first few weeks of life is as important as checking his vitals at birth.

While a foal is still in utero, his hooves are soft. The gelatinous *perioplic membrane* protects the mare's reproductive tract during the foaling process. Once a foal hits the ground, his hooves begin to harden. The perioplic membrane dries out and the hoof starts to transform into a sturdy horn-like material (fig. 8.1).

You might notice that the shape of a young hoof is different than an older horse's foot. The cone-like shape is wider near the coronet band and grows down to a narrower point where the hoof meets the ground. Over time, the hoof grows downward and fans out into the traditional hoof shape.

The first six months of the foal's life often determine his hoof and leg conformation as an adult.

8.1 The gelatinous-like membrane that surrounds a foal's hoof at birth is also called a "foal slipper."

Therefore, a plan for an early evaluation and a working relationship with a skilled farrier is essential for setting a young horse up for success (fig. 8.2).

Early Observation and Recognition of Problems

Eleven months is a seemingly long time to wait for a foal to arrive. Hopes, dreams, and aspirations come to fruition with a foal's entry into the world. By the end of a mare's gestation, everyone at the barn is bubbling with excitement. Ensuring the newborn and his mother are in good health is the priority. But within the first few days, it's important to take a step back and evaluate the foal's legs and hooves to rule out or identify any problems.

A foal's legs are unlikely to be straight at birth. It's also common for newborns to stand with a bit of a toed-out stance. The legs gain strength as the foal increases his activity level.

Premature foals have soft tissues in the joints and hooves that have not completely hardened and calcified as the structures do when a mare carries to term. On a radiograph, the tissues look like overcooked macaroni. Limiting exercise until the bony matrix toughens reduces the risk for injury, which allows the bones to harden so the hoof grows without further complications.

An early arrival can be stressful but can be easy to overcome. However, action is required if the horse is born with one or more conformation defects. The good news is that many can be corrected when identified and addressed early (fig. 8.3).

Some deformities are obvious at birth, while others are subtle and require regular observation. A few days

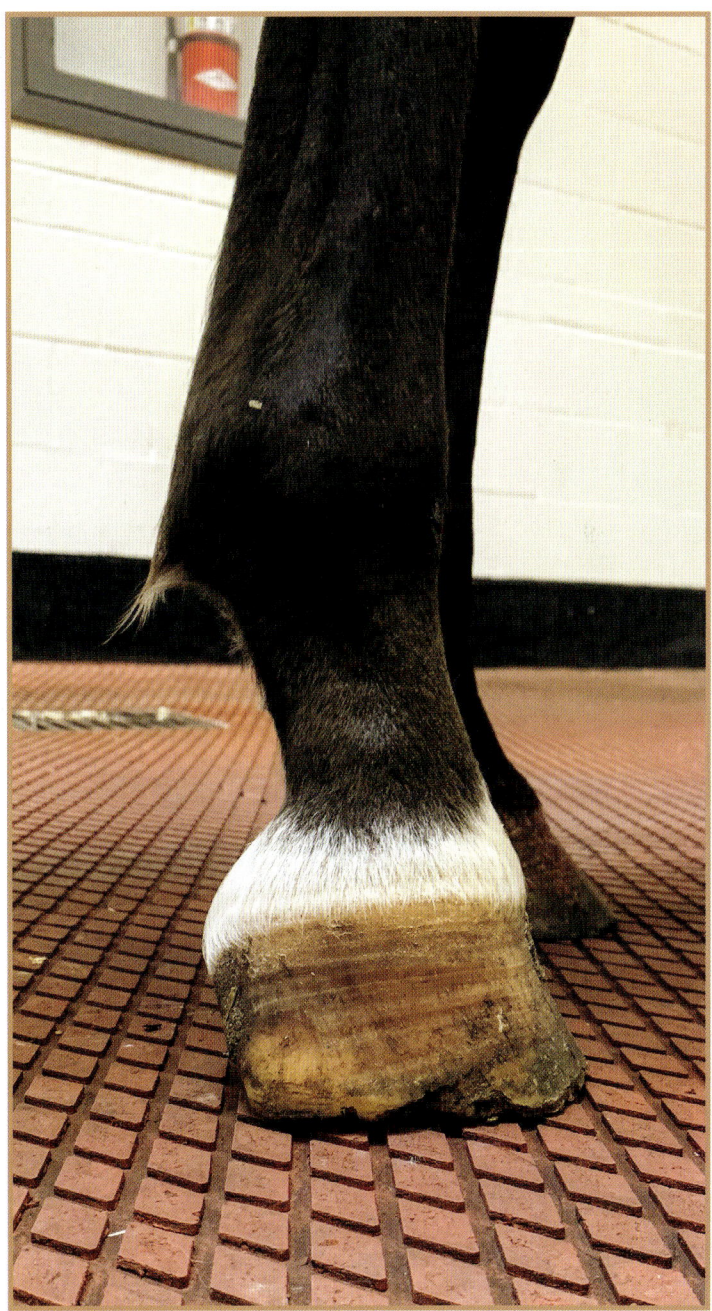

8.2 If a club foot in a foal is not corrected early, this photo shows the results. Now, only surgery will partially improve this leg.

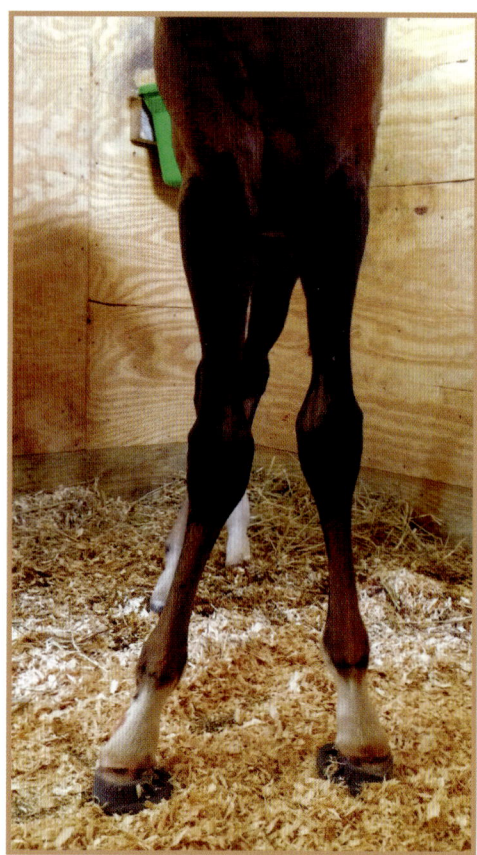

8.3 This foal has a severe base-wide, carpus valgus, a condition that must be addressed early in life. He is wearing glue-on medial support shoes to encourage straightness.

8.4 A high/low syndrome in the hoof is most noticeable while the foal is grazing. He consistently stands with the same leg pointed forward.

after the foal's arrival, take photos from the front, the side, and the rear. Stand the foal on a flat surface and as square as possible, which is much easier said than done. Repeat every few weeks to create a record of how the foal's conformation develops over time because an issue can crop up as time passes.

In Dr. Simon Curtis' book *From Foal to Racehorse*, he emphasizes that even foals born with normal hooves can develop problems when the youngster is not bearing weight equally on all four legs (fig. 8.4). Having a veterinarian or a farrier evaluate a foal as soon as one to two weeks of age gives you time to act. Some problems improve with exercise. Others will require special shoeing or even surgery to correct (figs. 8.5 & 8.6).

Limb deformities typically include joints, which means there is a limited timeframe for correcting an issue. The window of opportunity for influencing change to the leg and hooves is most successful when it occurs between four and nine months of age, the time when soft tissues begin to harden and lengthen.

There are three types of deformities in the legs: *angular*, *flexural* (p. 127), or *rotational* (p. 127). When these deviations are observed they are defined as *varus* or *valgus*. A *varus* deviation is usually at the fetlock, with the leg pointing toward the topline. Conversely, a limb that faces away from the midline has a *valgus deformity* (fig. 8.6).

What follows are common malformations that appear in foals.

Angular Limb Deformities

A limb that points away from the joint or toward the horse's midline is classified as an *angular limb deformity*. These occur when one side of the growth plate above the joint develops faster than the other.

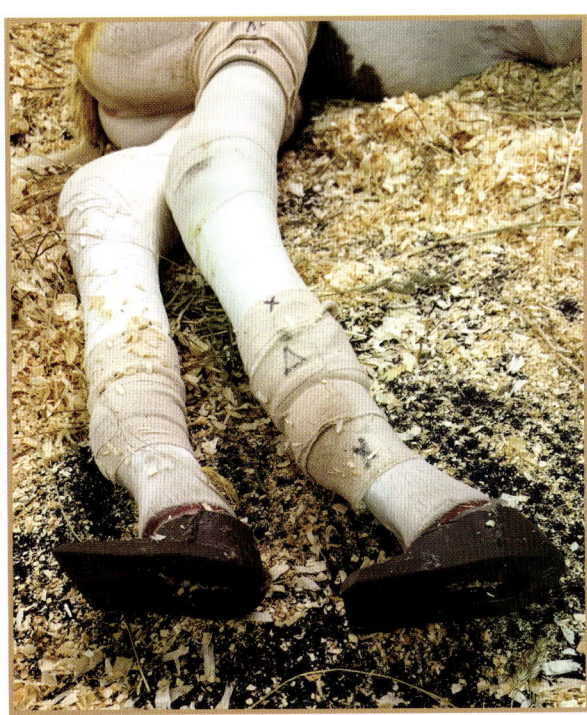

8.5 These glue-on heel extension shoes are used to help a foal with a weakness known as tendon flaccidity or laxity (see p. 126). Usually, after initial application, the foal has enough support to develop enough strength to stand properly.

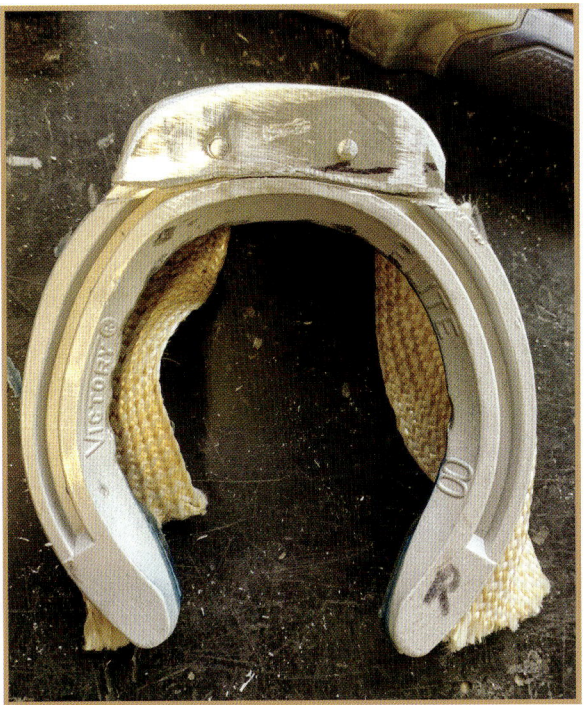

8.6 Toe extensions fabricated onto a glue-on shoe are used to support a hoof after surgery to correct a club foot.

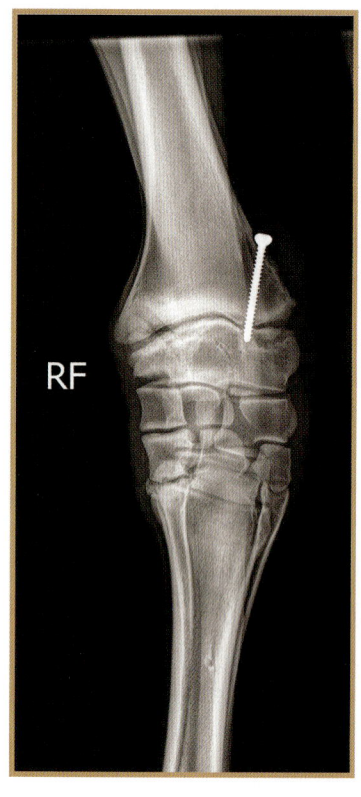

8.7 A transphyseal screw is placed in the growth plate on the opposite side of the deflected bone to slow down the growth.

An angular limb deformity occurring below the fetlock can be corrected within the first three months of life through trimming. However, work must start around one month of age. Waiting until day 89 to start an intervention decreases the chances of influencing straightness.

For mild deviations, corrective trimming every two to three weeks is sufficient. Glue-on shoes with support features can make the limb straighter in severe cases. When these less invasive interventions do not have the desired effect, surgery may be necessary before the foal hits a growth spurt. In these cases, surgeons place a screw in the growth plate to guide the joint's development (fig. 8.7).

Flexor Tendon Flaccidity

Foals are commonly born with muscle looseness, especially in the hind end. You might hear this referred to as a *tendon laxity*. This tends to correct itself as the colt moves about and gains strength. An extreme looseness in the deep digital flexor tendon (DDFT), which is found on the back of the leg, requires immediate intervention to avoid a long-term hoof deformity. Acting before the foal is a month old gives the best chances for correction.

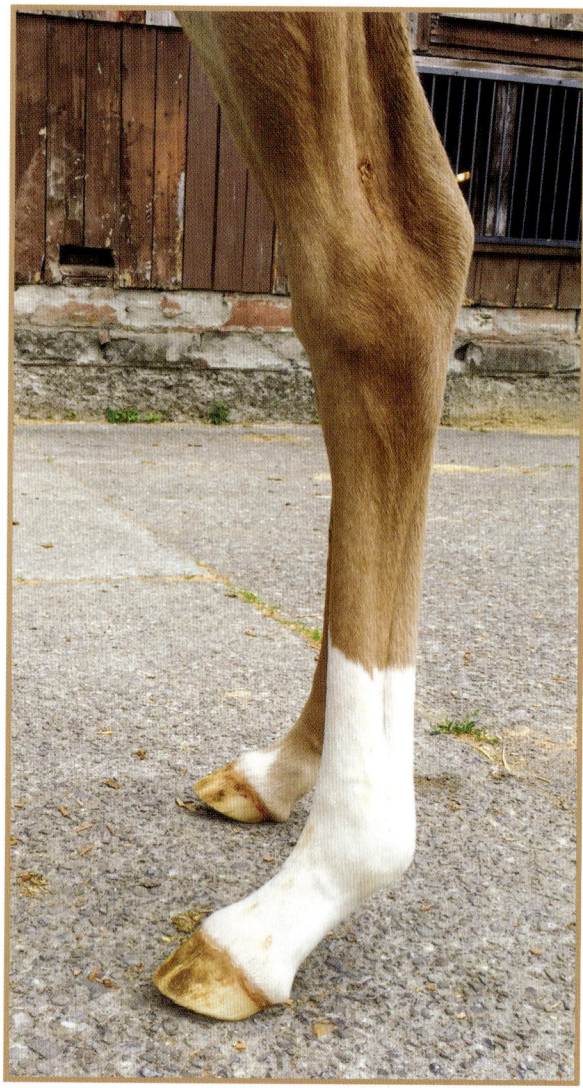

8.8 The toes are pointed up on this foal's hind feet, indicating tendon laxity.

A horse that stands on his heels with his toes off the ground displays the classic sign associated with excessive laxity. Premature, small, or sick foals may also be more likely to experience flexor tendon flaccidity (fig. 8.8).

Management strategies begin with controlled exercise and trimming. In more pronounced cases, glue-on shoes are also necessary. Depending on the severity, heel extensions are added to provide extra support so the muscle-tendon unit can shorten and strengthen (fig. 8.9).

Flexural Deformities (Contracted Tendons)

This deformity is the opposite of the one just described. In this case, the deep digital flexor muscle-tendon unit is "tight" or too short, making it impossible for a foal to fully extend his leg. This tension holds the joint in an abnormally flexed position. Flexural deformities can be present at birth or develop between two to four months (fig. 8.10).

The tendon cannot simply be stretched, so veterinarians and farriers must work together to create a plan for each foal. Often, restricted exercise, medication, splints, bandages, physical therapy, and diet changes are part of the treatment process. The drug tetracycline is a common choice for encouraging the muscles and tendons to relax. Surgery that cuts the check ligaments (the tissue that attaches to the DDFT below the knee) is used in extreme cases.

Knock Knees (Carpal Valgus)

Carpal valgus is an outward deviation at the horse's knee. This is considered an X deviation where the horse is narrow at the knee and base-wide at the lower limb. This is the most common leg deformity in young horses. It can occur in either one or both front legs and can be addressed with early trimming beginning around one month of age. The farrier is likely to

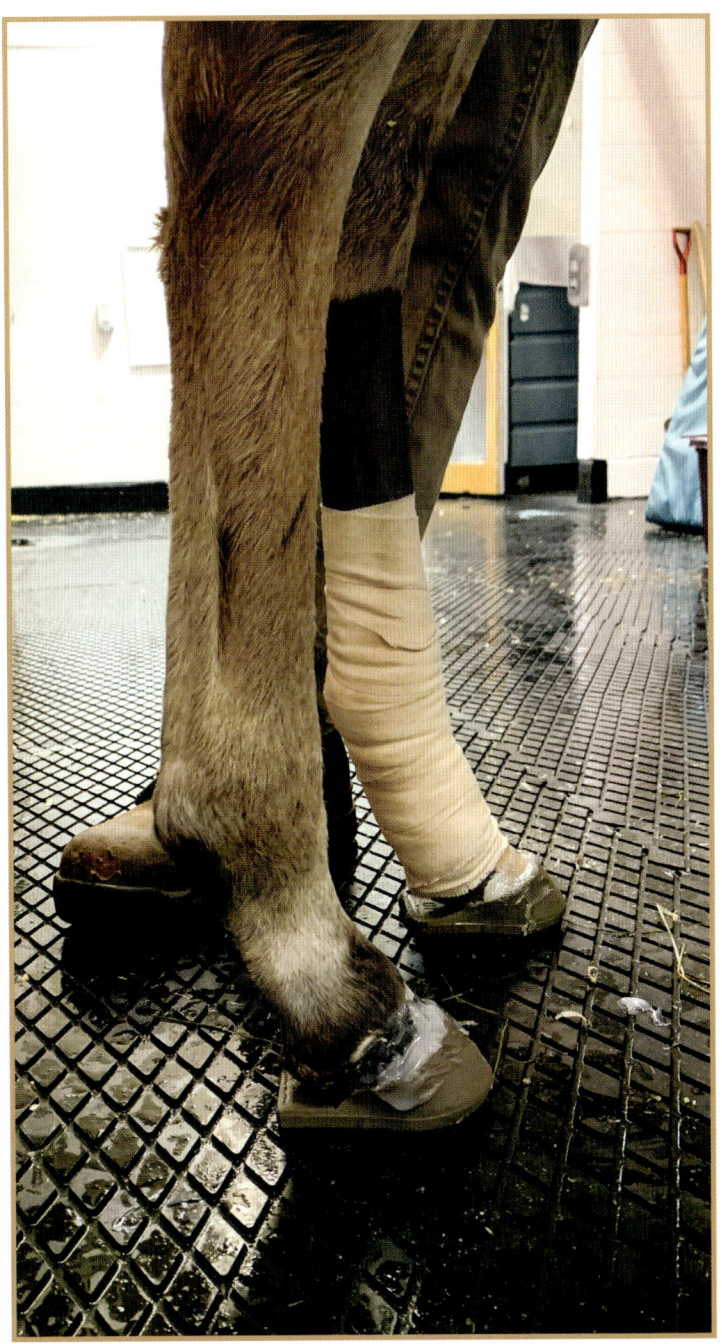

8.9 A hind tendon laxity supported with a Dalric heel extension.

8: HOOF CARE FOR FOALS | **127**

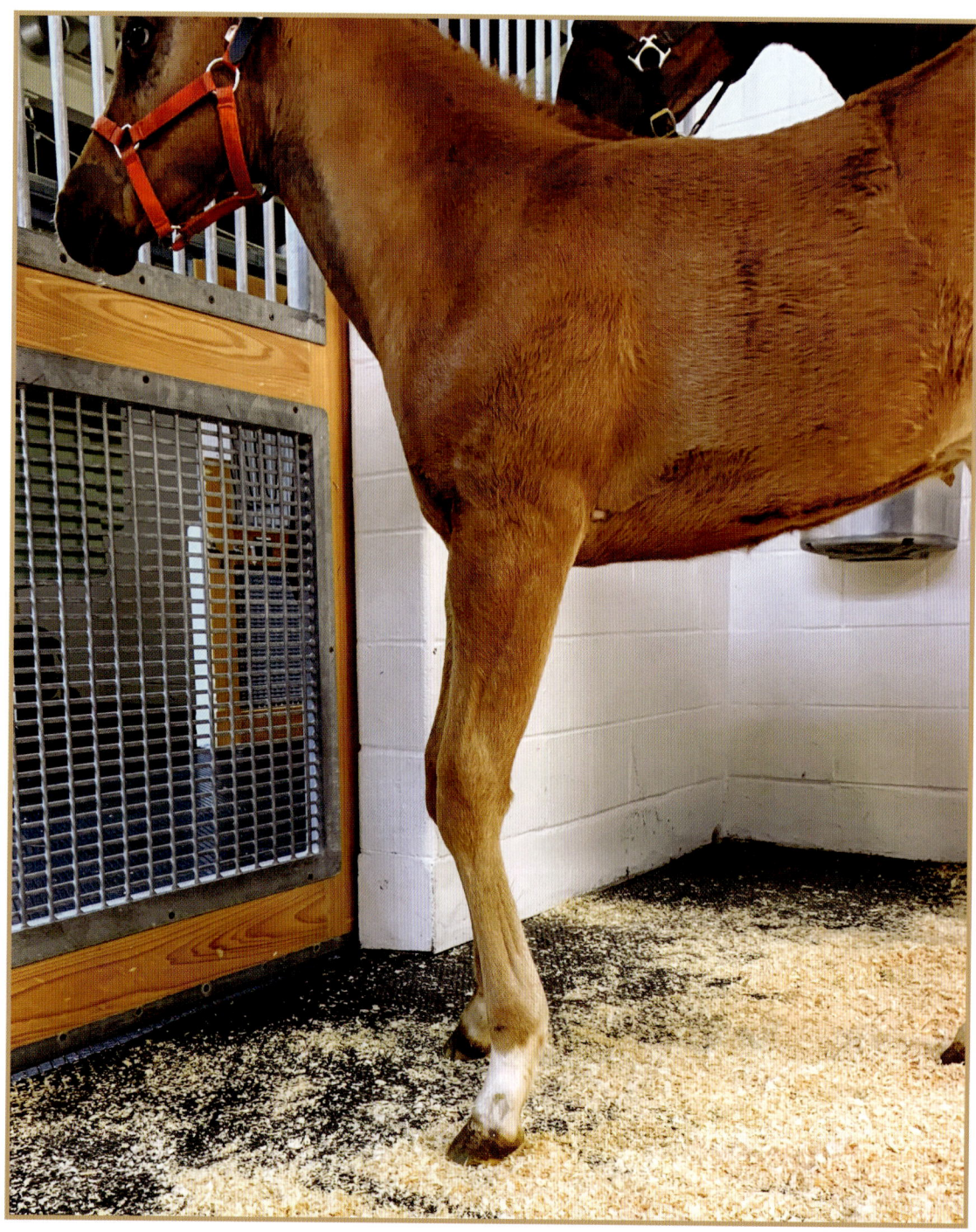

8.10 Contracted tendons, otherwise known as a flexural deformity or "over at the knees."

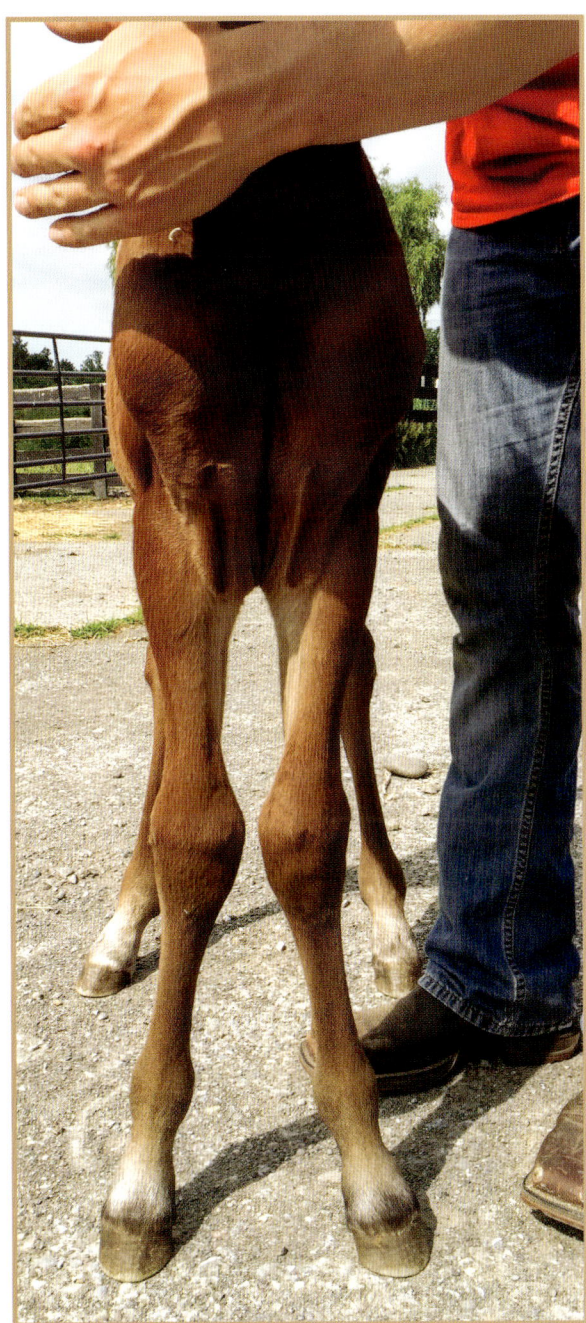

8.11 This foal is base wide and has a carpus valgus rotation, giving him a knock-kneed look.

8.12 Introducing foals to trimming early in life makes it easier to identify any deformities and prepares them not only for trimming but, eventually and if necessary, shoeing.

square the foal's toes with a rasp to remove the points and free up movement in the heels. Regularly trimming the length of the foot to the base of the frog creates a larger weight-bearing surface area (fig. 8.11).

Scheduling the farrier for monthly visits is recommended though every two weeks gives farriers more opportunities to follow the progress and monitor for signs of any other problems. Over time, trimming encourages the entire hoof to strengthen, allowing the horse to outgrow the condition (fig. 8.12).

Foal Monitoring Program—Observation and Recognition

Contributed by Normand G. Ducharme, DMV, MSc,
Cornell University Chief Medical Officer and Faculty Clinician

If you decide to have your mare(s) deliver foals, there are many management and surveillance protocols to establish. In your checklist of "things to do" is evaluating and recognizing if "crooked legs" are present early.

At the first week of life, you should evaluate the foal. Take pictures of the standing foal by aligning your cell phone camera with the toe of each hoof. Then snap a few of the foal walking toward and away from you. These serve as records for your foal and can be shared to your farrier and veterinarian. To quote Dr. Brett Woodie of Rood & Riddle Equine Hospital, we "make more mistakes from not looking than not knowing."

Crossing your fingers and ignoring it is not a good strategy. That is because early on, meaning a few days to a few weeks of age or after the appearance of the deformity, the majority of problems can be managed by change in exercise, such as turnout, glue-on shoes, and later on by corrective trimming. The goal is to avoid surgical intervention.

In general, there are three windows of opportunity for influencing correction in foal limb problems:

1 First few weeks of life: Noninvasive, simple activity restriction or increase, and farrier treatment (glue-on shoe) modalities are successful in managing crooked legs.

2 One to three months: Corrective trimming, splinting, casting, and systemic medications are used to influence limb development.

3 Two to seven months: Surgical intervention that affects growth plate imbalance. These are generally surgical procedures that target the imbalance of the growth plate causing the deformity.

As each window closes, the complications rate and morbidity rate increases. And at some point, in some conditions, the deformity is permanent. There is a risk of doing nothing. Monitoring the foal closely, ideally weekly, and focusing treatment in Window One is best. Ignoring early problems and hoping to address them in Window Three is a poor strategy as an aggressive approach will be needed to help the horse.

Depending on the severity of the limb deformity, the condition could affect the athletic potential, result in the need for lifelong farrier management, corrective shoeing, and decrease the sale and resale value of the horse.

The farrier and veterinarian have different strengths for identifying normal, abnormal, and the gray area in between. Although the veterinarian can perhaps make a more precise medical diagnosis sometimes with the help of imaging, the farrier is best at tailoring the treatment to the individual foal. Together and with you, they form an integral part of optimal guidance of what to do: when to only monitor and when to intervene with one or more treatment modalities. When treatments are not giving the expected results, the farrier and veterinarian working in consultation can indicate a different course.

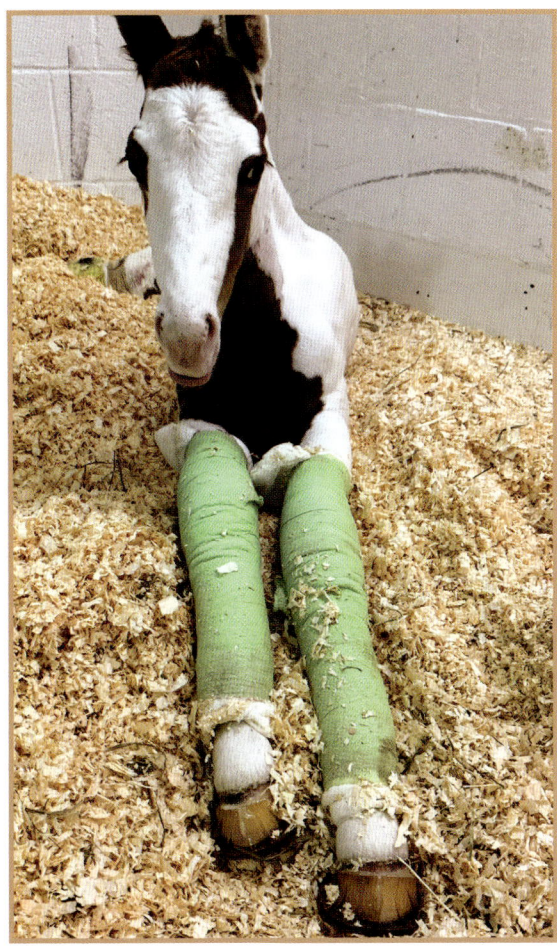

8.13 This foal had severe toed-in conformation. With the help of splints and medial extension shoes, the legs will straighten.

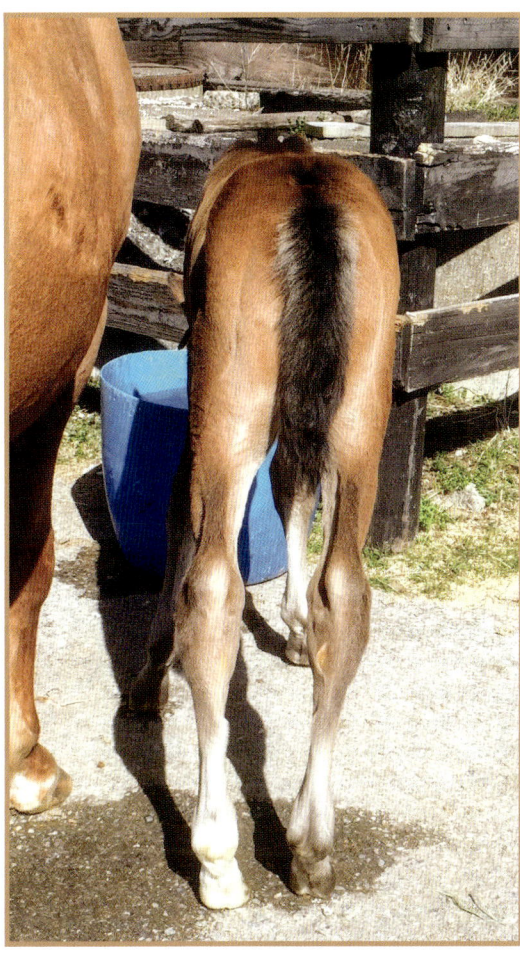

8.14 Observing a deformity like this left fetlock varus defect early is essential to increase the chances of correcting the issue.

Consequences of Inaction

Early observation, recognition, and intervention, when necessary, cannot be overemphasized. Being proactive is the best way to guarantee a straight-legged horse and protect the investment and time in raising a foal (fig. 8.13).

Paying attention to the development of a foal's legs from birth is the least expensive management approach but is often neglected (fig. 8.14). As time slips by, the growth plates ossify or "close." At that point, whichever axis is not plumb or aligned will remain in that position. Good farriery can manage the hoof to help with misaligned limbs, but it cannot fix anything as the first year slips away. The farther up the limb where there may be a misalignment, the less farriery can help the mature horse. (A foal does not grow nearly as much hoof wall as an older horse during the first few months, so it's essential to avoid over-trimming.)

An added benefit to regular trimming is that the foal gets used to handling and working with a farrier. Imagine what it is like to shoe a three- or four-year-old horse when little or no handling or trimming has been done.

The Role of Nutrition

The foal's natural conformation and genetics are only one piece of the larger picture. Nutrition can increase a young horse's chances of developing deformities in the legs. The American Association of Equine Practitioners (AAEP) believes that "the nutritional start a foal gets can have a profound effect on its health and soundness for the rest of its life. We can accelerate growth if we choose. However, research suggests that a balanced dietary approach, which supports no more than a moderate growth rate, is less likely to cause developmental problems."

Foals often hit a growth spurt between four to eight months of age. Rapid growth rates can lead to several conditions including:

Angular limb deformities: Foals that are "creep feeding," or have ready access to feed, may be taking in too many calories for the legs and joints to keep pace with growth.

Epiphysitis (physitis): This is a bone disease found in young, growing horses. It occurs when the growth plates are enlarged. Typically, this happens in the long bones of the horse's legs, such as the tibia, radius, and cannon bones. During this rapid growth stage, young horses may experience joint swelling and pain. It's still unknown what exactly causes epiphysitis, but horses that are overweight and fed high-calorie diets are at a higher risk.

Osteochondrosis (orthopedic disease): When the cartilage does not properly convert to bone, this is called *osteochondrosis*. Bone cysts, life-long joint problems, and bone fragments contribute to joint swelling, lameness, and poor performance. While there is still much to learn about this disease, a diet that is too rich and forces a horse to grow too fast is often to blame.

Hoof Quality Determined Before Birth

The likelihood a foal will have "good" or "bad" hooves is largely determined long before his arrival. It starts in the breeding shed. Breeding is a business, and like any enterprise, it is driven by money. Race earnings, show records, performance checks, and the cumulative winnings of a horse's offspring often drive the decisions for which horses are bred (fig. 8.15).

Profit isn't the only reason for breeding horses. Some prefer having control over the horses used in a sport of choice. For instance, a high-level polo player produces his prospects for the sole purpose of creating what he feels are superior horses for playing competitively and winning games. Still, others want a foal from a beloved mare or stallion.

Often, the horse's feet get overlooked when choosing a cross based on familial performance. The leg and hoof quality of the stallion and the dam supports or hinders athleticism, performance, and required maintenance.

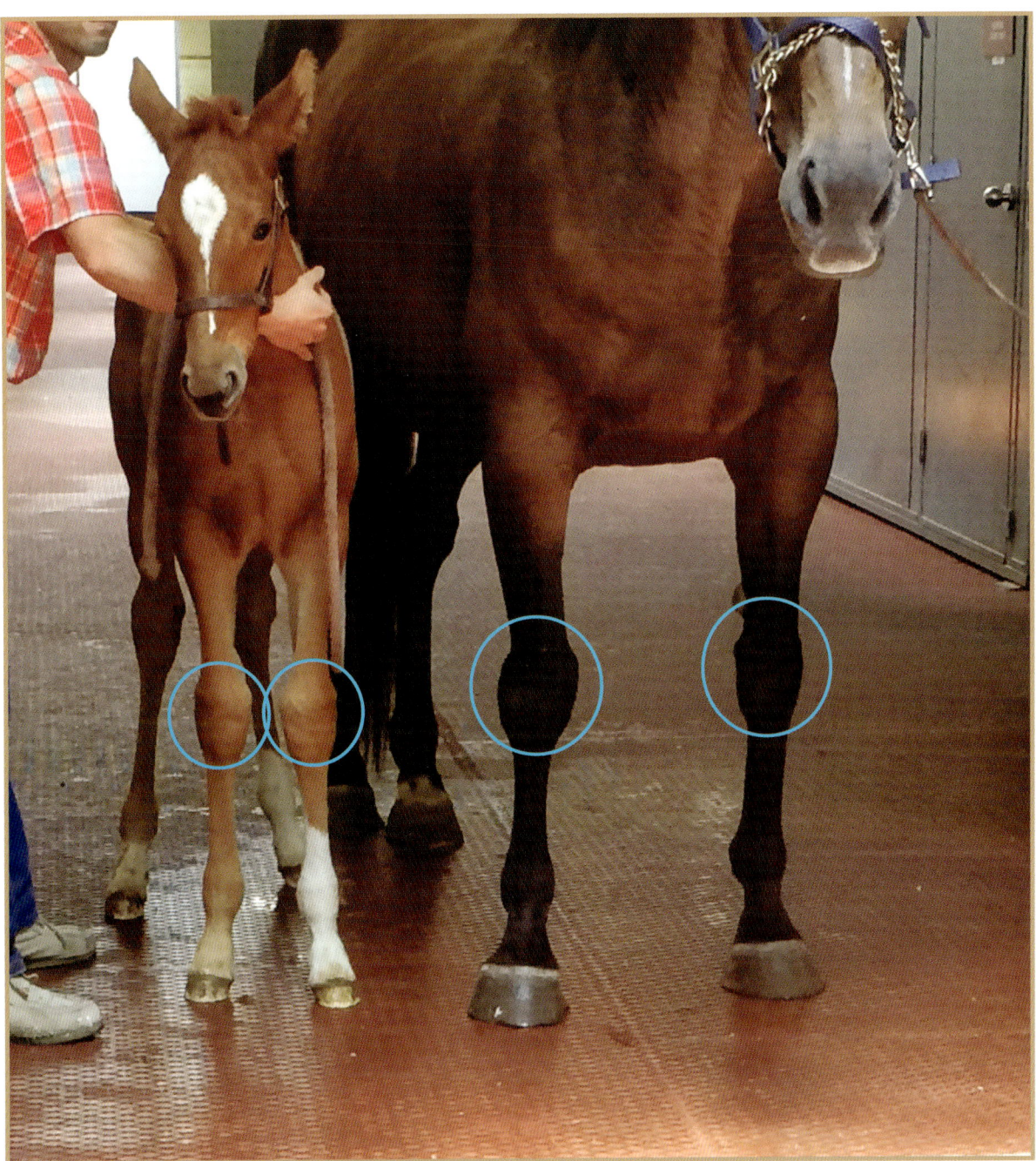

8.15 This mare and foal have the same conformational deviations on their right front limbs. Here we see a blend of "X-" and "Y-axis" deviations. Specifically, both horses are base-wide ("X-axis") and both horses have misaligned cannon bones in relation to their radius ("Y-axis"). Conformation defects are heritable.

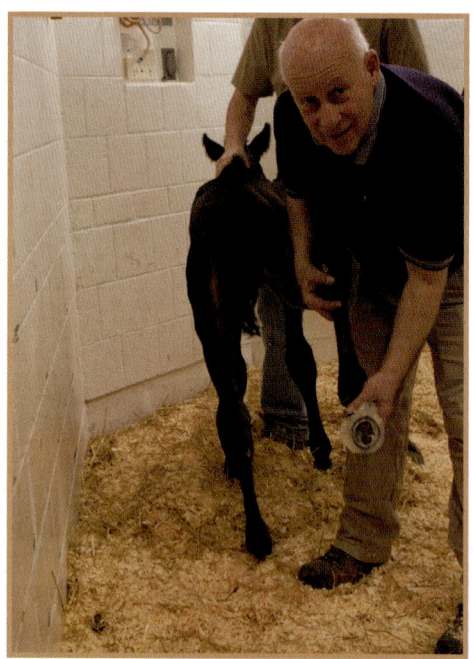

8.16 This Standardbred foal received glue-on shoes until his hind end developed enough strength to position his legs correctly.

8.17 Some limb deformities are obviously visible at birth while others show up a few weeks to months into the foal's life. Foals change rapidly, so regular inspection is necessary to stay on top of any changes. Most foals are base-wide, but will self-correct as their chest widens. To see angular limb deformities, you must observe the leg properly by standing to the side and in front of the foot to see if there are any deflections at the joints.

First, consider the stallion. Does a breed registration or a winning record make him a good match for a mare? It depends.

A Thoroughbred stud with crooked legs may be able to run fast for a short time. That same horse could not withstand the demands of other disciplines, and the reality is that many racehorses often find themselves in a second career.

Similarly, a cutting horse stallion may have the natural intuition to work a cow, but if his hooves are too small to support his body, he won't hold up for long. Crooked legs and small feet are both traits that can be passed along.

Mares are just as likely to pass along undesirable limb and hoof traits. Evaluating both horses in the equation (as we discussed in chapter 1, p. 5) gives a clearer picture of the resulting foal's potential weaknesses. In most cases, a pregnant mare does not require any more farrier work than normal. A trim every six to eight weeks keeps a mare's hooves in solid condition. Shoes may be necessary for mares with underlying issues, like chronic laminitis. The foal's weight may also cause foot soreness that can be relieved through shoeing, but such shoes are removed before foaling to avoid injury.

In any breeding situation, looking at both horses for structural correctness should come before emotion or profit to avoid debilitating (and costly) leg and hoof issues that can last a lifetime (fig. 8.16).

FROM THE FORGE
The Case for Farrier Visits for Foals

Early in my career, Harold Mowers was teaching the farrier program at Cornell University, and through his program I had many opportunities to work with young foals. It was interesting that few people were focusing on trimming foals back then. It's such a critical time in a young horse's life—a chance to make adjustments to deformed limbs before the growth plates close. I was impressed by Harold's attention to these horses, and his understanding of methods for correction before glue-on shoes were developed.

Soon I had a client of my own equally interested in hoof care early in a foal's life. John Valentino was a self-made millionaire who grew up in the streets of Brooklyn. Instead of finishing high school, he and a partner sold fruits and vegetables off a horse-drawn cart. When his partner was robbed and murdered, John took it over and parlayed that into a New York City business that supplies everything you see in a convenience store—soft drinks, cigarettes, candy, soda, and more.

John fancied racehorses so he bought 1,000 acres and established a high-level Thoroughbred breeding farm. During the 1990s, his farm was the top money earner producing New York bred horses. Two years into his operation, he asked me to visit. I'd heard he could be a challenge—a "my way or the highway" kind of guy.

He had just bought six weanlings at the Keeneland Sale in Kentucky, and their hooves were wearing unevenly on the abrasive soil of his farm. I shared this observation with Harold and my suggestion was to use a half horseshoe called a toe plate, to protect the hoof. This allowed the foot to grow without being worn away so that I could perform the necessary corrective trimming.

John also had a three-year-old, well-bred mare with a crooked front leg that was struggling in training. Her cannon bone was misaligned with her radius forcing her knee to deflect inward. The foot was trimmed the opposite way I would have done, so I pointed this out to John. After my own trimming and shoeing, her leg looked less crooked, and she moved more comfortably.

Those two instances helped me gain John's trust and respect, and I was the first one he called whenever he had a hoof or lameness problem.

Our relationship spanned 14 years, and although he was very demanding, working at his farm taught me the value of keeping records. John required that foals see the farrier within their first week of life. Then, foals were trimmed every two to three weeks for the first several months. Even if the horse only needed a few sweeps of a rasp to keep the foot straight, John was willing to pay for the work because it meant preventing larger issues from developing.

Photos and notes were taken at each visit to create a record of the changes in a horse's hooves and legs over time. This attention to detail had a big payoff—none of John's foals needed corrective surgery or therapeutic shoeing because problems were taken care of early and on a regular basis.

CHAPTER 9

What Can Possibly Go Wrong?

As in human medicine, not every farrier procedure turns out perfectly. Even with solid training, it is possible for trimming or shoeing to create lameness. Whether it is from lack of knowledge or simply an accident, a farrier can make a mistake.

The horse's hooves and legs are designed to absorb the loading forces of each footfall and transmit those pressures evenly. When the length of the hoof, the type of shoe, or hoof angle are incorrect for a horse, it will alter his movement, increase the risk of injury, and may be painful (fig. 9.1).

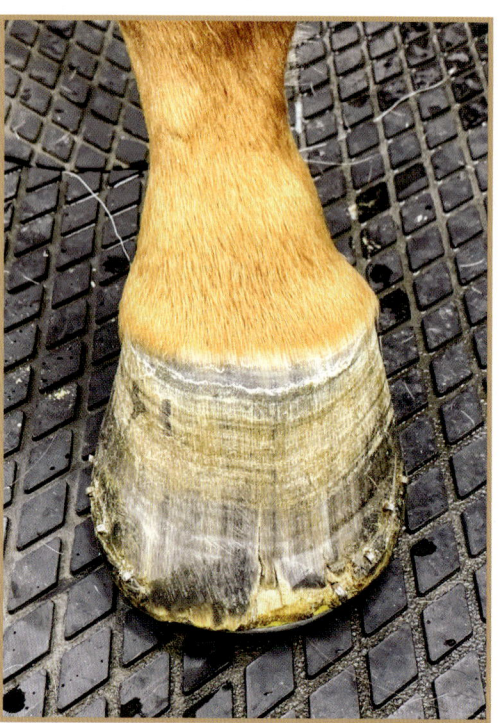

Skilled farriers make the average trimming and shoeing process look easy. But what makes good farriery so difficult is that there is no one way to trim and shoe—it is as much an art as it is a science. The practitioner must be able to visualize what he would like the horse's hooves to look like at the end of the job.

When all goes as planned, a thorough job can take an hour or less for a routine visit. The horse goes back to life as usual as if he had just walked out of a spa. A nip that is too short or a nail too close to sensitive tissues can leave a horse sore and lame (fig. 9.2).

9.1 This foot has a shoe that is too small, which inhibits proper nail placement. The clinches here were left too long. This weakens the shoeing and increases the risk for scraping the inside of the leg, creating opportunity for injury.

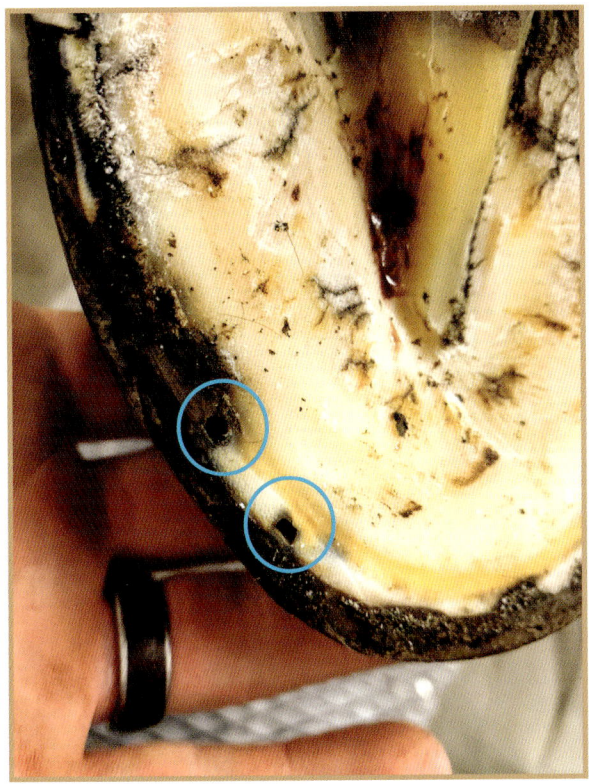 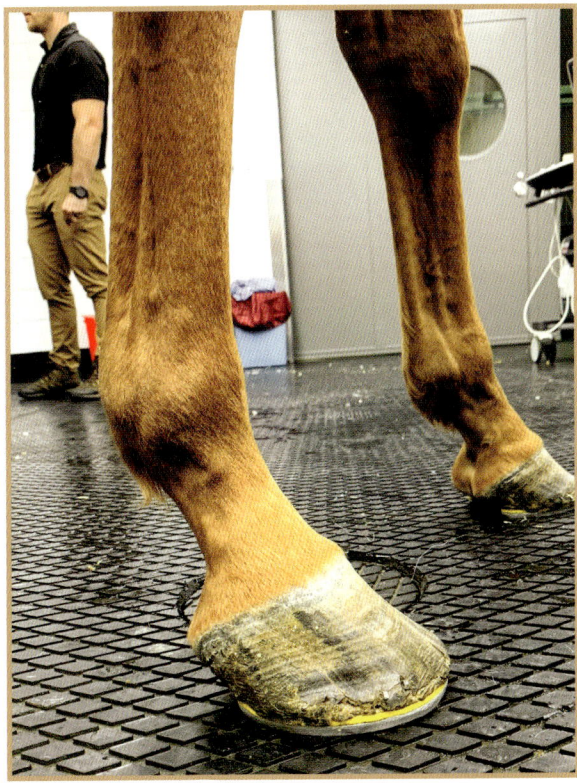

9.2 Two of three of these nail holes are inside the yellow line, which is the border between the sensitive and insensitive foot area.

9.3 The toes are too long on this foot, plus the underrun heels bring the foot too far in front of the leg.

It is only human to make mistakes, and it can likely be corrected within one or two normal shoeings. Repeated mistakes are what can end a horse's career.

Let's take a look at what can happen when these errors occur.

Common Farrier Mistakes

Incorrect Angles

Expert pool players know how crucial angles are to playing the game well. Without a proper line, the ball will never make it into the pocket. An angle is as critical in horse hooves as it is in billiards.

Generally, on the average horse, the front feet dorsal angle is close to a 50-degree angle in relationship to the ground. The dorsal angle of the hind feet is usually several degrees higher than in the front. This is an average—there is no perfect angle. As mentioned, the horse's hoof-pastern axis should align with his shoulder angle for ideal conformation. The "correct" angle is the one that keeps the horse's stance aligned and moving freely, even if it varies from the average (fig. 9.3).

9.4 These hoof walls have been excessively rasped, leaving no bearing surface on the hoof.

"Balance" is a buzzword, but it is often not well understood. The term describes how the bottom of the hoof makes contact with the ground and dissipates the force associated with movement. The combination of hoof angle and length influences how this transfer of pressure happens, and it is referred to as the *hoof-pastern axis*.

Horses' hooves that get too steep or too low-angled change this critical alignment, and the phrase *unbalanced feet* may be used. Too steep of a hoof angle is classified as *broken forward*, while one that is too shallow is called *broken back*. Either extreme deviation from normal puts excessive strain on the coffin and pastern joints—of course, there are always special cases that fall outside of the "normal" range.

Misalignment of angles increases the concussive forces a horse experiences in his legs. Uneven weight distribution overloads tendons and ligaments and can eventually change the bone structure. That bone changes in shape and density over time, producing formations called *osteophytes*. As we've already discussed, the term used to describe the process that happens when the bone adapts to the force exerted on it is "Wolf's Law."

Unbalanced feet can be one cause of suspensory or collateral ligament tears. These injuries are costly to correct because it requires veterinary care along with therapeutic shoeing until healing is finished. Injuries like this also tend to require several months of rehabilitation, all while the horse is out of work.

Even after the investment in healing, there will also always be a question of "what if?" What if that spot is weaker and more prone to another injury, or will the horse be able to get back to work?

Trimmed Too Short

Most of the time, horses feel no pain after a trim. Horses that are sore or "ouchy" may have been trimmed too short (fig. 9.4). In this scenario, there is too little distance left between the coffin bone inside the hoof capsule and the hoof surface that touches the ground.

The average-sized riding horse should have at least 8 to 10 millimeters of sole depth. Larger horses need a thicker sole depth to avoid tenderness. If it happens only

9.5 This shoe and pad are too small for the properly trimmed hoof.

9.6 The shoe on the right was too small for the horse's hoof, causing lameness. The larger shoe on the left was a better fit for the same horse. Cutting out the center of the pad alleviated extra pressure on the foot, and the horse returned to soundness.

once or twice, it can likely be corrected without long-term damage. Over time, repeated excessively short trims can create chronic lameness.

Properly fitted horseshoes can alleviate the discomfort a horse experiences when he has a shallow sole depth. Shoes increase the distance between the ground and the coffin bone, which relieves the pressure on the internal soft tissues (figs. 9.5 & 9.6). For some horses, this extra support is the difference between lameness and soundness. There is a myth that horseshoes numb the feet, and that sensation is what takes away the pain. This is an unsubstantiated claim.

Radiographs are the only way to truly see sole depth. However, it is impractical to X-ray every single horse. Over time, skilled farriers develop an eye for the internal structures and proper external angles. Farriers also use a *hoof gauge* that aids in measuring the external angles. Farriers place the metal tool up against the toe of the hoof. An arm on top of the tool hinges to the hoof wall, creating a visual measurement of the angles.

Toe lengths are typically measured from the hairline (coronary band) to the toe. Most horses should have the same toe length, side to side. However, unbalanced conformation or injury may produce uneven toe lengths.

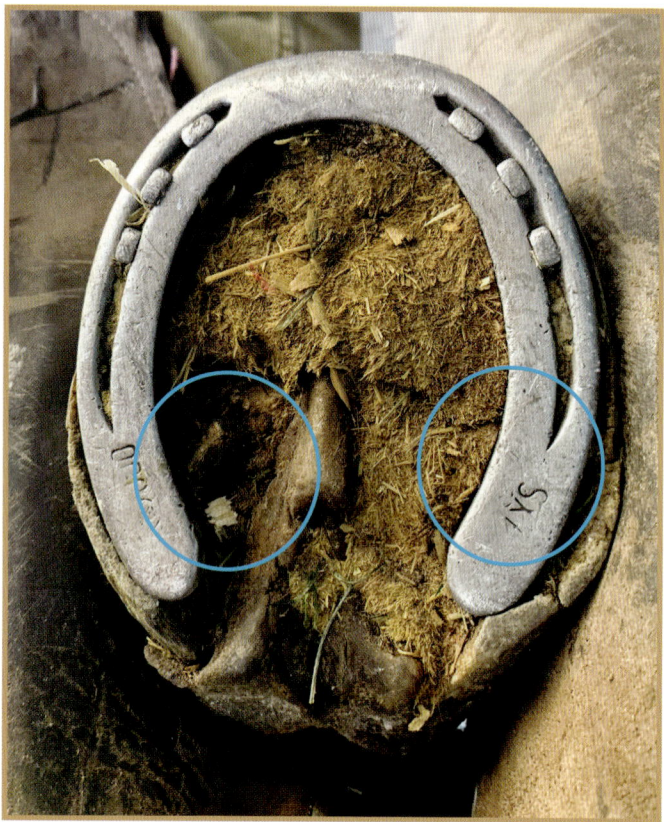

9.7 When the hoof grows out and is not trimmed in a timely manner it shifts the shoes forward off the heels.

Not Trimmed Enough

More isn't always better. Leaving too much hoof during a trim can also create problems. Long toes put extra strain on tendons. This incorrect trim can also increase the chance of chipping, breaking, and bruising. Sole abscesses and excessive pressure on the navicular bone and navicular bursa are more likely to happen in these situations.

Excessive Heel Length

As the hoof grows, the heel length increases, and the base of the heel migrates forward (fig. 9.7). This change creates a fulcrum on the downward forces of the leg. The pivot point causes the hoof to rock backward, forcing the horse to strike the ground toe first. The stabbing-like motion slams the heels into the ground rather than allowing the heel to land first and absorb the impact. Beyond poor movement, this motion interferes with blood circulation into and out of the hoof.

Some farriers choose not to trim the heels based on the theory that excessive heel length lessens strain on the deep flexor tendon. From a biomechanical standpoint, this is impossible. Leaving the heel too long can have the opposite effect, adding extra strain to the superficial flexor tendon and suspensory ligament.

There is also a misunderstanding that a higher heel angle allows a horse to move more quickly in speed events like roping, polo, and barrel racing, to name a few. This short-toe, high-heel angle creates a toe-first landing that can make horses more likely to trip or stumble.

Misalignment of Angles

The horse's hoof is three-dimensional. Most of the angles discussed so far only look at the hoof from the front

Not all horses that are sore after a visit have been trimmed too short. In locations with cold, snowy winters, shoes are often removed as the riding season slows. Simultaneously pulling the shoes and walking on hard footing can create soreness until the hoof toughens. A smart horse is careful about where he steps, but the ginger-footed placement may be misinterpreted as "my horse has been trimmed too short." Actually, the horse is simply being sensible—running over the uneven frozen ground can cause damage to internal hoof structures.

(*anterior*) and the back (*posterior*). The midline view, called the *lateral* or *medial alignment* is just as important. Chapter 6 (p. 93) describes how the medial/lateral alignment is based on an X, Y, and Z axis.

Trimming or shoeing that does not consider medial/lateral alignment can produce the same consequences as a horse that has poor conformation, such as *toe-in, toe-out, base-wide,* and *base-narrow*. Misalignment of the joints causes rotational deviations and a toe-in or toe-out stance. No horse is perfect and slight deviations are tolerable when the hooves are trimmed or shod regularly and correctly.

Nail Too Deep

Farriers must drive nails into the hoof to secure the shoe. There is a fine line between too deep and just right. It is possible for farriers to hit a blood vessel and have a "nail-quick." Like a dog's nails that have been clipped too short, it draws blood.

The area must be treated immediately to prevent an infection or lameness. Betadine, iodine, and peroxide are commonly flushed into the nail hole to discourage bacteria growth. Topical ointments with lidocaine are sometimes used to offer pain relief. Fortunately, when treated correctly, a nail-quick heals rapidly.

Wrong Shoe Size

The wrong shoe size can undermine good trimming. Modern horseshoes are measured by length and width, ranging in size from 000 to 4 depending on the manufacturer (figs. 9.8 A & B). Manufacturer records of horseshoe sales can give clues to the most common

9.8 A & B It may look like the shoe shown in Photo A fits the foot; however, it will not after the foot has been properly trimmed. With an appropriate trim shown in Photo B, the heels can be brought into proper position and it becomes apparent that the original shoe was too small. The shoe heel branch should extend to the edge of the hoof heel, whereas this one stops short. Also, the perimeter of the shoe is not wide enough for the entire hoof.

An Open Mind

Many of the students who enroll in the Cornell University Farrier course own horses and arrive with pre-conceived ideas about trimming and shoeing. One 40-year-old student was a lifelong horseman who competed in calf roping and team roping. Following the discipline style, he trimmed all his horses with a short toe and high hoof angle.

One of the first horses that arrived at the clinic while he was a student changed his perspective. That day's demonstration began with a lecture on the Golden Ratio method for guiding a trim. The horse had high heels that required a good deal of trimming. The student saw the nippers come out and gasped as the excess growth was cut away.

I asked the student about his concern. His response was that he had never seen that much heel cut off at once and worried it would hurt the horse. By using the Golden Ratio he saw how the trimming moved the heel under the horse's leg and improved her stance.

When the student showed up to class on that next Monday, he was excited to share that he tried the approach on his own horse prior to a weekend roping. He reported that the horse moved forward more freely and had a good "feel."

The payoff—his horse won each go-round with her fastest times that weekend. Other farriers were surprised when he confided his change in trimming and shoeing and attributed the win to those changes.

horseshoe sizes used. Sizes #0 and #1 fall in the middle of the curve, representing the largest number of horseshoes sold off the shelf. Frequently farriers make slight adjustments to improve fit, but these do not drastically alter the shoe size.

Note that it is better to trim a little extra heel length to slightly size down a shoe than to use a shoe that is too short. Too little heel support is considered to be a contributing factor to underperformance or lameness.

However, the standard distribution curve shifts when you look at individual breeds or types of horses. For instance, heavier-boned, larger-footed Warmbloods, on average, wear a large shoe with a wider web, ranging in size from a #2 to a #4. Conversely, lighter-boned, smaller breeds shift the size range down to #00 to #0.

Remember, there may be outliers that need a different shoe than what is typical for a breed or build. The various manufacturer's sizes are not an exact match. However, farriers use these little differences to fit individual horses more precisely.

Two factors determine which size a horse needs: his size and how big his bones are. When hoof-shoulder angles and shoe sizes are mismatched, this causes uneven movement and increases the risk for injury.

Horses with foot sizes inappropriately small for their body weight are more likely to develop soundness problems. Common issues are navicular disease or ligament tears that require costly veterinarian care and lengthy rehabilitation.

Fixing What Isn't Broken

There are legitimate situations where a different shoeing style is necessary. However, changing shoeing protocols

on a sound horse that is performing well is counterproductive. In competitive disciplines, there is the temptation to alter the trim or shoeing style based on how a champion rider's horse is shod. This is how horse owners began asking farriers for square-toe trims, which are helpful for some horses, but not all. Chances are that horse has a skilled farrier who is making decisions based on the individual horse (figs. 9.9 A & B).

9.9 A & B A neglected foot that has been allowed to grow too long (A), and what the same foot looks like when trimmed properly (B).

CHAPTER 10

Why Horses Lose Shoes and How to Limit Thrown Shoes

Chances are you've heard the ancient proverb, "For want of a nail, the shoe was lost…For want of a shoe, the horse was lost…." There is nothing more frustrating than having a horse throw a shoe. For riders, it means lost training time, and for farriers, it translates into last-minute scheduling changes. Besides the inconveniences, horses that chronically lose shoes can experience serious hoof damage or develop lameness.

It often feels like bad luck is to blame. Without fail, shoes pop off before an event or just after the farrier has been to the barn. Most farriers assume responsibility for premature missing shoes if it occurs within a few days. However, missing shoes are not necessarily the farrier's fault.

Some horses routinely lose shoes, while most horses never lose any. Experienced farriers agree that about 10 percent of shod horses randomly lose a shoe—and most often, it is a front shoe. There are three reasons horseshoes fall off:

∪ Farrier errors made while shoeing.

∪ Horse conformation flaws.

∪ Owner management mistakes.

Knowing the role people and animals play in the lost shoe problem can help in finding ways to reduce the occurrence of thrown shoes.

Shoeing Schedule

The widely accepted interval between shoeings ranges between four and six weeks. The time between visits depends on the season and where the horse lives. Hoof-growth cycles follow day

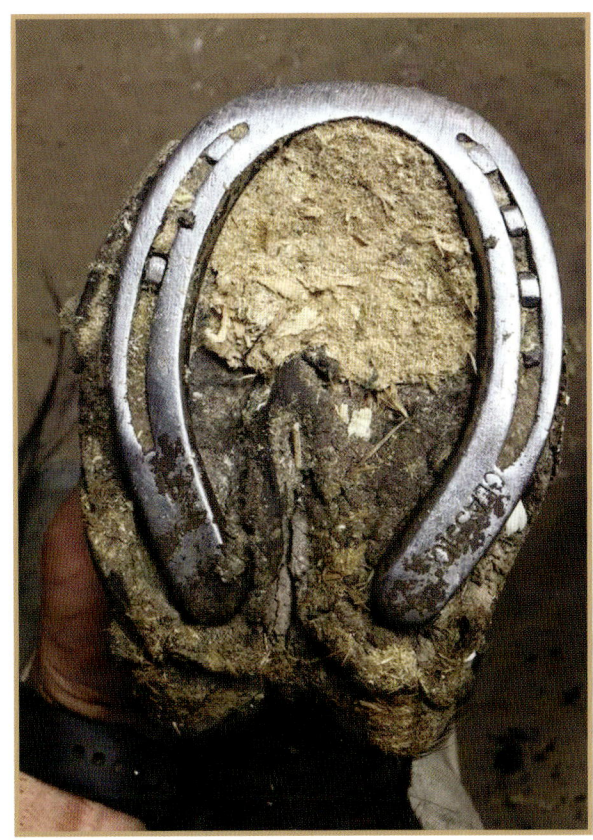

10.1 This horseshoe has shifted because it probably wasn't well fit to begin with and was left on the hoof too long before a trim.

length. Hoof growth increases in February as longer daylight hours triggers the hormonal activity to increase. This continues through the summer solstice and gradually slows in September. As daylight decreases, so does hoof growth as the horse puts more energy into hair growth to stay warm.

The type of work a horse performs also influences how frequently he needs to be reshod. Racehorses generally have the shortest intervals at three to four weeks. Performance horses average four to six weeks. Those in lighter or no work that may need shoes often follow a six- to eight-week shoeing cycle. Shoeing frequency for horses with a lameness, injury, or a therapeutic shoe is based on the individual situation.

A competition schedule may also determine the shoeing interval. Some riders do not want a horse shod right before competitions. These riders want to avoid a horse being trimmed too short or the chance of a bad nail making a horse sore. Competing on a horse that is at the end of the shoeing cycle raises the chance of a lost shoe during the event. It also places more strain on the tendons because longer toes increase the leverage on soft tissue.

As the hoof grows out, the shoes may loosen up, and the growth pattern of the hoof shifts the shoe position over time (fig. 10.1). Judging a farrier's ability only by how long the horseshoes stay on is a false evaluation of his skill. How a horse owner manages her horse, and her willingness to maintain a regular schedule is an important part of the equation. Waiting for the shoe to fall off before calling the farrier suggests the visits aren't frequent enough.

What Does a Proper Shoeing Look Like?

Fitting a shoe is a technical process. Farriers must make decisions that combine technical standards and the individual horse. Generally, shoes should be fit slightly wider than the widest part of the hoof and a bit longer than the point of the heel. This supports the leg and allows for a natural expansion of the hoof as it flexes.

Skilled farriers understand the proper fit for the horse's conformation and activity to prevent potential shoe-loss problems. Balanced feet will hold well-fit, flat shoes better throughout the shoeing cycle. With all the different shoe types, styles, widths, and punching (nail hole size and location) available, it is easy to select the appropriate shoe for any horse and customize it for a precise fit.

Any horse can wreck a solid shoeing job. The closer a shoeing job is to technical perfection, the more likely it is something can catch the heel and remove it. Farriers must decide how to balance correctness with the individual horse. A shoe with too much heel length is in jeopardy of being stepped off either by the horse himself or by pasture mates. Shoes that fit the hoof too tightly can pose a risk to soundness as it interferes with the horse's movement. When the shoes are too small, it eliminates the leg support shoes are designed to provide.

Beyond what the farrier can control, lost shoes are the responsibility of the horse owner, rider, or stable manager. The farrier should point out potential problems and provide guidance on how to minimize shoe loss, including suggestions for management changes.

Rider/Owner Errors and Environmental Factors That Lead to Shoe Loss

There's nothing more frustrating than dealing with lost shoes. The good news is there are a lot of things you can do to lessen the chances of this happening. Here's a list of situations within your control:

Problem: Poor conditioning. Unfit horses tire easily and move with a sloppy gait, causing interference, falling on the forehand, stepping shoes off.

Solution: Make sure a horse is well-conditioned for the work or distance.

Problem: Too much time in between shoeings. As the hooves grow beyond the shoes, the nails loosen and shift, causing cracks (fig. 10.2).

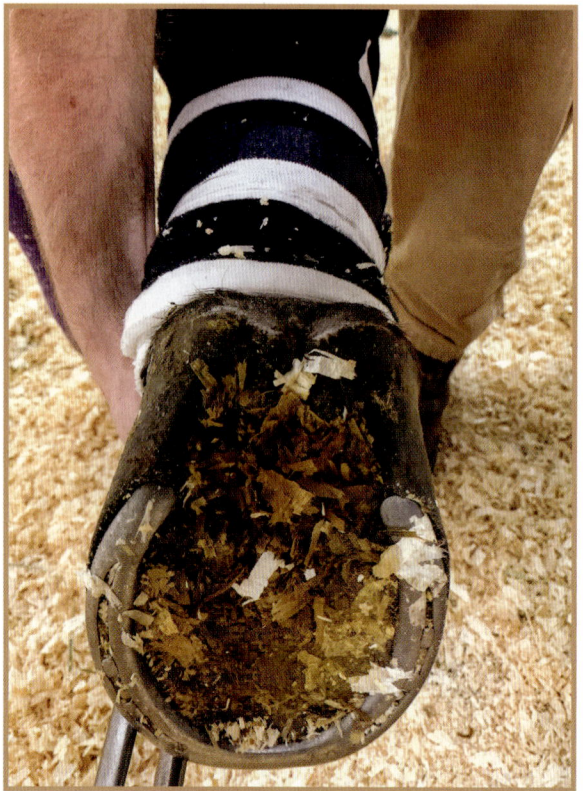

10.2 This is an example of a hoof where the heels are too long, the shoe too short, and too much time has passed between shoeing intervals.

Solution: Find the appropriate shoeing interval for the amount of hoof growth, which may change during different times of the year, and stick to it.

Problem: Poor paddock maintenance. Wet, muddy paddocks create soft hooves, which do not hold nails well. Contrary to popular belief, it is a myth that walking through mud alone sucks shoes off (fig. 10.3). What actually happens is that as a horse moves through deep mud, it creates a surface tension suction on the bottom of his foot. That suction creates a slight pause before the hoof lifts to step forward. The deeper the hoof penetrates the mud, the longer the delay before the foot lifts and steps forward. As the front leg struggles to lift, the hind feet swing forward, and the horse steps on the heels of a front shoe, thereby stepping the shoe off (fig. 10.4).

Allowing horses to drink or swim in ponds is another opportunity for shoe loss. A pond's sloping sides allow the hind feet to slide forward while entering the pond to drink or swim, again creating an opportunity to step off front shoes.

Solution: Improve pasture drainage and direct water runoff away from paddocks. Rotate pastures to cut down on muck and give shoes a better chance of staying put.

Problem: Pasture hazards. A loosely woven wire fence provides an opportunity for horses to stick feet through the fence when leaning over to graze on the other side, which can catch a shoe in the wire (fig. 10.5). Old equipment and other objects in the field can get stuck on a shoe and pull it off as the horse frees himself.

Solution: Check paddocks for risks and make repairs.

10.2 Slippery, muddy conditions cause horses to mistime their steps and overreach, often "stepping off" a shoe.

10.4 In deep mud, bell boots just flip up and provide no help in keeping shoes from becoming "stepped off."

10.5 Look closely and you'll see this fence "pulled off" two horseshoes.

Problem: Excessive foot stomping. A horse turned out during fly season can stomp his feet and pace excessively to rid his legs of flies. The frequent concussion loosens shoes and cracks hooves.

Solution: Bring the horse in during peak fly activity hours. Use fly repellents, fly boots, and sheets. Bell boots on hind feet prevent the inside of each hoof from interfering with the clinches.

Problem: Horse backs off the trailer too quickly, catching the heel of a hind shoe on the ramp.

Solution: Help to control your horse's speed as he exits the trailer.

Problem: Poor nutrition. Horses need a balanced diet that provides minerals and nutrients that support hoof growth.

Solution: Ask your veterinarian and farrier about feeding hoof growth supplements that are compatible with the horse's diet. Biotin, zinc/methionine, and other chelated minerals are associated with hoof growth.

Problem: Turning out incompatible horses. Chasing or fighting can create two problems. One is that the aggressor can step on the hind shoes of the horse he is chasing. The other fleeing horses may step off his front shoes trying to get away.

Solution: Strategically pair horses for turnout.

Problem: Stall-kicker loosens hind shoes or embeds them into stall walls.

Solution: If compatible stablemates cannot be arranged, hang rubber mats on stall dividers to reduce impact.

Problem: Poor saddle fit. An ill-fitting saddle inhibits shoulder movement, encouraging the horse to fall on his forehand. Both slow down the front feet making it more likely a hind foot will step on a front shoe.

Solution: Check saddle fit for proper position and pommel-to-cantle balance (see more on p. 155).

Problem: Cantering on the wrong lead while turning.

This brings the horse off balance as he overreaches to the outside of that tight circle, causing the horse to step on the outside heel of the front shoe.

Solution: Be aware of proper leads while turning at a canter. Counter-cantering in a controlled, collected manner is not problematic, but when the horse is moving in a disjointed way, it interferes with awareness of foot placement.

Problem: Trotting tight circles on the wrong "diagonal." At the trot, the horse's legs move in diagonal pairs. English riders rise into a posting position when the horse's outside front leg and inside back leg swing forward at the same time. Riding on the incorrect diagonal can unbalance a horse so that he steps on the heels of a front shoe.

Solution: Be aware of proper diagonals. Recognize and correct a wrong diagonal.

Problem: Rider asks the horse to make a quick start forward, then abruptly checks him. The horse's front end cannot get out of the way before the hind feet step on the front shoes.

Solution: Collect your horse and give clear cues for moving forward to avoid disjointed or false starts.

Horse-Caused Shoe Loss

The horse can be his own worst enemy. Conformation flaws and poor gait quality can sometimes be to blame. Here's a look at how the horse contributes to this challenge:

Problem: Base-wide conformation. When the front legs are too far apart, this often means the horse rotates his toes out. That "paddling" motion creates interference that causes a horse to step on the inside heel of a shoe (fig. 10.6).

Solution: The farrier trims the lateral toes lower than a traditional square balance. Bell boots can also be used to protect the shoes.

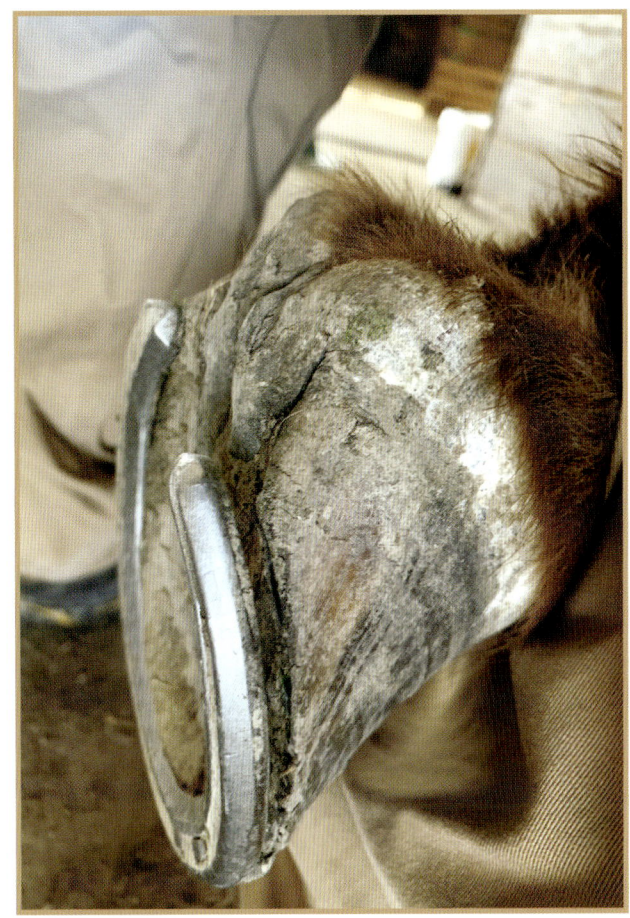

10.6 Interference caused by a conformation fault can spring a shoe.

Problem: Long-leg, short-back conformation. These horses frequently overstep, catching the heels of the front shoes.

Solution: The farrier may be able to slow the motion of the hind feet by using back shoes with extended heels. Using overreach boots may also help.

Problem: Base-narrow hind end. When the back legs are abnormally close, the feet brush against one another, creating an opportunity for stepping on the inside of the opposite shoe.

Solution: Farriers bevel or shape the inside branch of the horseshoe to reduce the surface area available for getting stepped on.

Problem: High-low conformation syndrome. A high-angled foot or a weakened shoulder inhibits a horse's movement on that side, and the heel of that shoe can be stepped on.

Solution: Trimming and shoeing designed to develop the weaker side is combined with rider-led exercises to build strength on the affected side.

Problem: Nervous, flighty disposition. A horse that is easily spooked is not concerned about foot placement as he either paces around or moves suddenly, often stepping on shoes. When a horse also has poor quality hoof walls and undesirable conformation, shoe loss will happen regularly. Anxious horses excessively wear shoes while stomping, pawing, and pacing.

Solution: Farrier work cannot change these behaviors. Working with a trainer or veterinarian may be necessary for anxious horses.

Farrier Errors Causing Shoe Loss

As I've already said, horseshoeing is more than a technical skill; it is an art. It takes training and practice

---

Lost Shoe Policies

Shoeing is expensive, and it's important to know your farrier's policy for replacing a thrown shoe. In my private farrier business, I reset a lost shoe within a month of the original visit. There is no extra charge if the shoe is available. If the shoe can't be found, the owner pays for the shoe replacement.

One client was upset when her horse lost a shoe two weeks after being shod. When I arrived at the barn, the shoe was unavailable. The client was unhappy about paying for a new shoe and pointed to my workmanship as the cause. The horse lived in a paved yard previously used for pigs with steel hog fencing made of square holes. I instructed the woman to walk the perimeter of the paddock to look for the shoe. Halfway around the paddock she found it bent and outside the fence. The horse had stuck his foot through the fence, caught it, and removed the shoe.

Moral of the story: Keeping shoes in place is a team effort between the farrier and the horse owner to match skill and management strategies to reduce lost shoes.

to develop. While most reasons for lost shoes can be traced back to the environment, the management, or the rider, farriers are human and can make mistakes that increase the risk for lost shoes (fig. 10.7). These are a few examples.

Problem: Hoof or shoe is not flat. In this situation, the shoe rocks on a high spot on the hoof, eventually loosening the shoe. A loose shoe will become a lost shoe.

Solution: Horseshoes must be perfectly flat. Hot-fitting and shaping are an aid a farrier can use to help produce perfectly flat hoof walls.

Problem: Horseshoes are too large or too small. Shoes that are too big for the hoof are easily stepped off. Shoes that are too small allow the hoof to grow over the shoe partway through the shoeing cycle. The shoe is then jammed up into the hoof, raising nail clinches, and loosening the shoe (fig. 10.8).

Solution: Choose an appropriately sized shoe.

Problem: Incorrect hind shoe modifications for the individual horse, such as extended heels or trailers. These adjustments are necessary to help with stance, gait problems, and enhance performance in specific

10.7 Most horseshoes become "lost" due to environmental conditions; however, farriers can also make a mistake in fitting and nailing on a shoe that may increase the chances for it to loosen or be thrown.

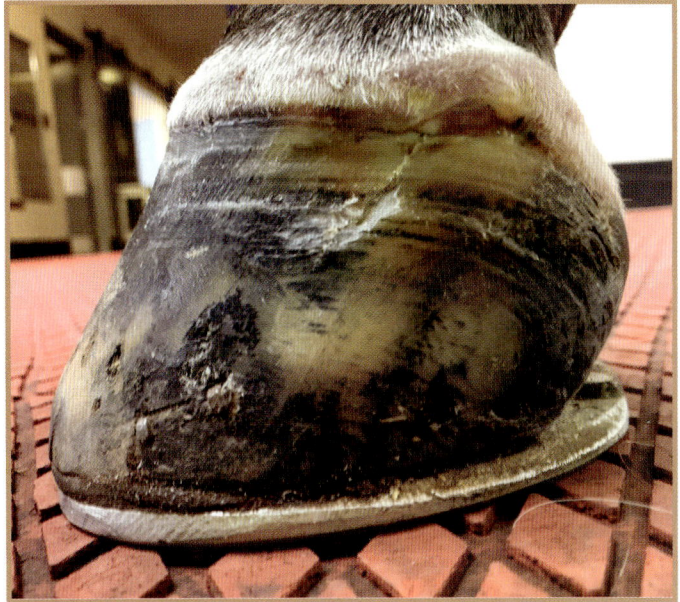

10.8 This shoe is way too large for the hoof it has been fitted to. When the shoe overhangs the hoof there is an increased risk for the horse himself, or a pasturemate, to step on the edge and dislodge it from the hoof.

disciplines but need to be sized with the understanding that this modification is vulnerable to being stepped on by other horses.

Solution: Recognize the potential challenges and plan turnout accordingly.

Problem: No clips when necessary. Horses that are performing lateral work, jumping, or stopping hard need clips to absorb the shear force exerted on the nails.

Solution: Use toe, side, and quarter clips to reduce shearing forces.

Problem: The shoe selected is punched too fine. Nail holes on fine-punched shoes are positioned closer to the outside of the shoe perimeter. Coarse-punched shoes position the nail holes farther in toward the middle of the shoe rather than the outside edge.

The hoof-wall thickness varies with hoof size, age, and breed. Nail holes must be aligned close to the white line to hold the shoe without splitting the hoof wall. Fine-punched shoes are for thin hoof walls, whereas coarse-punched shoes are used for thicker hoof walls. However, when the nail holes are too small, the nails cannot be driven deeply enough to hold the shoe and will split the hoof.

Solution: The horseshoe selected needs to allow for proper nail hole placement but also needs to cover the hoof wall.

Problem: An unbalanced trim. Unbalanced feet cause sloppy movement, creating interference that can step the shoe off.

Solution: Proper trimming.

Problem: Nail selection. Nails that are too small loosen prematurely. Slim nails without clips can shear easily in performance.

Solution: Select nails with the proper head size to fit the shoe nail holes.

Being Proactive

Horseshoes are an important part of routine maintenance for many horses. Most horses never lose a shoe, but those that do present a problem. Horse owners are unable to replace lost shoes themselves and are at the mercy of the farrier's schedule. Understanding how or why this happens gives you an opportunity to use horse-keeping skills that can reduce or eliminate thrown shoes (figs. 10.9, 10.10, & 10.11).

10.9 When this horse pulled his egg-bar shoe it twisted. As he stepped back onto the ground the shoe shifted, and he stepped on the clip. The shoe was removed quickly and replaced by the farrier so there were no lingering injuries, but stepping on a clip or nail can puncture the hoof in more severe cases.

10.10 When a drought lowered the pond shoreline, this horse owner found a lost shoe. It's a good reminder of why it can be best to keep horses out of ponds.

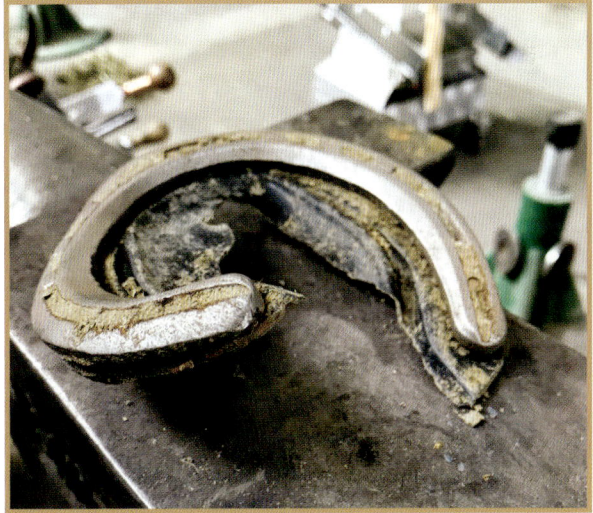

10.11 A horse that twists off a shoe can be at risk for stepping on the nails and creating a puncture wound.

FROM THE FORGE
A Rider's Influence

As an assistant polo coach and umpire for the Cornell University Polo Team, I am mounted right in the middle of the action. From this vantage point, I can see how well (or not) the riders are managing their horses. When a fastbreak happens, the horses explode forward to keep up with the ball. Often, I see riders lean forward with their legs slipping backward. As the horse is thrusting forward, riders snatch the reins to stay with the horses. In just a few seconds, the horse oversteps on a front shoe, ripping it off.

Riding in a balanced position and cueing the horse with enough notice to collect and respond helps reduce pulling shoes. No discipline is immune to the impacts of unbalanced riding.

Each July, there is a three-day, 100-mile competitive trail ride in Brookfield, New York. For five years, I worked the event, replacing lost shoes. Weather conditions varied dramatically from year to year. Sometimes it was dry, others wet. It wasn't uncommon for horses to lose a shoe on the hilly terrain.

Most riders gave me a spare set of previously fitted shoes so little time is lost shaping a new one. Then I stand at the boggy sections of the course, the area a horse would most likely lose a shoe, and replace it as needed. One year, a rider came through the first bog with a lost shoe on the right front. At the next checkpoint, the same rider came through missing the other front shoe.

As I reset the shoe, I suggested he sit up, not lean forward, and collect the horse to drive him through the tough terrain rather than moving in a strung-out fashion. He did not lose another shoe for the rest of the ride and admitted to feeling more in control when we met at the end of the course.

CHAPTER 11

The Horse Owner's Role in Hoof and Shoeing Problems

It can feel like "magic" when a farrier resolves a soundness issue or heals an injury. The farrier's expertise, care for the horse, and time invested in hoof problems create dramatic results. But even the most skilled farrier is not a miracle worker. He can't fix two critical factors—saddle fit and a rider's balance in the saddle. Both lead to hoof problems, soreness, increased frequency of pulled shoes, and behavior changes.

Farriers rarely get to watch a horse work before he begins to trim and shoe. In some ways, this means he is working blindly in response to your observation of a change in soundness or performance. By knowing what to look for and how to make changes to these elements you can support a farrier's work, which ultimately promotes soundness and peak performance in your horse (fig. 11.1).

Understanding Saddle Fit

Remember the pair of "super cute" shoes you bought on an impulse? The shoes were trendy but uncomfortable, and no amount of "breaking in" eliminated the spot that pinched a toe or rubbed a heel. And, that discomfort is the only thing you can think about when you wear them.

11.1 Skilled farriers start with basic, generic horseshoe designs that can be modified to improve a horse's comfort level and performance. This pile features a variety of shoes. Some include clips; others have extended heel trailers for added support.

11.2 Eye-appeal is the "icing on the cake" for a well-fitted saddle.

A pair of shoes that can leave you feeling sore is similar to what a horse experiences by wearing an improperly fitted saddle. Regardless of how expensive the saddle, or which company built it, your horse will notice when it doesn't fit correctly (fig. 11.2).

Saddle aesthetics often get riders most excited. However, what is hidden from view is most important to the horse—the tree. A tree is like a car engine—car owners rarely lift the hood to look at the engine, but without a well-built motor, the vehicle is useless.

A properly fitted saddle does not interfere with the horse's movement, and it should also help the rider keep a balanced seat. Of course, every horse is an individual, but there are common hoof and shoeing problems that can directly be related to poor saddle fit.

Traditionally, English disciplines have focused on saddle fit more than the Western world, but that is changing. Buying a specific saddle for every horse in the barn likely isn't affordable. Often riders tend to purchase similarly built horses, increasing the likelihood that one saddle can comfortably fit multiple horses. For example, many Western pleasure horses are similar in back length and shoulder angle. A skilled saddle maker has refined his craft so that one saddle can be used on multiple alike-built horses, easing the financial burden of buying numerous saddles.

Rub marks or uneven sweat patterns after a ride can suggest improper fit. The use of gel pads, riser pads, or any other extra pad, also indicates that the fit isn't perfect, although it's a common practice. Pads are an acceptable solution when other options are not viable.

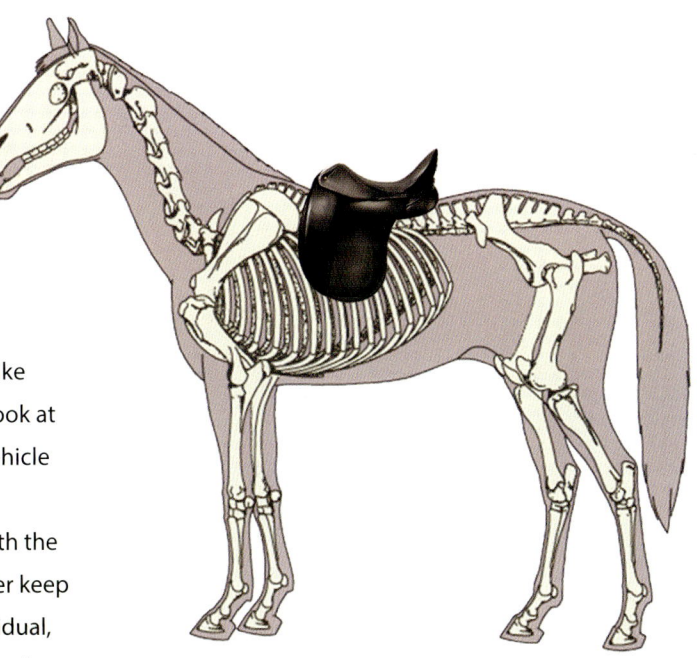

11.3 A well-fitted saddle rests just behind the shoulder blade as in the drawing, so it doesn't interfere with the horse's shoulder movement.

These are basic guidelines for determining if your saddle fits correctly.

Saddle Position

The saddle should sit behind the shoulder blade (fig. 11.3). A saddle that sits too far forward on the withers pinches and restricts the shoulders. This prevents the horse from fully moving his shoulder and front end. Consequently, the hind feet do not have enough room to land without striking his front hooves with his back feet. This is also known as "overreaching" or "forging." A saddle positioned too far back is equally problematic because it applies pressure and hurts the horse's back.

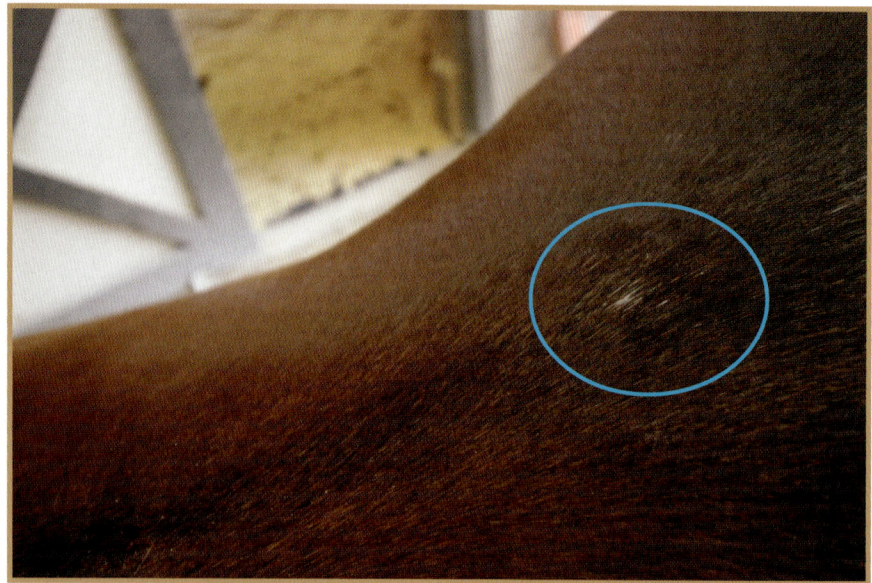

11.4 This small patch of white hairs is an indication that a saddle isn't fitting correctly. When not addressed, a poorly fitted saddle can create soreness.

Wither Clearance

The points of the saddle tree are shaped like a fork. There should be space to fit two to three fingers between the horse's withers and the saddle. This space gives horses the freedom to move. A narrow fork squeezes the shoulder muscles while a wide fork allows the saddle to rest on the withers, causing soreness and rubs. Both restrict flowing, forward motion.

White hairs or sores on the withers suggest the saddle is pinching the horse's withers and, if not corrected, this can also cause permanent injury to tissues and the spine (fig. 11.4).

Panel Pressure and Contact

The bottom side of the saddle should make equal contact from front to back. This helps spread the rider's weight evenly across the horse's back. Slide your palm under the saddle to feel for bridging or rocking, which suggest uneven contact points. When not corrected, back problems can arise and may lead to an altered stance and gait.

Pommel-to-Cantle Relationship

The saddle's cantle should be level with or higher than the pommel. The discipline you choose determines if (and how much) higher this relationship is. However, anytime the cantle is lower than the pommel, the saddle does not fit. This also pitches the rider backward in the seat.

Saddle Balance

The seat should be level on the horse's back (fig. 11.5). A backward tilt implies the gullet width is too narrow. This position creates excess pressure on the loins. On the other hand, a forward-leaning saddle means the gullet channel is too wide, which pinches the horse's shoulders. When the back of the seat is too high it takes you out of the correct posture because it drives your upper body forward and legs back, taking you out of the correct posture.

11.5 A & B This trained saddle fitter is using chalk to sketch a map of this horse's back so that when a saddle is placed on the horse's back he can see areas of the saddle that may cause sore spots or interfere with the horse's movement.

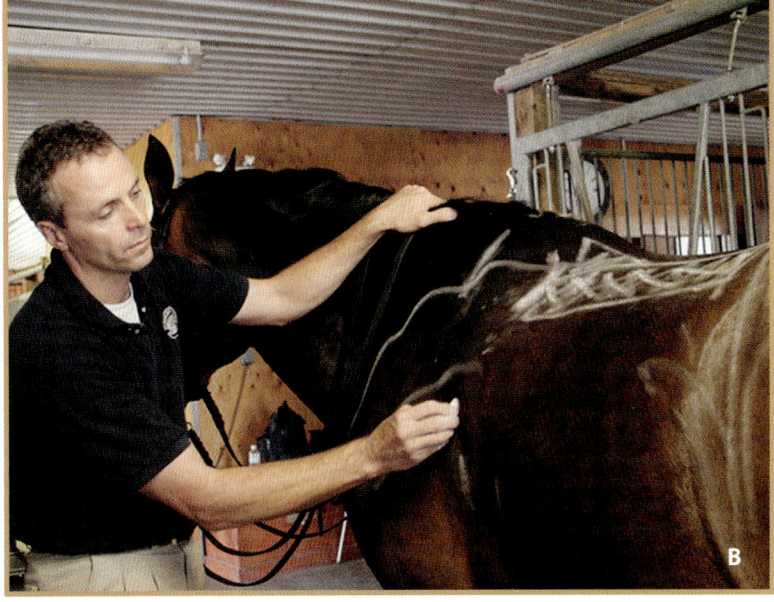

Channel Clearance and Gullet Width

If you look under your saddle, you'll notice a long groove down the center of the saddle. This is called the *channel* or *gullet*, and it's critical this doesn't contact the horse's spine. The saddle should only rest on the long back muscles as pressure on the spine causes dramatic movement problems. When the channel fits well, the horse's back in this area should be dry after a ride, signaling that airflow is moving through the space.

Saddle Length

Saddles are intended to rest behind the horse's shoulder. The saddle skirting should fit in front of the horse's last floating rib—his 18th thoracic vertebra. A saddle should never sit on the lumbar vertebrae. As the weakest structure in the back, they are not designed to carry significant weight (fig. 11.6).

11.6 It is critical to be sure the skirting ends before the floating rib to avoid uncomfortable pressure and stress on the area.

Rounded skirting often works well on short-backed horses to keep the saddle from interfering with the horse's hip movement. A saddle that is too long for the horse's back can cause hind-end problems that can be misinterpreted as shoeing problems when the skirting may be the culprit.

Tree Angle

The tree angle should follow the horse's shoulder angle to allow the shoulder to rotate up and back during a stride. When it does, the angle of your saddle's tree is correctly adjusted for your horse.

Signs That Signal Saddle-Fit Issues

Chances are, you know your horse better than anyone. Unless your horse is in full-time training with someone else, you can notice even the smallest changes in your horse's gait or behavior. Subtle changes in a horse's movement and willingness (or lack of) are often mistaken for behavior issues when saddle fit may be the root of the problem. These are a few signals that suggest improper saddle fit.

Lack of impulsion and refusal to extend gaits: A saddle with a fork that is too narrow for the horse pinches his shoulders. It also interferes with his ability to extend his scapula, a key structure in producing forward movement. Over time this can create lameness and injury because the consistent pressure or rubbing damages the tissues and bones beneath the withers.

Unwilling to turn in tight circles: When the saddle is too long for the horse's back, it blocks the spine's natural tendency to curve in the direction of the circle.

Refusals or runouts: Imagine trying to lift and propel your body over a fence wearing gear that pinches in one spot or another. Landing with pressure in a concentrated area is painful. Poorly fitted saddles create the same sensation in the horse's back. Sometimes this is misdiagnosed as hoof soreness when the pressure during landing is the reason for discomfort.

Saddling behaviors: Watching a horse's behavior while saddling offers clues to an improper saddle fit. For example, if the horse twitches or puts his ears back when approached with a saddle, it is likely the saddle may be causing discomfort. If you notice a change in your horse, asking your farrier to check out your saddle fit might be helpful. A farrier doesn't need to be a master saddle fitter, but he should understand the basic principles of saddle fit so that it can be considered in the equation. Since a horse's shape can change with age, muscle development, and overall fitness, it's entirely possible that a saddle that once fit comfortably no longer does.

Improving Saddle Fit

In a perfect world, each horse has his own saddle perfectly matched to his body type. In reality this is likely impractical. Investing in multiple saddles is costly, and fortunately, there are options for improving fit and making a saddle versatile enough to accommodate several horses.

11.7 A skilled saddle fitter can improve saddle fit by adding or removing wool in a process known as flocking.

One option is an adjustable tree. Adjustable trees function in one of two ways based on the saddle maker. The first is a multi-gullet system. Multiple gullet widths are included with the saddle purchase and can be swapped out based on the horse. The other adjustable tree style uses a small tool or key to turn a series of adjustment points within the tree to narrow or widen the space. There are also treeless saddles that mold themselves to the horse's back.

High-end dressage and jumping saddles use an adjustment method called flocking (fig. 11.7). Wool is inserted and manipulated to provide a precise fit and saddle balance with this approach. Flocking is done by a professional saddle fitter to ensure optimum fit and may need adjusting as the horse changes over time.

Pads do not fix saddle issues but rather enhance fit. Choosing the right saddle pad based on its thickness and size is crucial for obtaining a good fit and to fit the saddle to multiple horses. This is important in Western disciplines, which have a wide range of pad dimensions to choose among. Some horses also need wither pads to help address problems with the saddle fit over that area. It may be necessary to switch saddle pads at different times throughout the year as a horse's weight or fitness level fluctuates.

Recognizing an improper saddle fit is the key to knowing if there is a problem. Buying a saddle is more than an investment in tack; it's an investment in your horse's comfort, soundness, and hoof health.

Before finalizing the purchase of any saddle, ask to try it first. Most tack stores have an area where riders can sit in the saddle and determine if the seat, flaps, and fenders meet their needs. Some may even have a space on-site so a rider can bring a horse for a test ride. A trial period is often available so you can try the saddle at home for a limited time and return it (in the same condition as purchased) if it's not a fit.

Regardless of the discipline, the saddle should fit well behind the shoulder blade, or it will interfere with the horse's movement. First, place the saddle on the

11.8 A well-fitted saddle is comfortable for horse and rider.

horse's back without a pad. Slide one hand in along the panel from the front of the saddle to the back. The saddle panels shouldn't pinch, and it shouldn't be too loose.

Then, take a test ride with a clean pad. At the end of the ride, look for any dry areas on the pad or on the horse's sweaty back; both reveal poor fit. The exception is the spinal area. When the spine of the pad is wet, the saddle is placing too much pressure on the horse's spine.

The Rider's Role in Hoof Problems

Fitting a saddle to the horse is only half the equation. The saddle must also be comfortable for the rider (fig. 11.8). You can get the fit right for a horse, but it doesn't much matter if the saddle isn't right for the rider's balance. A rider in a saddle that is too small tends to tip forward in the seat to maintain balance. Similarly, a saddle that is too large forces a rider to work hard to maintain balance in the seat, shifting her focus away from the horse.

It can be uncomfortable, even hard, to admit that your role as a rider influences the horse's hooves. Not only does an incorrectly fitted saddle increase your horse's risk of injury, but an improperly fitting saddle also puts you in an unbalanced position. This impacts the horse's performance and can lead to movement problems and lameness. For example, a saddle that pitches the rider backward will eventually cause back issues, which will change the hind-end stance or movement.

A high cantle pitches the rider forward. When the rider leans too far forward, it throws the horse onto his forehand rather than encouraging him to drive from behind. In this position, the rider restricts and slows front-end movement. When this happens, the hind feet tend to overreach those slower-moving front feet, which will cause *forging*.

Forging is that clicking sound you hear when the toes of the hind feet hit the toes of the upward swing of the front feet. If the saddle is fitted correctly, but your balance is still off, it may mean it's time to take lessons or work with a trainer.

Even well-fitted saddles with skilled riders in the seat can shift when moving at speed, jumping, or in quick turns like those used in polo or cutting. This interference can impact your score and create sore spots. A breast collar, an over girth, or a belly strap may help this problem.

Weight Considerations

Aside from improper saddle fit causing a problem, the weight of the rider and the saddle may be too heavy for the horse. Here is one guideline for determining if this is the case:

1. Add the weight of the horse, the saddle, and the rider.
2. Divide this by the circumference of the horse's mid cannon bone.
3. Divide this by two, which equals a weight value.
4. Consider your results: Less than 75 is optimum. 75 to 80 is acceptable. Over 80 is questionable and may injure the horse.

Consider the Whole Picture

Riders and farriers often assume lameness is caused by a foot problem that was either caused by or can be remedied by the farrier. And farriers tend to focus on the shoeing aspects in their sphere of influence. It's human nature to correlate a lameness problem with a shoeing issue and blame the farrier.

However, understanding the whole picture is vital to recognizing problems beyond the hoof and how to handle them. Certainly, confirming correct trimming and shoeing is important. Still, it's equally useful to consider how saddle fit and rider balance contribute to gait faults, stance changes, obscure lameness, and lack of forward impulsion.

Appropriate, skillful shoeing needs to be done in concert with not only saddlery but bitting, dental care, nutrition, and training methods. The entire horse needs to be considered, rather than looking at his feet as an isolated part of the body.

FROM THE FORGE
Watching a Client Ride

A regular client mentioned that her horse was "clicking" at the trot. Farriers are taught to roll the toes and extend the shoe heels to slow the hind feet in this situation. It wasn't the answer, the horse was still "clicking" even with these modifications. It prompted me to ask if I could see the horse saddled and watch her ride. The problem was obvious—the saddle pitched forward on the horse's back. So, when the rider trotted off, she couldn't help but be forward too. This motion sent the legs rearward, and I heard the "click, click."

I asked if I could ride the horse. As soon as I sat in the saddle, it tilted me forward. I struggled to sit up straight with my legs under me as we trotted off. There was no clicking when I sat up, but it returned if I let the saddle push me forward.

It can be hard to admit that your saddle or riding position may be at the root of a problem. You invest a lot of time and money in tack, riding, and lessons. It can deflate the ego or put a dent in the budget, but considering these influences in certain situations could make all the difference in your horse's performance. It's also important to remember that farriers can't be responsible for circumstances outside their influence.

CHAPTER 12

Horse Behavior and Handling for Farriery

Imagine taking a toddler for his first haircut. As he squirms in the chair, the barber struggles to avoid jagged, uneven snips with the scissors. Horses that wiggle, pull back, or are simply impatient are like the young child at the hairdresser. An unsteady horse means a farrier may not be as precise as he would like. An unruly horse can be dangerous.

Bad behavior can create a negative experience that both horses and humans dread repeating. Remembering horse psychology—that the horse is a prey animal, primed to flee threats, and he can feel vulnerable when one leg is in the air. This alone makes it incredible that most horses willingly cooperate. Keeping that in mind, here's a look at how horse behavior and the handler's role in preparing a horse for the farrier contributes to creating a positive or an adverse situation.

What Happens When a Horse Doesn't Stand for the Farrier?

A balanced trim is the foundation for keeping a horse sound. A horse that jerks his feet away or dances during a trim makes it difficult for the farrier to make exact adjustments, which may impact performance. A horse that twitches or pulls his leg during shoeing increases the risks of injury to himself, the farrier, and the handler.

The farrier is susceptible to injury when bending over and standing beneath a 1,000-pound animal. During shoeing, nails are driven into a hoof and sharp points are exposed until the farrier can "clinch" or bend the edges over. Imagine a flailing hoof with a sharp point scraping against the horse's opposite leg or the farrier's hand. Glue-on shoes do not have sharp nails; however, an impatient horse that pulls his foot or stomps can shift or ruin the prep work before the adhesive sets.

There's a wide range of reasons a horse won't stand for the farrier—many manmade. Here's a look at common scenarios farriers experience, and solutions for helping these horses become comfortable with trimming and shoeing.

Problem: Lack of proper handling.

Solution: Introduce a foal to having his legs and hooves touched within the first few weeks of being born. Run your hands down the leg, use a soft brush on the area, and practice picking up a hoof. Older horses who won't stand for the farrier can benefit from this approach too.

Problem: Lack of respect. Just because a horse can be ridden does not mean he is respectful or has acceptable ground manners. Teaching ground manners has the most impact when a horse is still young, but a horse of any age can be taught to respect your space. Working in hand is as important as training under saddle. If the horse is dangerous or unruly, it may be necessary to get help from a trainer.

Solution: Spend 5 to 10 minutes each day practicing standing, leading, and picking up hooves. Even just a few minutes every day can greatly improve the horse's

12.1 A farrier assumes a level of risk every time he stands under a horse. A farrier will not tolerate an unruly or dangerous animal. Horses used to getting treats during daily grooming tasks, like picking out hooves, may beg during farrier work. It's best to wait until after the job is done.

willingness to stand for the farrier. Look for training exercises that teach your horse to acknowledge your "personal bubble." Standing within a foot or two of one another is normal, but the horse should not crowd you.

Problem: Treat "hound."

Solution: Treats can be overdone (fig. 12.1). A food-motivated horse may be more inclined to stomp or jerk his legs from the farrier's hand in search of treats. Even if the horse doesn't pull his leg away, wiggling to beg makes the farrier's job harder. Save the snacks for when the farrier's work is done rather than dispensing them like a vending machine throughout the visit. Find other ways to reward the horse for good behavior throughout the process.

Problem: Distrust of farriers or strangers. Horses that have been mistreated may be wary of new people—including farriers.

Solution: Help the horse gain confidence by introducing new visitors slowly. Choose a location where your horse feels most comfortable for an introduction and avoid spaces that make the horse feel trapped. If you have the luxury of being at a barn with multiple horses requiring frequent farrier visits, arranging a time for an informal "meet and greet" without any work can get the relationship off on the right hoof.

Problem: Flies and other biting pests. Bugs are pesky enough to make even a "good" horse flinch. Holding or tying up a horse for shoeing out in the sun is like inviting bugs to a feast. Flies will take advantage of an easy target, and the blazing heat of the sun's rays turns on the sweat, making everyone uncomfortable.

Solution: Choose a location that attracts fewer flies and apply a repellant just before the farrier begins his work. Remember, a farrier must bend over underneath your horse to do his job. It might seem useful to spray a horse's legs when the bugs show up but give your farrier the courtesy of standing up first to avoid getting sprayed in the face. Fans can also be useful in controlling flies while a farrier works.

Create Positive Farrier Experiences

Horseshoeing/trimming large animals is potentially dangerous enough that one horse can temporarily injure a farrier or even end his career. Poorly behaved horses put the owner or handler at risk and can hurt himself in a battle with a farrier. Most horses that have regular hoof care do so without serious mishaps. But horses are animals, and there is always the potential for a situation to arise no matter how docile the horse is.

Recognizing opportunities to create a positive experience avoids problems and creates positive situations, so neither the horse nor the farrier dread their time together. This starts by considering basic herd dynamics—horses rely on herdmates to feel safe. Take a few minutes to bring pasturemates into the barn and keep all horses together until the farrier is finished. Allowing a nervous horse to stand in an area where he is around others or can see other horses helps alleviate anxiety.

Positive experiences don't happen by accident. Set up a suitable area for trimming and shoeing without distractions or hazards. Some farriers require having a handler hold the horse. Others don't mind working on a horse that is safely tied. Ask the farrier for his preference and ensure the horse is trained to stand tied before assuming all will be well. Breakaway clips are necessary to allow for a quick release if the horse spooks or pulls back.

Your horse may not verbally talk with you, but that doesn't mean he isn't communicating. Watch your horse for signs of fear, aggression, or nervousness. Depending on the horse, it may signal he is not ready for trimming or shoeing, or it may mean taking a short break to help him feel more comfortable.

Common Causes of "Bad Behavior"

Is It Pain?

It's human nature to blame the horse and jump to the conclusion that there is a behavior issue. In some cases, pain may be at the root of the problem. Discomfort can manifest in many ways when shoeing. An abscess, a chronic injury, or a sensitive sole, especially during a laminitis event, can make it difficult for a horse to stand on three legs. Old age, injuries, arthritis, and poor conformation that interfere with flexibility in the knee, shoulder, hock, stifle, or hip may also be causing the resistance. Bodywork like massage and chiropractic have helped resistant horses stand better for shoeing.

Basic stretching exercises can loosen stiff legs, making it easier for the horse to hold up his leg for an extended period of time (fig. 12.2). These are two simple stretches to try with your horse:

Exercise 1: Stand just behind the horse's shoulder and pick up the hind leg on the same side. Gently pull the leg toward you. This stretches the hamstring and other muscles in the back end and prepares the horse for resting his hoof on a stand while the farrier works.

12.2 Use gentle stretching exercises to help stiff horses feel more comfortable during a farrier's visit.

Exercise 2: Stand at the hindquarters facing away from the horse's head. Pick up the leg as if to clean a hoof. Slowly walk a few steps away from the back end to create a stretch. Loosening these muscles keeps the horse limber. The motion also stimulates the range of motion and position farriers use during trimming.

Horses should have good manners but ruling out underlying problems and those unrelated to the hoof should always be prioritized. It's also important to acknowledge the horse's limitations. Certain conformation issues like base-narrow front legs make it difficult for the horse to hold his legs in a proper shoeing position without discomfort.

Arthritis, especially in the hocks, can make the process uncomfortable. You may notice these are times a farrier uses a hoof stand with a leg cradle to provide extra support and relief during trimming and shoeing.

Owner Actions That Cause Behavioral Problems

Bad horse behavior can also directly result from a nervous owner anticipating an action that hasn't happened yet. The horse looks to the "herd" for cues of danger. In this case, the "herd" is the handler. When the person holding the horse is nervous, she is suggesting a possible threat.

Recognize your presence influences your horse and how this plays into his natural prey instinct. Learning to control your feelings may take time and practice. In the short term, asking someone more comfortable to hold the horse can help the situation.

Barn Management That Contributes to Behavioral Problems

Well-managed stables have a dedicated area for a farrier to work. In an ideal scenario, the space is quiet and close enough to other horses to avoid separation anxiety. In a public stable, farriers often set up at the end of the barn aisle. The activity of horses or people coming and going can be a major distraction for some horses. Set the horse up for the best possible experience by finding a less busy space to keep the horse focused on the task at hand.

Dogs are as much a part of some barns as horses. It's not uncommon for dogs to be as at home in the barn as inside the owner's home. Dogs hover, waiting to snatch a hoof clipping as a tasty treat. However, dogs must stay out of the farrier's way to keep everyone safe. Rambunctious or aggressive animals should be kept out of the barn until the work is done.

Farrier Attitude That Causes Behavioral Problems

Shoeing is stressful and physically demanding. Providing top-notch customer service, dealing with emergencies, difficult horses, and demanding clients can lead to burnout. A good day can easily turn bad when an unpredictable horse strains a farrier's back or pulls a nail into a hand. Horses sense that frustration and can respond with worse behavior. But stopping even for 5 or 10 minutes, can be enough for everyone to regain composure and resume in a better frame of mind.

Sedative Solutions

Calming medications serve a purpose in specific trimming and shoeing situations. Horses may be in excruciating pain, and without pain relief, are unable to stand for the farrier. For example, sedation can be supportive in therapeutic hoof situations or horses dealing with a lameness not directly associated with hoof care. A horse with shivers has no control over his reactions, and a tranquilizer keeps the horse comfortable during farrier visits. Other horses may be so unruly that sedation makes them safer for the people involved (figs. 12.3).

However, tranquilizers *are not* a quick-fix, cure-all for bad behavior. While there are situations when sedation is used, it is important to understand the drawbacks. First, while sedated, the horse is not learning to become more accepting of the work—the horse is simply forced

12.3 Sedation is not a quick fix for horses uncomfortable with farrier work but is necessary in some instances to keep the horse and farrier safe. This mini stood for the farrier to trim her front feet but bit and kicked out when trimmed on the hind. After several attempts over multiple visits, the veterinarian was on-site to give the horse an injectable sedative.

into compliance. Second, some horses react to the drug. Under sedation, horses are still aware of what is happening around them and can "wake up," kick out, or spook without warning. The reaction may be sparked by a simple action—such as someone walking behind the horse. The motion translates into a perceived threat because the sedated horse isn't aware of a person in that space.

The most common medications used are either a gel or an intravenous (IV) cocktail. The oral gel must be prescribed by a veterinarian who provides specific instructions to the horse owner for its use. Even though the gel is as easy to give as a tube of dewormer, it is up to you to administer the drug, not the farrier, as the prescription is written to you, the horse owner.

Legally, only licensed veterinarians can administer injectable sedatives. Vets have the training and expertise to monitor a horse's vital signs for any adverse effects. Coordinating schedules between the vet, farrier, and owner (or handler) means extra work scheduling appointments.

As with any drug, there is a risk for serious medical complications. When a horse hasn't been sedated properly, the result can be anaphylactic shock, severe allergic reactions, and even death. When veterinarians administer the medication, they must first confirm the horse is in good health and have additional drugs to counteract negative reactions.

A Horse-First Approach

Thinking like a horse and understanding herd behavior and physiology can go a long way in helping horses overcome fear or dislike for farrier work. First, consider how the horse's size and build can influence comfort during trimming or shoeing. While larger horses may be okay when a farrier lifts their leg higher, ponies and shorter horses have a harder time with this position, and it can make them feel unbalanced.

In response, horses naturally raise their head and neck and shift their weight. This is an intuitive reaction among all horses—even those that have never had an issue with farriers. Humans tend to see this as "bad behavior" and reprimand the horse, which encourages him to raise his head higher, making him less balanced, feeding an unproductive cycle.

The veterinary field has increasingly adopted a new approach focused on reducing the horse's stress during a visit. The method is known as *cooperative care* or *protective care* and gives the animal the option for choosing when and how to interact in the procedure. The method is widely used in farrier interactions with wild horses and zoo animals. The focus is on increasing safety while reducing fear. It gives the animal the choice to allow the start of a procedure and when to stop.

A barrier is placed between the farrier and the horse with an opening where the hoof can be safely reached. This allows the horse to walk and move away as he feels uncomfortable and return on his own terms. The enticement to cooperate is positive reinforcement. Initially, many are skeptical but the approach can calm horses faster than any other technique, allowing cooperation to be "shaped."

If you haven't seen the process, it is easy to imagine that this will take forever, but in practice, it actually takes very little time and is easier because the horse is more comfortable, and everyone is safer.

12.4 Introducing foals to farrier work begins at a young age through farrier visits and regular handling of the legs.

Training Horses for Shoeing

Training for shoeing starts with preparation for trimming. Because foals need to be observed during the first few weeks of life, and possibly earlier if there are noticeable deformities, basic handling starts at that time (fig. 12.4).

Short, daily sessions spent touching or brushing legs, leading, and standing pay dividends in the future. Teaching the horse to hold his hoof up for increasingly longer periods of time teaches patience. The stretching exercises mentioned on p. 168 are one way to introduce the position and sensation a horse experiences during a visit from the farrier.

Some horse owners expect farriers to teach horses to accept trimming and shoeing. Not all farriers are willing or capable of training. Farriers should be experienced horse handlers, but training horses is a different skill. A farrier understands that working with inexperienced horses is part of the job and would not expect a horse owner to introduce her horse to the tools and smells of the trade, but he has every right to expect the horses have a basic level of respect for people.

Graduating from trimming to shoeing follows similar principles. When done correctly, horses do not feel pain from the horseshoe nails because the hoof is made of a hard material, much like your fingernails. However, it does take time for a horse to get used to the sensation of a farrier pounding on his hoof. Some horses also need time to get used to the smell and smoke of a hot shoeing. Forcing an untrained horse to stand still and behave for a new

12.5 A & B Regularly pick up and clean all four feet for good hoof care and to prepare the horse for the farrier (B). Basic handling skills set a solid foundation of respect in all areas of horse ownership, including farrier visits (B). Teaching a horse to lead, respect his handler, and remain calm walking to and from the barn prepares him for farrier care.

set of shoes without prior preparation is unfair to both the horse and the farrier and can result in a bad experience for both.

Use this pre-shoeing checklist to evaluate your horse's readiness for his first shoeing (figs. 12.5 A & B):

- Can you pick up and clean all four feet?
- Can you lead the horse?
- Does the horse cross-tie or straight tie?
- Does the horse threaten to kick, or kick out when you reach for the hind legs?
- Does the horse bite?
- Is the horse in pain?

FROM THE FORGE
Tales from the Field

On a remote polo field at Cornell University, a group of horses was turned out for summer, and that is where I would shoe them. The horses stood tied to the shady side of a trailer for trimming and shoeing. All were well-behaved and used to being tied while I worked, so I never had a problem. Except for that one time…

During one visit, the trailer was being used off-site. A pipe gate was the only place in the field to tie to—something I would only do with horses I trusted. I tied two horses to the gate and stood between them. As I bent over to start, the roan rubbed on the gate. It caught on his halter and lifted the gate off the pegs. Not a problem until the horse realized the gate was attached to his halter. My helper remembers looking up and seeing two horses running backward while I ran toward them, trying to release them. The horses broke their lead rope snaps then just stood there. Luckily, no one was hurt.

A similar experience happened during a visit to two retired Cornell University polo horses bought by a beef farmer. Usually, a student worker caught and held the horses. On one visit, the student was unavailable, and the horses were tied to a steel gate at the back of the pole barn.

I parked far from the horses anticipating what might happen next. As I slowly approached, one horse pulled violently. The gate popped off the pegs and flew over my head, forcing me to duck.

The horse ran, trying to flee the gate chasing him. He blindly headed for my truck and hit the back end. Then he slid alongside the truck body, pulling the gate against the rear of the truck pinning himself there. He caught his breath and, still attached to the gate. He decided to jump it.

Catching both front feet in the gate, he flipped. Now the gate was on the ground in front of him and he just stared at it. The cheap snap should have broken but didn't, so I crept forward and cut the lead rope with my knife. The horse was uninjured but shook up. Needless to say, I got the owner to hold him and required someone to be present for every visit.

It can be a matter of personal pride for a farrier to finish the job on a horse he has started. And horse owners can put pressure on a farrier to finish when a competition is looming or a schedule is limited.

Early in my career, a chestnut mare stood unusually still with a glassy look in her eyes. As I positioned myself to reach for a hind leg, this mare shrieked and sent both legs right by my head. The air snapped in front of my face. Undaunted, I reached for that hind leg again with the same results. Obviously, it was dangerous to continue, but the owner needed the horse finished because her daughter had a 4-H show coming up.

The woman called her husband to help. He had little patience for horses and used a nose twitch to restrain the mare. I could feel the tension building. I put her leg down, stepped away, and said the horse was too dangerous to work on. The husband said, "If you were any kind of real man, you would finish the job!" I later learned this horse kicked and broke the leg of the previous farrier.

I've run into other mares with this same behavior throughout my career. Talking with veterinarians has revealed that hormonal imbalances or cysts on the ovaries can cause this type of reaction because of the pain, even though it is unrelated to the hoof or legs. There is not any training that resolves a problem like this, and further veterinary attention is necessary to help these horses.

CHAPTER 13

Becoming a Better Consumer of Farriery

It's not uncommon to hear (or have) complaints about farriers. Finding one is only a piece of the challenge—keeping one can be just as hard. The farrier is booked, fails to show for an appointment, neglects to return a phone call, or "disappears" altogether. The search begins and takes many forms, from posts on social groups for advice asking fellow horse people and veterinarians for recommendations.

The reality is some farriers are simply unprofessional. And, well-qualified farriers are in short supply, especially in certain geographic regions and disciplines. But in many cases, there are underlying reasons a farrier drops a client. From a farrier's perspective, these are a few factors that he uses to decide to keep or let go of a customer.

Dangerous Conditions or Badly Behaved Horses

Farriers are independent business owners. A farrier chooses who, when, and where he is willing to shoe a horse. Horseshoeing can be a dangerous occupation and he cannot put himself at risk of an injury.

Making excuses for poor behavior does not go well when the person trying to shoe or trim the horse is being tossed around or kicked. Plus, it is impossible to perform quality hoof care when dealing with a moving target.

Most horses are responsive to training and stand well for shoeing, but this needs to happen before the farrier appointment. Most farriers will not train horses to stand well for shoeing, and instead encourage horse owners to work with a trainer. If the horse requires extra time for shoeing, the farrier appreciates a heads-up so he can schedule the stop accordingly.

Know-It-All Clients Who Micromanage

For the relationship to work, there needs to be mutual respect. Most farriers appreciate when a horse owner is interested in understanding the mechanics of her horse's feet.

Asking questions and talking about shoeing choices creates a valuable partnership that best serves the horse. When the interest turns into an inquiry that doubts the farrier's expertise, the relationship breaks down, and you may find yourself searching for someone new.

No, Slow, or Poor Payment

You wouldn't go to the grocery store or the gas station and ask for a discount or the option to pay later. Farriers, too, expect full payment at the time of service. There are always exceptions. Some clients and farriers work together so frequently that a monthly agreement may be possible, but it's imperative to have this conversation up front.

As an independent business owner, a farrier relies on prompt payment to cover his own medical and liability insurance. Many opt out of disability insurance because of the expense, so if he gets hurt and can't work, he doesn't get paid.

Running a business also means farriers have other fixed costs to prepare to shoe your horse. This ranges from supplies like shoes and nails to vehicle payments, travel expenses, and more. Since shoeing is required on an ongoing basis, as a horse owner, it is important to budget for the service and refrain from asking for credit, discounts, or extended terms.

This is the farrier's "salary." He relies on prompt payment not only to cover business expenses but also to support his home life. Repeated bounced checks, refusal to pay, or multiple delayed payments impact his ability to pay his own bills. As much as he might like you and your horse, it just doesn't make financial sense to continue.

Loose Horses

Catching horses is not the farrier's job and potentially puts him in an unsafe situation. Numerous farriers have been seriously injured while attempting to bring in clients' horses. Whether it is the horse himself or a protective herdmate that is to blame, asking the farrier to bring the horse in for a visit invites the opportunity for harm.

There's another reason farriers groan when pulling up to the barn to find the horses outside. It's inconvenient. A farrier has multiple appointments booked and plans his schedule based on efficiencies. Trying to catch horses (especially those not wanting to be caught) can be time-consuming and make him late for his next appointment.

Think how you would feel if you were the next customer, waiting a few minutes to a few hours for him to arrive.

Muddy Horses

Safety and efficiency aren't the only reasons farriers appreciate clients who bring in the horses in advance. Muddy, wet conditions make for a dirty job. Imagine putting your hands or tools on a mucky mess or having caked dirt flake off as you're trying to work.

Not only is there the "ick" factor, but it is difficult to be precise when mud is caked or dried on the hoof.

Bringing your horses in early enough to dry and brush off the dirt will support a lasting relationship with your farrier.

Poor Working Conditions

Chances are your employer provides amenities that make it easier to perform your work. Good lighting, an ergonomic chair, room to move around are all part of the employment agreement. You wouldn't tolerate an employer who doesn't provide the basics.

Your barn is the farrier's office. There are farriers, who like a vet, have their own shop. In these situations, as we've already discussed, the client hauls in for an appointment, giving the farrier complete control of the area. However, the majority of farriers work out of their truck. So, farriers rely on you to provide an adequate area for them to work.

To do a proper job, the farrier needs a reasonable work area. Start by providing him access to a flat, well-lit, roomy space with good ventilation. Make sure the ground is level, and dry—uneven, muddy ground is a guarantee for substandard work.

This workspace could be inside or out but consider how the weather may influence comfort. Shoeing horses outside may be pleasant in some climates on some days. However, working in the hot sun, rain, snow, or wind is unpleasant for all involved.

Regardless of where the farrier sets up on-site, make sure the area is free from clutter and stored equipment. Busy barns should consider setting up a designated space away from others coming and going to minimize distractions. If you truly want to make friends with the farrier—make the area easy for him to access his truck,

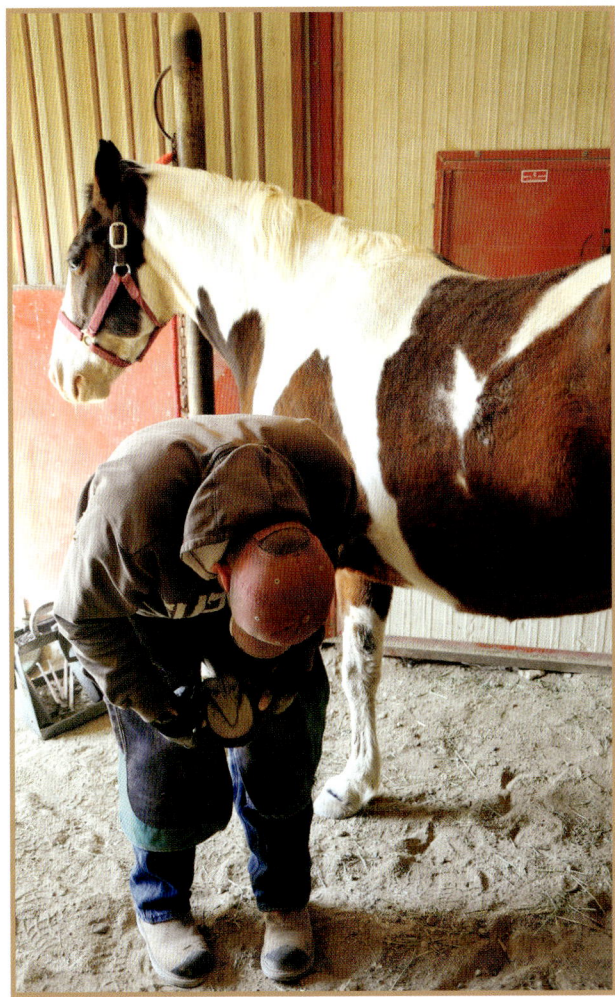

13.1 Provide an area for the farrier that is level, out of the elements, and free of clutter.

which will make it easy for him to reach his supplies (figs. 13.1 and 13.2).

Choosing a space that is inside where fans are used can provide relief from bugs. Biting flies transform normally good horses into difficult ones and marginal behavioral problems into impossible situations.

13.2 Finding a shady place out of the flow of traffic offers a farrier a place to easily set up his mobile shop and get to work in a safe setting.

Inconsistency

Think about how frustrating it is when someone cancels plans on you last minute. The first time it happens, you understand there may be a valid reason. Second and third occurrences make it clear it's a pattern. There's no way to recover the time spent waiting or making adjustments for a last-minute change.

Routinely canceling appointments or repeatedly delaying a visit until an "emergency" will not help your relationship with the farrier. It will happen occasionally, and for valid reasons the farrier will understand, but when it becomes a habit, don't be surprised if you're looking for a new farrier.

Expecting the farrier to be available on a moment's notice for routine calls is also not a good strategy for endearing yourself to him. Farrier schedules are usually booked solid. Failing to stay on a schedule has implications for your horse too—it increases his chances

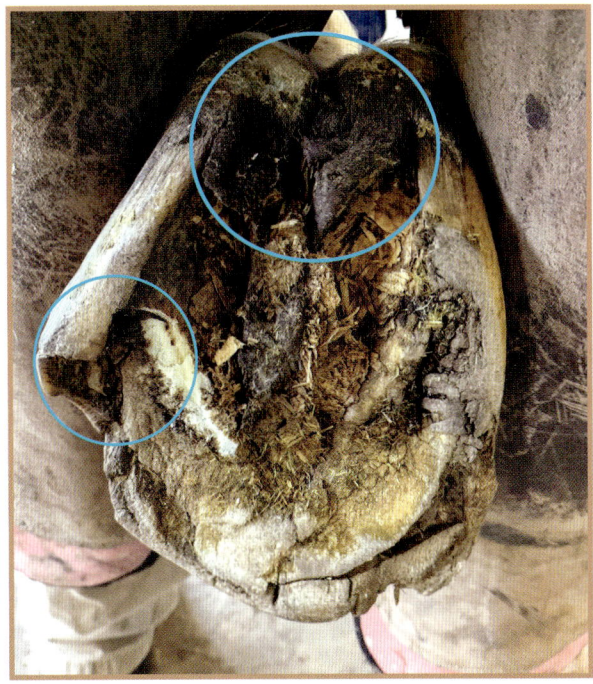

13.3 Failing to keep a horse on a regular schedule can lead to severe hoof problems like this that a farrier can't fix immediately. This hoof was not trimmed for nearly a year. As the hoof grew the wall became brittle and chipped. The heels are also collapsed here, meaning the area around the frog is too narrow.

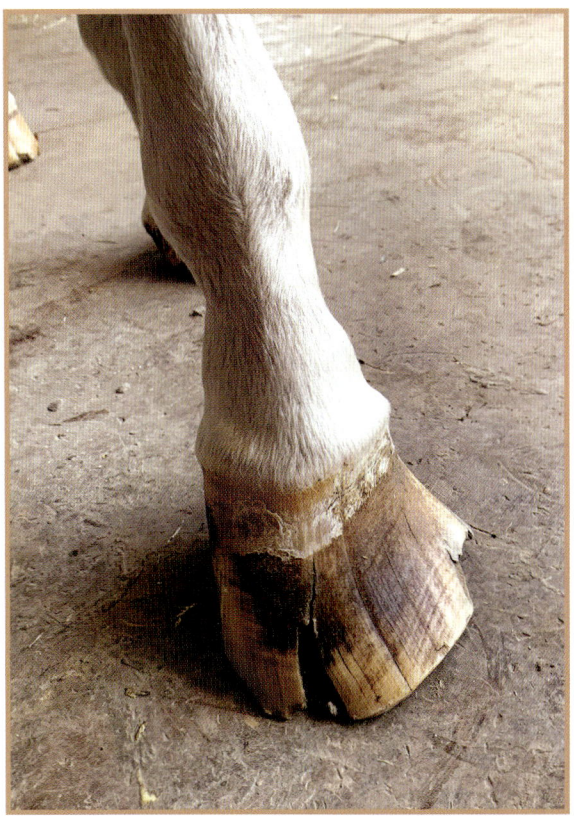

13.4 This hoof is the result of poor conformation coupled with neglect. The uneven loading causes hoof cracks in specific places. Not trimming often enough will cause the cracks to expand, while the hoof develops flares.

of losing a shoe. Inevitably, it is always right before a show or trail ride. Waiting to call for an appointment or stretching the schedules can interfere with your horse's work, and depending on the farrier's schedule, make it difficult to fit you in.

Skipping Management Recommendations

In some cases, farriers make specific suggestions for management changes to ensure the shoeing works best for the horse. That might mean limiting turnout, which may be inconvenient. Failing to follow recommendations and having to "fix" the same problem repeatedly is frustrating when a farrier is trying his best to serve the horse (figs. 13.3 &. 13.4).

Switching Farriers Often

Hiring a new farrier is sometimes necessary to serve the best interest of the horse. It may be as simple as an emergency, a relocation, or a discipline switch. In other cases, personality clashes or disagreements may be valid reasons for finding a new farrier. However, some horse owners try to save money by frequently switching farriers. You wouldn't switch dentists every time you need your teeth cleaned, so why do that with your horse's feet?

What You Can Expect

Any or all the scenarios described are sound reasons for farriers to "quit" certain clients. But it is a two-way relationship, and it is reasonable for you, the horse owner, to ask a farrier to meet certain expectations. Farriers are also guilty of having poor business practices that make it difficult for clients to do business.

This list highlights what you can expect from a professional farrier who is committed to running a good service-based business. If the person you're using isn't holding up his end of the relationship, it is time to move on.

Prompt, Clear Communication

Staying in touch is easier than ever via phone, email, or text message. However, good communication extends beyond being responsive—it's also about explaining shoeing decisions and answering questions in terms you can understand. As the one paying the bill and caring for the horse, it is important to know as much as possible about your horse's hooves, especially if he has problems.

If a farrier is unwilling to answer questions or becomes defensive during a respectful, well-intentioned conversation, it can be a signal it's time to find someone else. You're paying for a service and deserve explanations, whether they are out of curiosity or necessity to care for the horse.

Lateness

Time is precious for everyone. Just as a farrier expects clients to be on time, you should expect the same, within reason. Remember that he operates out of a mobile office. There is the possibility that traffic or an unforeseen event unexpectedly changes his schedule, but there is a difference between an unpredictable event and chronic tardiness. It's not unreasonable to expect an update from the farrier if a delay arises so you can plan accordingly.

Poor Horse Handling Skills

Horsemanship is a skill that is the mark of a good farrier. Those who use a calm, steady demeanor help keep the horses comfortable and agreeable to work on.

If you stop and think about it, it is quite remarkable that most horses patiently stand for trimming and shoeing. The horse's legs are everything to the horse. The simple act of picking up a hoof takes away his first defense strategy and, in some cases, can seriously threaten his ability to balance. Finding a farrier who can put a horse at ease is critical to a strong, long-lasting relationship.

Unprepared

Routinely arriving without the right supplies indicates it's time to find someone else. A well-stocked truck means he can complete the job in one visit. He must also have the knowledge and ability to work on a specific breed or within a discipline to properly trim and shoe the horse to support your goals.

Disinterest in Continuing Education

Ongoing professional development demonstrates the farrier's commitment to his trade. Although some of the basics of horseshoeing have not changed, there are innovations, new research, and new products that offer possibilities for specific cases. There is always something to learn in this profession. One highly regarded farrier once remarked, "I hope I live long enough to learn all I need to know!"

It's okay to ask about his involvement with continuing education events. Many of the most successful farriers attend local, regional, or national workshops. Networking with other colleagues and veterinarians to share case studies and compare outcomes and observations are often valuable ways a farrier expands his knowledge.

Certification or accreditation is not required of farriers and isn't always indicative of expertise. However, those who volunteer to do so demonstrate an added level of commitment to the profession. Those who choose to become a certified farrier through the American Farrier's Association (AFA) or the International Association of Professional Farriers (IAPF) have passed an extensive written exam and several practical exams to demonstrate proficiency at both forging horseshoes and shoeing. Advancement through certification levels demonstrates a more extensive knowledge of anatomy, function, pathology, and advanced shoe-making techniques.

Learning is not just for farriers. Horse owners, too, can benefit from attending workshops about horseshoeing. Cooperative extension agencies, veterinarians, and tack stores offer budget-friendly, often free opportunities that improve general hoof-care knowledge.

Quality of Work

It's easy to evaluate quality in the clothing, electronics, and other products you buy. The feel and functionality offer clues to the level of craftsmanship. Understanding a "good shoeing" is a bit more difficult for horse owners to discern.

Lameness can be the most obvious sign of a "bad job" when the horse has good feet and no existing soundness issues.

But what does a "good job" look like?

While farriers aren't required to attend a certification program, the AFA score sheet for the Certified Farrier Exam offers a good explanation. The exam is divided into three sections: hoof preparation, shoe fit and preparation, and nailing/finishing.

Hoof preparation: The job starts with trimming the hoof to the appropriate angle and toe length for the horse's conformation. This also means the feet are balanced medially/laterally, and the feet are aligned under the horse's legs. It is critical that he leaves adequate sole depth and frog contact with the ground. All edges of the foot must be smooth and hoof walls are trimmed to a uniform thickness.

Shoe preparation and fit: In general, the shoe width should be twice the hoof wall thickness. This arrangement guides proper nail location. The fit around the heel should leave room for the natural expansion of the hoof. The shoe should have no sharp edges or hammer marks and the shoe should have sole relief to avoid any sole pressure. The certification exam requires farriers to fit the shoe to the perimeter of the hoof with a shorter toe length. In practice, it is recognized that reducing toe lengths on deformed feet may not be recommended.

Nailing and finishing: The shoe is placed exactly where intended, with no extra hoof wall protruding over the edge. The end goal is that between a proper trimming and appropriate shoe fit, the shoe stays in perfect position between visits (fig. 13.5). Nails should not be beyond the widest part of the hoof and should exit at one-third the height of the hoof wall in a straight line. Clinches should be uniform, short, and smooth, with no rough edges. The hoof wall should also be smooth with no rasp marks.

There will be times farriers and clients don't see eye to eye. It's an uncomfortable feeling for both and the horse is the one stuck in the middle, and in some cases, it is in the best interest of all involved to part ways.

The most successful relationships are symbiotic. The scientific term "symbiosis" in science defines this as a phenomenon that occurs when two dissimilar organisms partner for a mutually beneficial result. In the barn, this results in a sound horse. Both parties have different expectations—horse owners want quality work in a timely manner, and farriers desire a good work environment and payment from the horse owner. By working together, the ultimate result can be achieved—a happier horse.

Basic Hoof Care Skills for Horse Owners

There is no substitute for having a skilled farrier provide regular trimming and shoeing. A handful of horse owners want to trim or shoe their horses and choose to enroll in basic classes or learn from a skilled farrier.

Chances are you rely on a relationship with a professional farrier, which is considered best practice for most horse owners. However, there are a few hoof-care skills

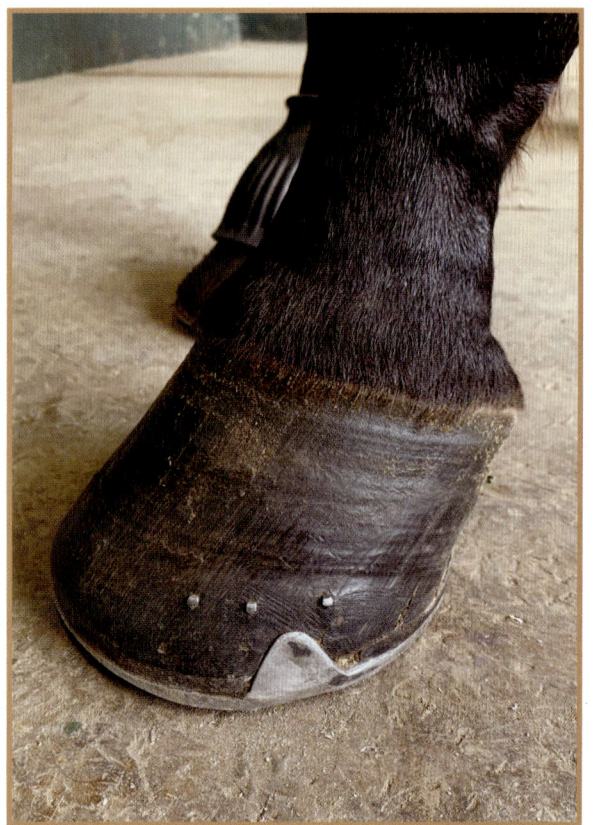

13.5 This is an example of a well-done shoeing job that started with a solid trim, well-fitted shoe, and precise nailing and finishing.

that you can perform between visits to support your horse's hoof health.

Pulling a Shoe

A loose shoe interferes with the horse's balance and increases the chances for a hoof injury if the shoe shifts and creates an opportunity for stepping on protruding nails. Be sure to dismount if you notice a loose shoe while riding.

Conformation, specifically hoof angles, can also play a role. Front feet with long toes and low heels are more prone to the shoes loosening and getting lost. In addition, the mechanics of a long-toe low-heel stride creates pressure that pushes the shoe from the toe to the heel with each step. This sets up an opportunity for the back foot to overstep, land on the tail of the front shoe and partially pull it off.

This can happen in any breed, but Tennessee Walking horses tend to be more prone. This breed's natural gait places the hind footfall in the exact front prints of the front hooves, which increases the chance of stepping on the back of the front shoe.

Unfavorable environmental conditions like mud, deep snow, a small stone wedged between the hoof and shoe, or simply waiting too long between visits can loosen the nails or partially remove a shoe. And because horses seem to be experts at finding (and making) "trouble," it's possible for a horse with good feet and routine farrier care to have a loose shoe. So, whether it gets caught on a fence or simply from a rambunctious romp in the paddock, you need to be prepared to respond until the farrier arrives.

Fortunately, a shoe that loosens isn't likely to significantly impact overall hoof health. The biggest issue occurs when the shoe is part way off and twisted or shifted out of position. It's possible for puncture wounds to occur when nails are still in a shifted shoe and the horse steps on it. This can open an entry point for bacteria to create an infection or abscess.

If a shoe is left dangling and the horse steps on it, the nails might also pull off more hoof material. Pulling a loose shoe and knowing how to remove it helps reduce the risk of damage to the hoof.

Whether trail riding, around the barn, or in a competitive arena, all horse owners should be ready to pull a shoe in an emergency.

Start by having a basic set of farrier tools handy in the barn—a farrier's rasp, shoe pull-offs, or a pair of long-handled nippers. You can purchase these supplies at most farm and tack stores, or your farrier may be willing to sell his old tools. A claw hammer can substitute for nippers or pull-offs to remove the shoe from the hoof in an emergency.

Picking up the horse's hoof to pull a loose shoe is different from lifting one for cleaning. It'll likely feel awkward to handle a hoof in this way, so it's important to know where to position yourself.

Chances are your farrier uses a hoof stand to position the hoof, not an item horse owners tend to have. Acceptable alternatives include a cinder block, a stout tree stump, or a similar object free of sharp points that can injure you or the horse. You can also use the inside of your leg as support.

When working on the front feet, stand at your horse's shoulder and face the same direction—be sure that your back is toward the hindquarters. As you pick up the hoof, rest it on your inside thigh.

When working on the back feet, get next to the hip and face the horse's head, bringing the leg to rest on your inside thigh. Once you're in position:

1. Rasp the nails to thin out the metal (fig. 13.6). This makes it easier for the shoe to fully detach while reducing the chances of breaking off a chunk of the hoof wall. Use the smoother, fine gauge side of the rasp. The rougher side skips over the nails and digs into the hoof material. Make a sweeping motion across the front of the hoof. Use firm, consistent pressure but don't overdo it or risk digging into hoof material. Hoof nippers can also be used to snip the nail heads off and loosen the clinch if a rasp is unavailable or too hard to use.

2. Next, turn toward the horse's rear end to hold the leg properly to pull the shoe. Grab a pair of nippers

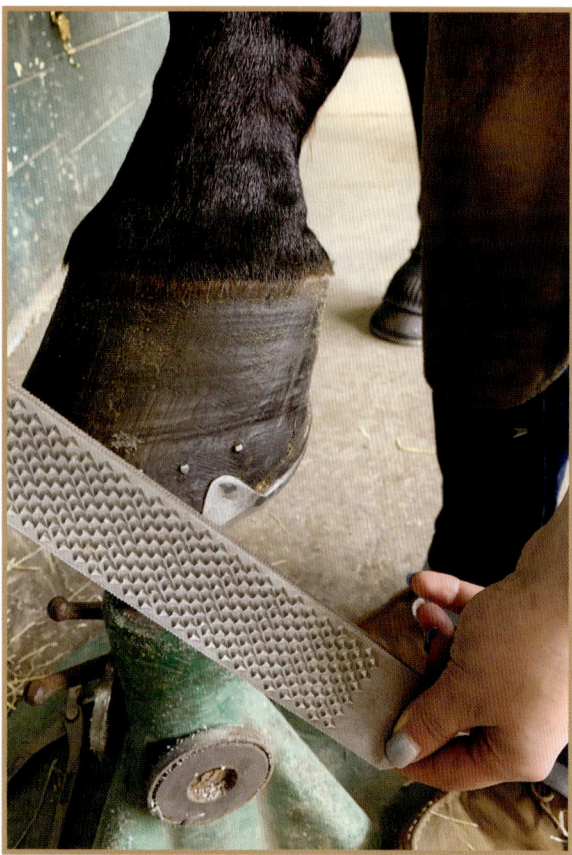

13.6 To "pop" the shoe off, use the rasp to thin out the nails to make it easier.

13.7 Gently wiggle the nippers like wiggling a loose tooth to separate the shoe from the hoof.

or shoe pull-offs. Start at the heels and insert the nippers or shoe pull-offs in between the shoe and hoof. With firm, steady pressure, "work" the shoe as if you're wiggling a loose tooth. Move the nippers back and forth, pulling in an opposite diagonal motion for the best success (fig. 13.7).

Repeat on the opposite heel and work around the hoof until the shoe is entirely off. Keep the pressure steady and firm and take your time to avoid bruising the sole or damaging the hoof wall.

In a pinch, a claw head hammer can substitute. Pull the hammer with one hand instead of pushing as you would with farrier tools to pry the shoe forward. Keep the hammer between the hoof and shoe, loosening as you go.

In many cases, that's all you need to do until the farrier can reset it. Pulling a shoe prevents a major injury, and a sound horse is just fine in the interim. However, if the hoof is damaged or a nail penetrates the hoof, it might be necessary to involve a veterinarian. Should this happen, clean debris from the hoof and apply a protective wrap until the vet or farrier arrives. Use cotton pads or gauze to cover the sole of the foot and use duct tape or adhesive vet tape to create a "boot-like" structure around the outside of the hoof. A baby diaper wrapped with duct tape or vet wrap is an easy-to-use alternative to bulkier materials.

Rasping a Hoof

Another way to get involved in your horse's hoof care is learning how to use a rasp. Used correctly, the rasp removes flares, smooths out small chips, and cleans up a

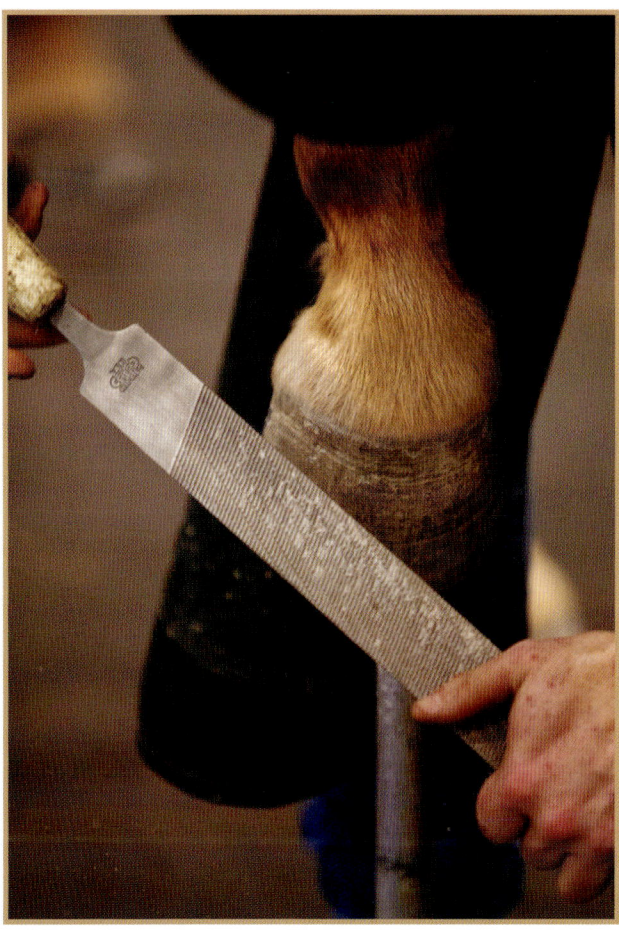

13.8 If you're interested in pitching in with your horse's hoof care ask your farrier how you might be able to use a rasp to smooth out uneven edges between visits.

hoof after a pulled shoe until the farrier can get there for a trimming and shoeing (fig. 13.8). Talk with your farrier and share your interest in how this can help support your horse's hoof health before jumping in.

Properly using the rasp starts with knowing how it is made. Rasps are two-sided. One is coarse, the other fine. One end is rounded, the other pointed side is called the "tang," where a wooden or rubber handle can be added. The handle is used to push the rasp, and the butt guides or pulls the rasp across the hoof.

Like a kitchen grater, the rasp has different patterns notched into it. The coarse side has six to eight teeth in a row, with each row offset from the next. The smooth side has cuts made in opposite directions for a sharper cutting edge.

The rasp is used in a left-to-right motion. Visualize this movement as you're pushing and pulling a rasp across a horse's hoof. Your farrier wears chaps to protect his legs and you may want to consider that too. It's harder juggling the hoof and tools than giving yourself a manicure, but these four steps can help you get started.

1. Remove debris with a hoof pick.

2. Pick up the hoof and make a downward stroke from heel to toe, keeping the rasp as flat as possible. Avoid applying uneven pressure in any single spot.

3. In a singular motion, begin at the heel and move to the toe. Pick up the rasp to reposition rather than dragging it back over your file marks.

4. Run the rasp around the front of the hoof following its round contour to smooth off minor chips.

CHAPTER 14

Who Is the Modern Farrier and What Training is Required?

In most professions, a person begins his career at the "bottom" and progresses to higher positions over time. Horseshoers start at the bottom and stay there—well at the bottom of the horse anyway. Don't let the bad anatomy joke fool you. While farriers are not climbing the corporate ladder, there are countless opportunities for basic and advanced training that allows a farrier to hone his craft and become recognized as an expert.

Before modern times, young boys, often with a family member who was a blacksmith, were compelled to work in the shop, often in harsh conditions. In England, these youngsters were forced into blacksmithing apprenticeships to gain a skill and earn a wage that would help support the family. Despite the demanding work environment, rookies achieved a level of knowledge and expertise that is only possible with hands-on experience. Fortunately, working conditions began improving and evolving too (fig. 14.1).

Today, the European training process requires a specific number of apprenticeship hours and a certification test. This has created a pipeline of well-trained blacksmiths and established a standard set of guidelines that define good farrier work.

14.1 The farrier trade is often passed from one generation to the next. Here a farrier is showing a young boy how to use a hammer to flatten a piece of steel on an anvil.

14.2 Certification tests require that farriers hand-forge horseshoes to specific specifications. Events are held at farrier conventions and horseshoeing schools throughout the year at a number of locations across the country.

In the United States, there is no required training or testing process. Quite literally, anyone can pick up a rasp, nippers, and shoeing hammer and advertise as a farrier. Obviously, this approach is not recommended for safety and welfare issues.

On the positive side, the flexibility offers greater opportunities for an individual to find a training option that fits his lifestyle—either through an apprenticeship or schooling. The flip side is that without a consistent curriculum, there can be dramatic variability in the skills and the breadth of knowledge among farriers. This too has its upsides—granting room for innovations that have changed the lives of horses—but can also have its drawbacks in making sure an individual is prepared to trim and shoe.

Learning how to shoe horses well enough to earn a living is one of the hardest endeavors a person has ever tried. It takes complete dedication and focus to master and combine the technical skills needed to become a well-rounded farrier (fig. 14.2).

What Training Do Farriers Receive?

There is no quick way to become an experienced, well-trained farrier. Author Malcolm Gladwell explains in his book *Outliers* that it takes 10,000 hours of practice to master most skills. Breaking that down over time is the equivalent of nearly five years of consistent 40-hour workweeks.

In Great Britain, a four-year apprenticeship is standard for farrier training, though other European countries have varying requirements ranging from two to four years. The training includes a blend of on-the-job work experience with a Master Farrier, theoretical training, and a certification exam. As a result, the system has created a process that emphasizes blacksmithing and serves as a recruitment tool to bring interested individuals into the industry.

In the United States, a typical 16-week course totals 640 hours. There are currently about 60 farrier schools in the United States, according to the *American Farrier's Journal*, and the programs vary in length from as little as a two-week short course to more in-depth 16-week programs. At one time, there were nearly 100 schools.

Cornell University launched its farrier program in 1914 and has the oldest, continually operating farrier-teaching program in the United States. Like the Cornell University Farriery Course, some are attached to a vet hospital. This offers students exposure to specialty shoeing and rare cases. Other programs are hosted by a skilled farrier who has spent a lifetime honing his skills. Individual training programs accept students without a high school diploma or GED, while others require these as basic qualifications. The American Farriers Association (AFA) offers a listing of select training programs if you're interested in learning more (americanfarriers.org/page/schools).

Although most farriers have traded in a full blacksmith shop for a truck outfitted to travel to the client, apprenticeships remain a viable option for a new farrier to learn the business and advance his skills to the next level. Working alongside an established blacksmith, apprentices receive in-depth training on all aspects of hoof-care work (fig. 14.3).

In the United States, informal apprenticeships have provided valuable opportunities, and sometimes self-directed learning was a necessity. The working cowboy is one example. A ranch hand had to learn to shoe his horses from watching others and through trial and error to keep his horse sound for work. Over time, ranch hands

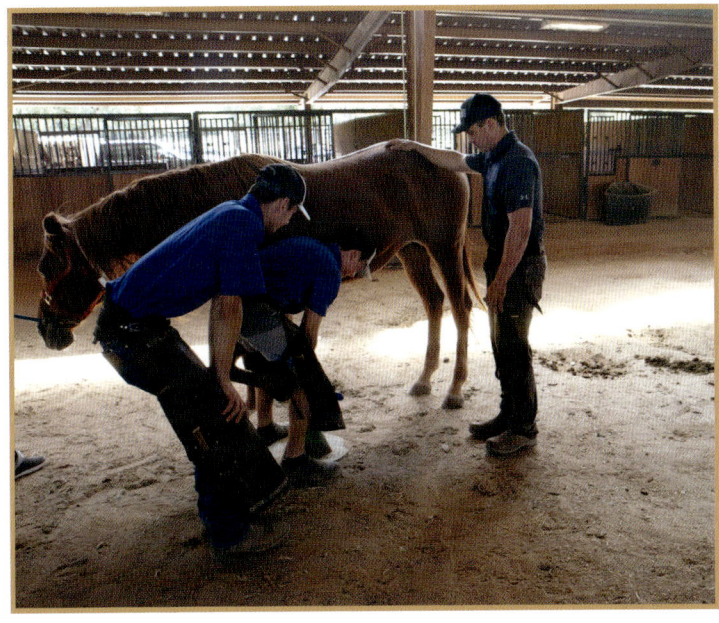

14.3 Apprenticeship and mentorships offer farriers opportunities to learn the hands-on skills and experience the business side of the trade. Here, two young apprentices work on trimming this hoof under the watchful eye of an experienced farrier who is guiding them in their training.

began shoeing horses for the public, and the phrase "cowboy shoeing" was coined.

Increasingly, modern farriers are college graduates who have likely taken science or business classes before trimming and shoeing horses. Veterinary medicine students are also becoming increasingly common in farrier-training programs. An individual may decide medicine isn't his chosen path and switch careers. Or he decides to take a farrier program to expand upon his knowledge as a DVM to become a vet who specializes in hoof care.

What Does It Take to Be a Farrier?

The individuals who are most successful as farriers have a desire to work with their hands and with horses; they have a horse background before picking up the tools. This does not mean a farrier must be an expert rider. Instead, he needs experience handling and leading horses. Some individuals gain this experience working at a breeding facility. Others come from a specific horse setting, be it in the show-horse world or trail riding.

Horseshoeing is a hands-on profession that requires a lot of knowledge, long hours, and physical strength to perform the task. The career isn't like learning how to change and rotate tires at an auto repair store, which can be taught and mastered quickly. Farriers must have the training to understand the mechanics of equine anatomy and put that into practice through the actual work of trimming and shoeing. Technical skills are only a piece of the equation. The profession also requires business savvy as most farriers work for themselves and treat the practice like a company, not a hobby.

Working as a farrier means being a member of the trades, a field that has experienced significant worker shortages. Arguably, good hoof-care professionals are in high demand like other skilled tradesmen including plumbers, masons, and electricians. The farrier industry estimates that there are roughly nine million horses in this country and an estimated 32,000 to 35,000 farriers working full and part-time across the United States, with the average farrier regularly shoeing 200 to 250 horses.

Advanced Training

Investing in ongoing professional development highlights any person's commitment to improving for the sake of tackling more complex work or delivering higher quality services. The same is true for farriers who regularly attend clinics and seek out information about advancements in the field. In some locations, veterinarians and farriers meet periodically to jointly work on a case and share observations from the field. This offers the opportunity to learn from one another and work through complex cases.

Optional advanced training can lead to certification. Several organizations have established a credentialing system that allows farriers to continue progressing in their work. For example, the IAPF sponsors discipline-specific certifications such as dressage and hunter-jumpers so that farriers can develop expertise within a specific niche. The certification process involves multiple tests that evaluate a farrier's skills as it relates to forging horseshoes that follow precise specifications.

The AFA offers three levels—the Certified Farrier (CF), Certified Tradesman Farrier (CTF) and Certified Journeyman Farrier (CJF) (fig. 14.4). As a farrier advances

14.4 Certifications are one way farriers can continue to enhance their skills and knowledge of fundamental and evolving shoeing practices. Farriers are given specifications for building a shoe and then most show the finished product to an examiner for evaluation and feedback.

Here's a look at the variety of advanced credentials your farrier might have earned.

AF = American Association of Professional Farriers Inc (AAPF) Accredited Farrier

APF = AAPF Accredited Professional Farrier

AF-I = AAPF Accredited Farrier with Foundation Credential

APF-I = AAPF Accredited Professional Farrier with Foundation Credential

ASF = FITS Advanced Skills Farrier

AWCF = Associate of the Worshipful Company of Farriers

CF = American Farriers Association (AFA) Certified Farrier

CF = FITS Certified Farrier

CJF = AFA Certified Journeyman Farrier

CJF I = BWFA Certified Journeyman Farrier I

CJF II = BWFA Certified Journeyman Farrier II

CME = BWFA Certified Master Educator

CMF = BWFA Certified Master Farrier

DVM = Doctor of Veterinary Medicine

DWCF or **DipWCF** = Diplomate of the Worshipful Company of Farriers

FWCF = Fellow of the Worshipful Company of Farriers

RF = Guild Registered Farrier

RJF = Guild Registered Journeyman Farrier

EE = AFA Educators Endorsement

FE = AFA Forging Endorsement

TE = AFA Therapeutic Endorsement

A word of caution— a person can attend continuing education events or earn multiple certifications and still be a terrible horseshoer, so there must be a balance between training and ability.

> **FROM THE FORGE**
> ## Eye of the Beholder
>
> In the 1970s, the county called me for jury duty. The dates of service overlapped with that year's American Farrier's Association (AFA) National Convention, where I was speaking and managing the tradeshow booth for Mustad.
>
> When I reported to the courthouse, an older, stern judge was presiding over the case. He lectured on the seriousness of service and emphasized he did not accept most requests for exemption. Serving was a civic duty. It came to my turn to talk with the judge and request a delay due to a pre-planned trip. I explained the location and the purpose for attending and he began asking me questions about my farrier business. Then he asked, "You willingly do this? Run a business that requires the hardest, dirtiest work?"
>
> He laughed at me and explained he grew up in a blacksmith shop, one run by his grandfather, father, and uncles. Law school was his ticket to a less physically demanding job, and he claimed he never wanted to see the inside of another blacksmith shop. I wished my family was in the business, and he couldn't get away fast enough.
>
> He ended the conversation telling me that because I have "the worst, most demanding job," he'd strike me from the jury rolls. I have never received a summons since!

through the program, he is expected to make increasingly complex shoe styles. Earning the highest level—certified journeyman—takes at least an hour of daily practice. That might not seem like much, but on top of a full day's work, burnout and fatigue can creep in. Pursuing certification is as much a testament to stamina as it is about skills.

Farrier certifications are a bit of an alphabet soup so understanding the credentials your farrier may have takes a bit of learning.

Equine Podiatry Specialty

Many general horse-care practices and specialties have evolved out of advancements in human medicine. Hoof care is just one area benefitting from this spillover. Equine podiatry is a relatively new field that has evolved over the last 20 years. Equine podiatrists use advanced diagnostics such as digital radiography, MRI, and video gait analysis to provide optimum foot care. Like human foot doctors, equine podiatrists receive focused training for recognizing, diagnosing, and treating hoof problems.

This overlap adds to a long-existing gray zone between a farrier's work and that of a veterinarian. Many times, the two must work together to resolve foot problems. An equine podiatrist must have training in both areas—farriery and veterinary medicine. Equine podiatrists tend to work out of a dedicated facility, such as a veterinary medicine university, or large veterinary medical practices like Rood & Riddle and Hagyard Equine Medical Institute. Depending on the arrangement, the podiatrist may be on staff or an independent farrier with whom a relationship is developed.

Ultimately, equine podiatry unites the art of farriery and blacksmithing with the medicine and science of the veterinary profession to provide care for hoof injuries, infections, abnormalities, wounds, and foot-related lameness.

Chances are you will never have to work with an equine podiatrist as horses with good conformation, and "normal" hooves are well-served with routine trimming and shoeing. However, it's nice to know there is an area of expertise within the industry to help with lameness, injury, and illness to support an afflicted horse.

Farrier Competitions

Another way a farrier can refine his skills is through blacksmithing competitions. In these contests, he must forge shoes to exact specifications within an allotted timeframe. The public is welcomed and encouraged to attend. These live demonstrations offer an inside look at what it is like for a farrier to use a forge to build a set of horseshoes to specific specifications.

If you've never seen a live forging contest, add it to your bucket list! Watching a competition is thrilling and intense (fig. 14.5). It's not uncommon to see sweat rolling off a farrier as he works in the heat to shape the shoe, to see a competitor get tired or burn up a shoe in the forge without enough time to restart.

When the timer goes off, judges inspect each farrier's work. The shoes are graded based on several factors. Competing farriers not only have the chance to win cash prizes, but the judge's feedback offers insights into his work for continuing professional development. Top finishers can even earn a spot on a team that travels to international competitions.

14.5 Blacksmithing competitions are exciting to watch and push farriers' skills as they compete against others from across the country and around the world. Rood & Riddle Equine Hospital hosted this specific event known as the World Horseshoeing Classic at its Lexington, Kentucky, facility.

2020 FARRIER BUSINESS PRACTICES SURVEY
What Farriers Are Charging (Both full-time and part-time farriers)

Region	Trim 4 Feet Only	Trim, Set 4 Keg Shoes	Trim, Reset 4 Keg Shoes	Trim, Forge & Set 2 Bar Shoes	Set Therapeutic, Specialty Steel, Aluminum Shoes	Trim, Forge & Set 4 Handmade Shoes	Repair Moderate Hoof Crack	Extra Charge for 2 Pads, Packing	Trim & Set 4 Aluminum Shoes	Trim & Glue-on 4 Shoes
National	$49.60	$147.23	$145.64	$155.34	$163.42	$133.51	$68.53	$40.36	$164.45	$276.45
Northeast	$54.84	$186.08	$184.35	$193.59	$185.00	$142.86	$81.00	$58.38	$209.35	$379.12
Central	$46.20	$147.50	$143.83	$143.46	$166.25	$152.00	$65.74	$37.07	$165.37	$283.04
Southeast	$44.66	$146.49	$144.78	$157.24	$172.18	$134.50	$64.02	$42.33	$156.54	$305.49
Southwest	$49.66	$132.40	$133.52	$142.73	$161.25	$112.63	$55.35	$43.13	$151.96	$212.50
West	$48.59	$124.31	$121.72	$141.35	$132.14	$112.08	$71.48	$41.07	$145.96	$205.00
Far West	$55.00	$136.18	$135.86	$144.19	$155.16	$139.11	$70.17	$36.32	$149.53	$226.61

14.6 The cost you can expect to pay for trimming and shoeing varies based on where you live and the type of services you horse needs.

There are a few forging and horseshoeing events hosted by various organizations. The World Blacksmith Competition (WBC) is one example. The WBC hosts competitions in multiple locations in North America, including the Calgary Stampede in Canada. The AFA also includes a competition at its annual conference.

Depending on the event and the class entered, a farrier must craft certain types of shoes within a set time. Other competitions pair a farrier with a specific horse to shoe. And others are part of a two-person team working on a draft horse.

The Cost of Shoeing

Experience and expertise factor into the fees a farrier charges for his services. As an independent businessperson, he sets pricing to account for investments in training. That doesn't mean hiring the most expensive farrier is the best option for your horse, but it can reflect a proficiency aligned with the goals for your horse.

Costs vary geographically and are based on the complexity of the shoeing with therapeutic and advanced techniques, naturally increasing the price. A 2020 survey by the *American Farrier's Journal* compiled pricing provided by 600 farriers across the country. Here is a snapshot of the typical cost based on location and service as of 2020 (fig. 14.6).

Who Is the Modern Farrier?

Painter Norman Rockwell is famous for his knack for capturing iconic snippets of daily life. His nearly 50-year career started in 1916, and he soon became world-famous for painting images of an idealized America. The blacksmith's shop was no exception. In his painting titled the "Blacksmith Shop," he recreates the concentration, skill, and brute strength required to build and shape a horseshoe from raw metal.

The nostalgia of "simpler times" is in sharp contrast to the significant advancements in blacksmithing and farriery since the turn of the twentieth century. Modern farriers must still possess the fundamentals that have been a part of the trade since its inception. Still, the knowledge and tools available now offer a deeper understanding of general hoof care and the diseases and conditions that can arise.

As society has changed, so too have the people who work in the field. Men still make up the majority of farriers at 83 percent, and women represent 17 percent of hoof-care professionals. The average full-time farrier travels 523 miles to work on an average of 38 horses each week, according to a 2020 survey by the *American Farrier's Journal*. The chart above right offers insight into the general farrier demographics (fig. 14.7).

While some farriers choose to work with one type of horse exclusively, others have clients from different backgrounds. Many farriers work on horses performing in multiple disciplines. The types of horses that farriers choose to work on typically depend on the needs of
the local horse-owning population, personal preference, and additional training or certification within a specific area.

A Glimpse at the Typical U.S. Farrier
(Full-time and Part-time)

Farrier Categories	Full-time Farriers	Part-time Farriers
Age	48	46
Male	83%	76%
Female	17%	24%

14.7 Women are increasingly working as farriers.

Female Farriers

As just mentioned, women only account for about 17 percent of all farriers in the United States, but participation has increased steadily since the 1970s. In 2018, the Cornell University Farrier Course accepted its first 100-percent female cohort. In 1972, the College received its first application from a woman. Her name was Toni Hanna. She knew her interest in horseshoeing was unconventional and often discouraged, and that access was restricted.

Toni was a skilled horsewoman who had experience and references but worried her gender would prevent acceptance. She arrived for the interview with her hair tucked under a baseball cap and an Ace bandage secured around her midsection to disguise her gender from then-instructor Harold Mowers. She easily met the entrance requirements and enrolled in the program.

On the first day of class, Harold refused to accept her presence and threatened to resign. The Veterinary College administration convinced him to let her stay because it was predicted she would likely drop out in a week.

A Look Inside Cornell University's Farriery Course

Farrier school is hard, physical work. It takes strength and stamina to stand under a horse and work on a hoof. The Cornell program is 16 weeks long, which is longer than most other schools. Class kicks off at eight in the morning Monday through Friday and ends around 4:30 to 5 p.m., meaning students are clocking a solid eight-hour day.

The training is a mix of hands-on observations and lectures. Students benefit from being at a veterinary hospital where a wide variety of cases are sent on referral for specialty work on diseased and injured hooves (fig. 14.8).

The program encompasses far more than technical skills. The curriculum teaches students how to develop strength and the hand-eye coordination necessary for trimming and fitting shoes properly. A student with hands-on experience before class has these basics, so he is pushed to build up additional stamina. A farrier can't make a living shoeing one horse a day and must work up to seeing a decent number daily until he finds a sustainable case load for his business goals and lifestyle.

In the United States, high-school "shop" classes used to teach the basics of operating power tools, but that isn't a guarantee anymore. While a person may come into our program with some apprentice or mentoring experience, he needs to learn how to weld and drill holes efficiently. I call this part of the program "arts and crafts" and require students to punch nail holes, weld, grind, and finish shoes on the workbench (fig. 14.9).

14.8 Clinics that invite students and working farriers provide an opportunity to work on a specific case and talk through approaches to trimming and shoeing. This workshop was hosted at Cornell University to provide students and farriers from across the region an opportunity to advance their knowledge of horse movement and trimming practices.

14.9 Shop skills, which were once taught in most public high schools, are an important part of the training process.

Toni's desire to become a farrier and charming personality proved she was not a quitter. Within the first week, she convinced Harold his preconceptions were inaccurate. He became a mentor and friend and even built a portable coal forge for her truck, doing all he could to help her learn and become appropriately equipped to start her own business.

Toni was among the women who were groundbreakers. About the same time, Ada Gates Patton was also an inspiration for aspiring female farriers. Her family tree traced back to Henry Burden, the first to mass-produce horseshoes, and the Vanderbilts. While her family owned horses, the prize-winning equestrian was first a socialite, model, and actress.

Ada settled in Vail, Colorado, in the early 1970s and was frustrated by being unable to find a farrier. So, she enrolled in an Oklahoma-based horseshoeing school. On the first day of class, she discovered she was the only woman in the program. That training is reported to have gotten her "hooked on hooves."

In 1978, she became the first and only woman (as of 2022) to be a licensed journey farrier to shoe Thoroughbred racehorses in the United States and Canada through the International Union of Journeymen Horseshoers. She also served as the farrier liaison for the United States Equestrian Team during the 1984 Olympics.

Both women were trailblazers in the industry.

14.10 There is no one single skill that farriers can master to excel; it takes a combination of skills that are learned through continuing-education clinics.

But above all else, these ladies demonstrated what it takes to become a farrier—persistence and desire.

What Farrier Training Means to Horse Owners

Horse owners need to recognize that most people who become farriers view it as a career or a professional endeavor, not a hobby. Becoming a farrier involves learning and using separate skills all at once (fig. 14.10).

First, there is horsemanship, which includes handling, anatomy, conformation, and diseases. Then there are the actual hoof trimming skills necessary to work in harmony with anatomy and conformation. Skills related to blacksmithing and fitting therapeutic or synthetic shoes are needed. Plus, studying discipline-specific shoeing applications is part of the process.

14.11 A & B Hands-on trainings are available across the country giving farriers ample opportunities to hone and advance their skills. This particular event was held at a horseshoeing school in the Midwest during the winter months, a tradtionally slower time of year for trimming and shoeing.

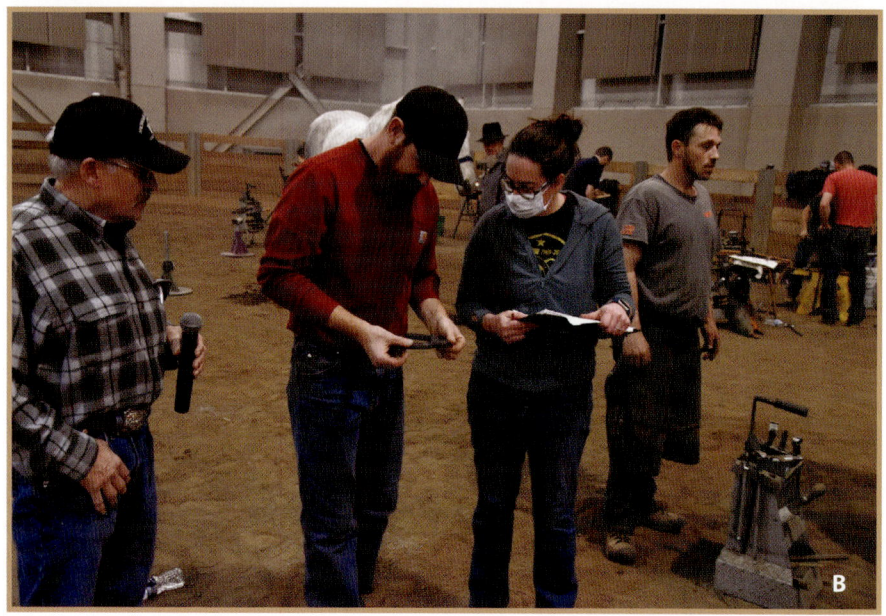

14.12 Demonstrations and clinics are not only for professionals. Look for events sponsored by your farrier or veterinarian to better understand the skills your farrier uses.

It's also helpful to understand how even the "easy" jobs can take a physical toll on the farrier's body. Many farriers retire or move on to other jobs after about 20 years due to injuries, fatigue, and burnout from constantly working in a stooped position beneath 1,000-pound, sometimes fractious animals.

Because there are no formal requirements to do this work, farriers must have the self-discipline to be successful at it, including voluntary participation in continuing education. There are endless opportunities for learning in clinics sponsored by manufacturers, suppliers, universities, and more (figs. 14.11 A & B). Horse owners should be aware of these opportunities and support participation, and farriers should appreciate clients who see the value of continual learning to provide the best hoof care work (figs. 14.12 & 14.13).

14.13 Farriery is as much an art as it is a skill that requires a commitment to lifelong learning. This desire to always learn is a big reason I work in the industry. Here I am, on the left, leading a roundtable discussion with the use of cadaver legs as part of my participation in the annual International Hoof Care Summit.

FROM THE FORGE
How Shoeing *May* Have Saved My Life

During the late 1960s, the Vietnam war was reason to worry if you were an 18-year-old male. Attending college gave many young men an alternative to being drafted through a 2-S student deferment. I planned to go to college to become a veterinarian, avoiding the draft was secondary.

In 1968, I was a junior at Cornell University and the draft rules changed. The new rules allowed you to give up a student deferment and enter the new year's lottery, which included all 18- to 25-year-olds, based on your birthday. I decided to go in this first large pool, hoping for a "safe number." I traded in my 2-S status and became a 1-A status, which meant I was eligible for the draft. My lottery number was 228 and seemed reasonably safe. If my number was not called within the first year, those turning 18 in the next year would receive lower numbers, reducing my chances of getting called up.

Friends and classmates chose the same strategy. However, many were assigned low numbers and left college for the Army. Being shipped overseas to fight and possibly die certainly caused a lot of worry. The war had heated up and the Army was going through the numbers fast, so I thought they would get to my number before the year ended.

Seeing the fear and panic amongst my fellow students did not give me confidence about fighting in a jungle halfway around the world. I decided that if I was going to war, I wanted to be with the toughest soldiers—the Marines. As the draft numbers approached 200, I picked up my paperwork to enlist. At the time, I was shoeing horses several afternoons a week after class. I got the paperwork started but did not get done shoeing early enough to turn it in on a Friday.

That following Monday, as I was driving to the recruitment station the news announced that the Department of Defense was stopping at 195. That meant the next year would start with all the new numbers for the new 18-year-olds, giving me a higher number and less chance of being drafted.

The Vietnam War tallied 58,220 US military fatal casualties, according to the National Archives Vietnam War U.S. Military Fatal Casualty Statistics. Many more soldiers were permanently injured. I knew some of these people, and I could have been one of these had I gone.

If I had not been delayed from getting my paperwork in by having horses to shoe, who knows what would have happened if I had joined the Marines (fig. 14.14).

14.14 Presenting at the International Hoof Care Summit, sharing all he has learned through a decades-long career.

CHAPTER 15

The Future of Farriery

Today's modern horses have emerged because of the "baby boom" generation who invigorated a surge in horse ownership after World War II. Before then, horses were mostly used for transportation and by the military rather than for show and recreation. In the more than 75 years since then, sophisticated sports and activities have evolved, as have the health and hoof care available (fig. 15.1).

The future is always just around the corner. Farriers and equine podiatrists, like most in the industry, are always looking toward what is on the horizon to best serve the horses of tomorrow. Some things have not changed at all—even the modern horse needs old-fashioned, common-sense horsemanship, despite how the uses, venues, and breeding have changed.

While the principles of farriery are similar to those used over the last 200 years, the materials, knowledge, and methods significantly advanced (fig. 15.2). The aim of farriery has always been to keep horses sound and healthy in order to keep them in work.

15.1 Horseshoes have evolved to meet the changing uses of horses from work to showing and recreation.

15.2 Steel is still the most commonly used material for making horseshoes, but aluminum and plastic materials have evolved to provide enhanced performance and soundness based on a horse's individual needs.

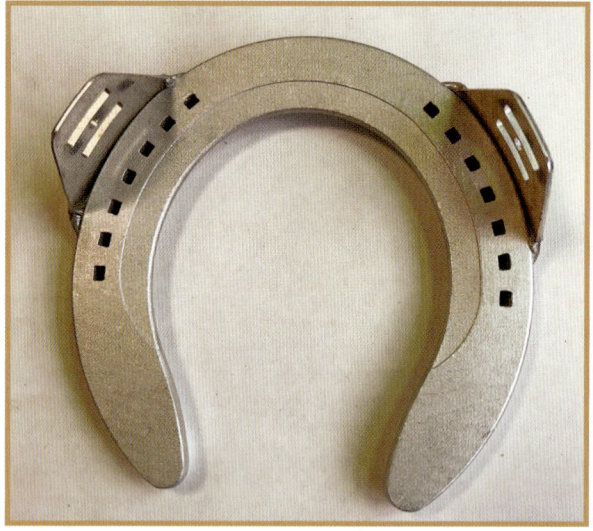

15.3 Through research and anecdotal evidence, farriers and equine podiatrists are finding new ways to modify horseshoes to best serve the horse. One example is this aluminum shoe that can be attached with glue on the side tabs and partially nailed on.

The Rise of Technology in Shoeing the Modern Horse

In some cases, modern technology has proved what our ancestors knew intuitively but could not document. The modern horse benefits from advanced diagnostics and medical treatments as well as improved methods of preventing lameness (fig. 15.3).

Not too far in the past, radiographs were rarely used for farriery and hoof disorders. In the twenty-first century, portable digital radiography and advanced imaging with MRIs and bone and CT scans make it possible to efficiently capture an inside look at the hoof structures. It is now possible to radiograph untrimmed hooves and take new radiographs post trimming in real time to assess proper balance and length. Smartphones and widely available mobile internet connections allow veterinarians, farriers, and horse owners to communicate about diagnoses, treatments, and outcomes.

"Behind-the-scenes" technology in the farrier industry has helped the production of horseshoes and related products become more diverse and of higher quality. Computers are used to design horseshoes and run the machines that produce the shoes. Even the components for the horseshoe manufacturing machines are produced by computer-guided machine tools.

It's also possible to scan the trimmed feet and send the information to a computer connected to a 3D printer to produce any combination of width, thickness, type, and features of an appropriate horseshoe exactly as programmed. Currently, 3D-printed horseshoes only

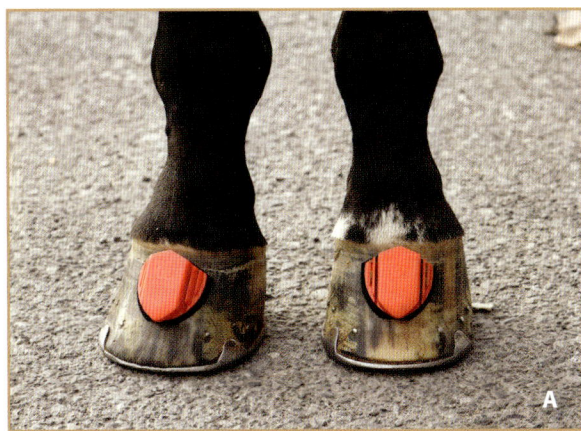

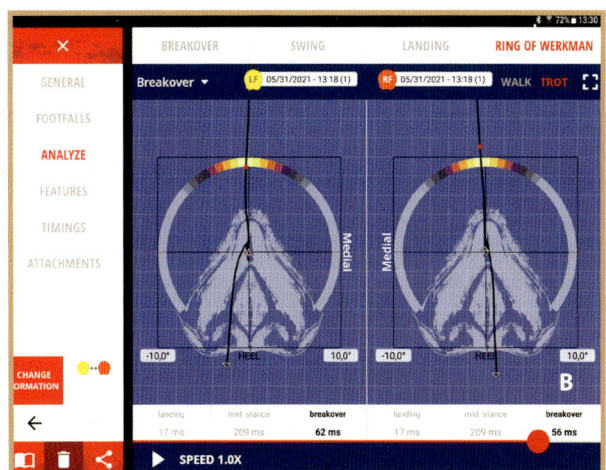

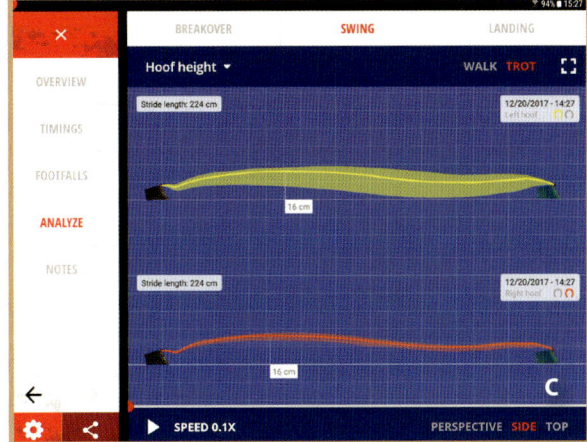

15.4 A–C Motion sensors provide precise data on the angle at which a horse's hooves are striking the ground. This information informs trimming and shoeing decisions.

use non-metallic materials and are not practical for wide-scale use, but they do offer another option. The 3D printing process will likely continue to improve and become less expensive and more widespread over time.

It's interesting to imagine what Henry Burden, who made the first horseshoe machine in 1838, would think of today's horseshoe production.

Gait analysis tools like the Werkman Black motion tracking technology and the Equinosis Q Lameness Locator® provide an objective analysis of gait problems and lameness. These technologies capture and document data for future comparison on an individual horse and for the benefit of all horses with similar situations (figs. 15.4 A–C).

Unfortunately, using all this technology will likely exponentially increase the time and expense of shoeing the horse. Not every horse is a candidate for these procedures. However, when there are problems, the more objective information available leads to a successful outcome.

The danger of the increased usage of this technology may be that too much reliance on it will remove the hand-eye skill of trimming and shoeing. Shoeing horses well is an art. The technology should be available to augment the process, not become the process.

And maybe horse breeders have an opportunity to learn from the dairy industry. Dairy producers use

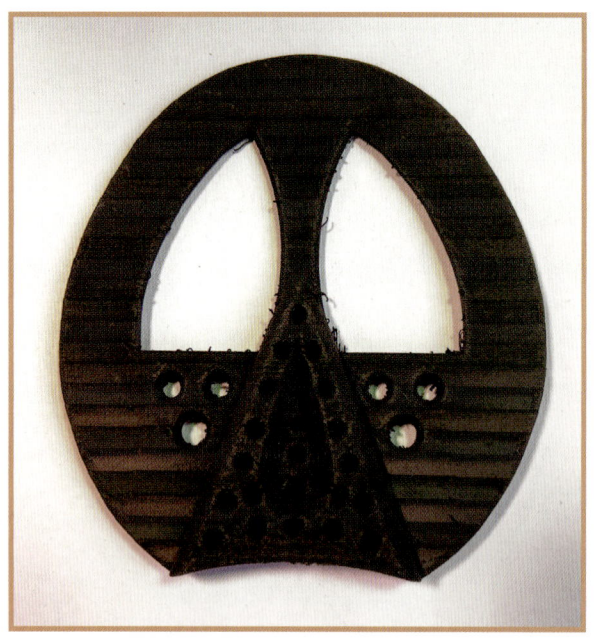

15.5 Advancements in technology like 3D printing are finding their way into horseshoeing. A 3D printer can create a pad like this to exact specifications.

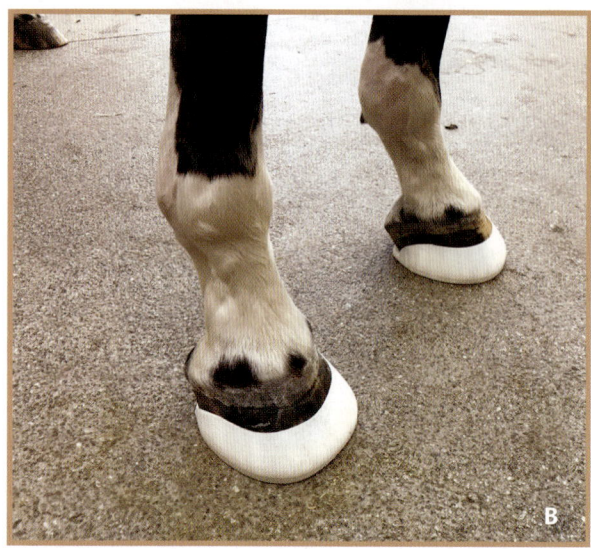

15.6 A & B Another example of how technology is evolving the farrier trade are 3D printed shoes, custom-made for an individual horse. Prof. Dr. H. Brommer and the farriers J. de Zwaan and G. Bronkhorst, Utrecht University, The Netherlands, collaborated to design the therapeutic shoe shown here.

genomic testing to improve milk production and cull out less desirable conformation traits. Could horse breeders use the same techniques to develop better legs and feet in horses? This is just one area researchers and scientists are working on.

Predictions for the Future

In the timeline of the "modern horse" defined here (post-WWII), the farrier profession has rapidly progressed (fig. 15.5). The once shortage of quality horseshoes, tools, equipment, and knowledge has transpired into a wealth of available resources (figs. 15.6 A & B). The gas forge is one of the biggest game-changers the profession has seen as traditional coal forges have been replaced with

15.7 The portable propane forge has given farriers the freedom to take their shop on the road.

15.8 A class of future farriers learning the trade at Cornell University Farrier School.

portable propane (fig. 15.7). And in the not-too-distant future, electromagnetic induction for heating metal horseshoes will become more commonplace.

Metal horseshoes will likely remain the preferred choice for shoeing most horses due to their simplicity and the varieties available. But the skills that require extensive practice to make handmade horseshoes may decline as forging is replaced with a manufactured facsimile.

The future of farriery may best be served with the standardization of farriery teaching programs and qualifications. This effort will require collaboration between individual states, a task that at this point has been too enormous to tackle.

The bottom line is that although shoeing a horse has become easier with well-manufactured horseshoes, related products, and information technology, the process continues to be a hands-on job. With all the great support available, shoeing horses will always be a demanding profession, both physically and mentally (fig. 15.8).

FROM THE FORGE
My Why

If it isn't already obvious, farriery is a challenging career—one that is tough on the body and is certainly one that can leave a person covered in dirt, sweat, and maybe even urine or manure by day's end.

Nothing was going to stop me during my first years of learning to shoe. Not the cuts and blisters on my hands, certainly not the grime, sweat, and manure. Not even the uncooperative and dangerous horses deterred me—I had to do this work.

But why? It all started with a basic desire to become a better horseman. Little did I know this endeavor would become an obsession and my life's work. For many who have entered this profession, shoeing horses becomes a calling that transitions from achieving a personal goal to a professional endeavor and, eventually, an act like breathing that one simply has to do to exist.

Cowboy movies and TV shows planted a seed within me. But growing up in New York City's South Bronx meant mounted police horses were what I saw most often. My family spent summers on Long Island's north shore, and my father took me for pony rides at a local stable on the weekends.

At age five, the pony rides progressed to trail riding almost every weekend. By the time I was 10, our family no longer spent summers there, so my parents looked for a sleepaway camp. We found a place in Northeastern Pennsylvania called Camp Huskee, which would set the direction of my life.

Camp Huskee was an eight-week summer camp. Horses were the main attraction. My first real goal in life became an obsession to get into the "Horseman Group." This opportunity paired campers who demonstrated a strong interest in horses with a specific mount for the duration of camp.

In 1963, I earned a spot in the "Horseman Group," a great triumph for a city kid. That year—a moment that changed my life forever—was the first time I saw a farrier shoeing a horse, and I was fascinated.

A Texas cowboy who worked at the ranch soon taught the camp owner's son and me how to trim and shape hooves under his guidance. Then, I was invited to join the riding staff where I would be helping teach riding and increase the shoeing work I was doing. Throughout high school and into college, I spent summers at Camp Huskee shoeing horses, eventually taking on responsibility for a herd of 30 horses.

I started my college career at the State University of New York at Farmingdale from 1966 to 1968 as an agricultural science major and transferred to Cornell University where I graduated with a Bachelor of Science in Animal Science in 1971. However, one day I found the Farrier Shop on the backside of the Veterinary College, stuck my head in the door, and the most amazing thing happened.

Harold Mowers was working on a shoe at his forge beneath a massive horseshoe display created by the famous farrier Henry Asmus on the wall, and right then my career choice changed. I instantly realized that I knew very little about shoeing horses but was eager to find out more. Little did I know that 42 years later I would teach others about shoeing horses in that same shop.

Before enrolling at Cornell, I was absorbed in shoeing horses; however, I really did not grasp the depth and breadth of what was captivating me. I was shoeing camp horses on my own and had mastered some difficult cases. My shoes stayed on; the horses traveled okay; what more could there be to this? Soon it became my mission to learn all I could about horses, their feet, and how to help them—and in fact, I've never stopped learning.

Many people who have become successful at shoeing horses have perseverance, a love of horses, and are determined. The farrier profession is full of men and women who have put in the hard work, sweat, and tears to serve in this unique profession.

There is nothing else like it.

For Further Information

Numerous excellent resources exist where you can find additional information about horseshoeing for the modern horse. These are a few of the sources we recommend.

American Association of Equine Practitioners: The AAEP is an organization designed to improve the health and welfare of the horse by supporting ongoing research and professional development for veterinarians of all disciplines, including equine podiatrists. Use the search feature to find many articles on general equine health and those that specifically relate to hoof care and horseshoeing. The dedicated "Horse Owners Tab" takes you to a page that helps you "Get-A-DVM" or "Find a Veterinary Dental Practitioner." You can also access the "Ask the Vet" archives and find veterinarian responses to questions about therapeutic farriery. Visit the website at: *www.aaep.org.*

American Farriers Association: The AFA website has a plethora of information for hoof care professionals and horse owners alike. A page on the website specifically designed for horse owners includes a link to the American Farriers Association YouTube Channel, which features highlights of the annual convention, trimming and shoeing principles, and hands-on demonstrations. The site also has a "Find a Farrier" directory to help you find a farrier in your area. For the professional, the website includes information about certification, access to professional development opportunities, and a directory of farrier training programs. You can find out more about it at: *americanfarriers.org*

***American Farriers Journal*:** Farriers and equine veterinarians looking for the latest in hoof care and horseshoeing methods presented alongside the important industry fundamentals will find in-depth, hands-on insights and developments. If you're a professional farrier or veterinarian interested in hoof care, you'll want to check out the magazine at: *www.americanfarriers.com.*

Anatomy of the Equine: For a look at detailed anatomical photos, you'll want to check out this website. Talented farriers Jenny Edwards and Paige Poss partner to create information for horse owners, farriers, and veterinarians to better understand the inner hoof structures. Find this unique resource at: *anatomy-of-the-equine.com.*

Equine Podiatry: Created by equine podiatrist Stephen O'Grady, DVM, MRCVS, this website provides in-depth information and technical details related to equine podiatry. He is recognized as an expert in therapeutic farriery, and he is a member of the International Equine Veterinarians Hall of Fame. Visit him at: *www.equinepodiatry.com/podiatry.html.*

Farrier Program at Cornell University College of Veterinary Medicine: As the oldest, continuously operating farrier training program, the Farrier Program at Cornell University provides aspiring farriers with practical, hands-on skills to help keep horses healthy and sound. Through its affiliation with the University veterinary hospital, students also experience a broad range of therapeutic and challenging cases to help them prepare for what they might see while caring for client horses. If you're considering becoming a farrier, take a look at: *https://www.vet.cornell.edu/education/visitor-professional-programs/farrier-program*.

International Association of Professional Farriers: The IAPF is an organization committed to promoting the farrier industry through knowledge and skills earned through continuing education. Farriers can also earn certification through the association's credentialing process and find a listing of training programs available throughout the country. IAPF also offers a detailed section on the website especially designed for horse owners where you can find many articles on a wide variety of hoof care topics. Articles range from general hoof care to diseases and conditions, shoeing techniques, and much more. Find them at: *www.professionalfarriers.com*.

National Museum of Horseshoeing Tools and Hall of Honor: The museum was originally created as a private collection featuring one-of-a-kind tools and products used for shoeing horses. The extraordinary collection honors the traditions and progress of the horseshoeing trade and includes a Hall of Honor to recognize farriers, companies, and products who have had a lasting impact on the industry. For the full in-person experience, visit the museum in Stockyards City, Oklahoma, or learn more at: *horseshoeingmuseum.com*.

Schleese Saddlery: Jochen and Sabine Schleese own and operate Schleese Saddlery to help horse owners better understand saddle fit and how it impacts horse and rider anatomy. The website is packed with educational materials, videos, and advice to help riders find the right saddle fit for horse and rider. The saddle specialists are known for gender specific saddles that are ergonomically designed to match the different hip and pelvis angles between men and women equestrians. Learn more from the Certified Equine Ergonomists at: *https://schleese.com*.

The Worshipful Company of Farriers: Founded in 1356, the WCF is the oldest continually operating farrier organization in the world. The organization was started to promote equine welfare in regard to farriery. It continues to do so today by upholding high standards of farriery in the United Kingdom and offering its exams abroad. Learn more at: *www.wcf.org.uk*.

Podcasts: Farriers, equine podiatrists, and industry experts host informative podcasts that cover a wide range of hoof care topics. This is a selection of those you may want to explore:

- Farrier Focus by Butler Professional Farrier School
- The Hoof of the Horse by Dr. Simon Curtis
- AFJ Podcast by the *American Farriers Journal*

Recommended Reading

This is a list of books that have been invaluable to me during my career as a farrier and that have informed the knowledge that is presented in this book here.

Butler, D. PhD, CJF, FWCF (2004). *The Principles of Horseshoeing (P3)*. Crawford, Nebraska: Doug Butler Enterprises, Inc.

Butler, D. PhD, CJF, FWCF (1998). *Shoeing in Your Right Mind*. LaPortte, Colorado: Butler Publishing.

Curtis, S. J. PhD, FWCF (2018). *The Hoof of the Horse*. Newmarket, Suffolk, UK: Newmarket Farrier Consultancy.

Curtis, S. J. PhD, FWCF (1999). *Farrier–Foal to Racehorse*. Newmarket, Suffolk, UK: Newmarket Farrier Consultancy.

Miller, M.E MD, CJF, FWCF (2010). *The Mirage of the Natural Foot*. Huntsville, Alabama: Michael Miller.

McShane, C. and Tar. J.A. (2007). *The Horses in the City*. Baltimore: Johns Hopkins University Press.

Lungwitz, A. and Adams, J.W. (YEAR). *A Textbook of Horseshoeing for Horseshoers and Veterinarians*. London: JB Lippincott Co.

Loving, N. S. (1997). *Conformation and Performance*. Ossining: New York: Breakthrough Publications.

Acknowledgments

My editor and co-writer, Katie Navarra, made the compiling a book of this scope possible. Without her effort, I would not be able to accomplish such a task alone.

We describe farriery as a blend of art and science; however, there are other essential components. Horsemanship is an indispensable ingredient, along with being able to withstand the rigors of this work. Shoeing horses successfully for nearly 60 years does not just happen; it takes guidance from mentors to develop from just a worker to a skilled artisan who can make a difference for horses. Another essential ingredient is the friends and family that support this lifetime endeavor.

My career would not be possible without the following individuals that have contributed to it:

The Hartung family who owned Camp Huskee where my horsemanship training began and where I first learned to shoe horses with the help of Chris Hartung. Chris stood over me while I trimmed and shod my first horses. Every summer for several years, Chris and I worked together shoeing the camp's horses, often learning the hard way.

Harold Mowers, Resident Farrier at Cornell University College of Veterinary Medicine, 1965–1976. Harold provided amazing technical knowledge that took me from being a basic horseshoe installer to understanding how horses move, how conformation works, and how to forge my first horseshoes.

Dr. Doug Butler, who was inspirational in so many ways to me as a person and as a farrier.

Marshall "Buster" Conklin, Resident Farrier at Cornell University College of Veterinary Medicine from 1976–1991. He was an amazing role model, farrier, and friend.

Doug Pokorney, farrier and one of the best friends I ever had. Every farrier should have a buddy like Doug to talk over the everyday problems of shoeing horses for a living.

Dr. Norman Ducharme who offered and convinced me to accept the Head of Farrier Services position at the Cornell University College of Veterinary Medicine. He taught me that just because something has not been done before, that does not make it impossible to do.

Mustad Hoofcare Group: I was fortunate to become the first Farrier Technical Consultant in the United States for Mustad horseshoe nails in 1976. My association with this company provided countless opportunities to travel, meet other farriers, and learn.

The American Farriers Association: For providing the format for learning and comraderies amongst farriers.

I must also acknowledge all the farriers who I have made friendships with and the clients who have trusted me with their horses. I have shod horses for a handful of people for nearly as long as I have been a farrier. They also happen to be my best friends and teammates playing polo. Danny and Janet Scheraga, Jan Suwinski, (the "Green Team"), and David Eldredge. Shoeing your horses over these years has allowed me to develop consistency and try new techniques.

Betsy Keller, best friend and partner. Horses brought us together. Betsy, you have supported me in all my endeavors and strived to make me a better person.

Gloria Kraus, my mother, who despite her fears of what tragedies might happen to me doing dangerous work, always supported my career.

Kermit Kraus, my father, who taught me that no matter how hard you are ever knocked down, always get back up. An essential trait to have when shoeing horses.

Index

Page numbers in *italics* indicate illustrations.

Abscesses, 102–3, *102*, 108, 120, *140*
Abusive practices, 71
Accessories. *See* Calks; Pads; Studs
Accreditation, 181
Adhesives, 25, 54, 56–57
Age, of horse, 9
Aluminum shoes, 23, *25*, 55, *70*, 79, *202*
American Association of Equine Practitioners, 119, 132
American Farrier's Association, 181, 190, 192
American Pharoah, 52
Angular limb deformities, 125–26, *125*, 132
Apprenticeships, 187, 188–89, *189*
Arabian horses, 9, 66
Arenas. *See* Footing
Arthritis, risk of, 86, *88*, 91, 96, 97, 106
Asmus, Henry, *48*, 207
Autoimmune responses, 104–5

Back injuries, 97
Balance
    geometric, 35–38, 99, 142
    of horse, 36–37, 96
    of rider, 163
    of saddle, 158
    in shoeing, 60, 138
Bar shoes, 40, 106, 110
Barefoot hoof care, 4–19, 20, 54
Barn management practices, 169
Barrel racers, 67

Bars, of hooves, 50
Base-narrow conformation
    assessment of, 90, 91, *92*, *95*, 96–97, 99
    in foals, *124*
    shoeing considerations, *88*, 150
Base-wide conformation, 90, 91, 94, *94*, 97, 149
Behavior, 99, 150, 160, 165–71
Bell boots, *147*, 148, 149
"Big Lick" gait, 71
Blacksmiths and blacksmithing. *See also* Hand-forged shoes
    competitions, 193–94, *193*
    vs. farriery, 73–74
    history of, 28–30, 63–64, *73–74*
    practitioner demographics, 195
    tools of, 75, 204–6, *205*
Bone, damage to, 72, 91, *92*, 115–16, 138
Bony growths, 103–4, *103*
Borium, 14, 44
Bow-legged conformation, *87*, 95
Brazil, case study in, 99
Breakover, 35, 38–39, 63
Breed show guidelines, 65–66
Breeding considerations, 7, 85–86, 132–34, 203–4
Brommer, Harold, 53, *204*
Bronkhorst, G., *204*
Bruising, 41, 50, 52, 62, 107–8
Burden, Henry, 28, *29*, 197
Burns, Curtis, 60
Butler, Doug, 89

Calks, *6*, 28, 62, 67
Camped out conformation, 97

Canker, 104–5, 108
Canter, 118, 148–49
Capewell Horse Nail Company, *27*
Carpal valgus, 127, *129*
Carriage horses, *48*, 65. *See also* Standardbreds
Caudal support, *42*, 62
Cavalry, horseshoeing and, 28–29, 83
Certification, 181, *188*, 190–91, *191*. *See also* Education and training
Champagne, Wes, 52–53
Chapman, Burney, 45, 121
Civil War, 28–29
Clinches, *18*, *136*, 151, 165, 182
Clinics, 54, 190, 196–99, *199*
Clips, 33–34, *33–34*, 71, 79, 152, *153*
Closed-heel shoes, 40, *40*, 49–51
Club feet, 60, 96, *96*, 106, 116–18, *123*, *125*
Clydesdales, 108
Coffin bone
    breakover role, 35
    damage/defects in, 14, 50, 105–6, *105*, *114*, 115–16
    location of, 38
    low angle of, 40
    trimming considerations, 138
Cold climate hoof care, 15, *15*, 41–42, *42*
Cold-fit shoeing, 77, *77*, 82, 84
Collaborative care, 171. *See also* Vet-farrier partnerships
Communication, *101*, 118–19, 121, 130, 180
Competition, 65–71, 72, 145, 154, 193–94
Concussion, effects of, 104, 138
Conformation

assessment of, 89–99, *89–92*, *94–97*
defect severity classifications, 87–89, 94
defects in, 59, *89*, 98–99, 118, 123–25, 132–34, *133*
hoof care implications, 2, 7, 14, 18, 85–86, 149–50
proportion and balance in, 36–37
term definitions, 93
Conklin, Buster, 121
Continuing education. *See* Education and training
Contracted heels, 60, 106–7, *106*
Contraction, of hoof, 55
Copper sulfate, 117
Cornell University
Equine Drug Testing program, 17
farrier program and resources, 46, *46*, 76, 142, 189, 195–96, *206*, 207
Corns, 50, 107–8, *107*
Coronary band, *18*, 59, *87*
Coronitis, 108, *108*
Corrective shoeing, 10, 18, 42, 98, *111*
Counter-canter, 118, 148–49
Cow-hocked conformation, 39, *94*, 96
Cracks, 58, 96, 99, *102*, 109–10, *109*. *See also* Quarter cracks
Credentials. *See* Certification
CT scans, 120, 202
Cuff style shoes, 55–56, *56*
Curtis, Simon, 124
Cushing's disease, 111
Cutting, 68, 134

De Zwaan, J., *204*
Deep digital flexor tendons, 37, 52, 115, 126–27, 140
Dermatitis, interbulbular, 110–11
Desensitization, 81–82
Diagonals, in posting trot, 149
Disciplines, shoe design for, 63–71
Disposition. *See* Behavior

Distractions, managing, 168, 169, 177
Draft horses, *46*, 64, *65*, 68, 77, *94*, 108
Dressage, 32, 60, 62, 97
Driving, *48*, *65*. *See also* Standardbreds
Ducharme, Normand G., *101*, 130
Duckett's Dot, 37
Duration of work, in WIDTH protocol, 5, 7

Education and training, 54, 187–92, 196–97, *198–99*, 199, 206. *See also* Certification
Egg bar shoes, 40, 49–50, *50*, 108, 114
Ehrmann, Doug, 58
Endurance riding, 9, 63, 68–69
Engagement, of hind end, 97
English riding/performance, 72, 157
Epiphysitis, 132
Equine Drug Testing program, 17
Equine metabolic syndrome, 111
Equine podiatrists, 121, 192–93
"Euclid's Elements," 35
Europe, farrier training in, 187, 189
Eventing, *31*, 44, 66–67
Extended heels, 39
Extensor tendons, 37

Fans, for ventilation, 79, 80, 167, 175–80
Farley, Dave, 72
Farriers. *See also* Farriery
best practices for, 150–52, 190
vs. blacksmiths, 73–74
client relations, 175–81, 182
demographics, 194–95, *195*, 197
education and training of, 181, 187–93
fees charged by, 14, 194
health consideration, 79, 80
mistakes by, 136–43, 169
partnerships with vets, *101*, 118–19, 121, 130, 192–93
roles/responsibilities of, 180–82
skill set, 20, 196–99, 203

Farriery. *See also* Farriers
as business, 194, 199
as calling, 207
competitions for, 193–94
technology in, 202–4
tools of, 83, *83*, 177–78, *177–78*, 184, 196, *196*
Fencing, shoe loss and, 147, *148*, 150
Feral horses, 10–11, 14
Fetlocks, 35, 88, 121, 125, *131*
Fibonacci sequence, 36
Fire risk, from hot-fit shoeing, 81
First aid kits, 115
Flat feet, 25, 114
Flat shoes, 30
Flexor tendons. *See* Deep digital flexor tendons
Flies, *14*, 18, 148, 167, 177
Flocking, of saddles, 161
Foals
glue-on shoes for, *28*, 45, 60, *125*, 127, *134*
high/low syndrome in, 118, *124*
hoof care for, *129*, 135, *172*
hoof characteristics, 122–23, *122*
limb deformities in, 98, 123–34, *124–29*, *131*, *134*
monitoring and observation of, 123–25, 130
premature, 123, 126
Footing, 61, 72. *See also* Traction
Forehand, falling on, 96, 148, 163
Forges, 75, 81, 204
Forging. *See* Overreaching
Founder, 112
Fox hunters, 69
Friesians, 108
Frog, support of, 40, 42, *56*, 114–15
From Foal to Racehorse (Curtis), 124
Front end, conformation defects in, 88–89, *92*, 94–96, 118
Front pattern shoes, 30, *31*

Fullering, 62
Full-swedge shoes, *70*

Gait
    analysis of, 72, 203
    asymmetrical, 119
    correction of, 63
    phases of, 55, 72, 99, 107, 108, 119
Gaited horses, 63, *63*, 65, 70–71
G-bar shoes, 40
Genotypes, 86
Gladwell, Malcolm, 188
Glue-on shoes
    about, 25–26, 53–54
    application of, 25, 54, 56–57, 77
    for foals, *28*, 45, *125*, 126, 127, *134*
    hoof preparation for, 57, 60
    vs. nailed shoes, 45, *202*
    types of, 55–57
    uses of, 69, *113*
Gluteal injuries, 97
Golden Ratio, 35–38, *35*, *37*, 99, 142
Grass, traction considerations, *6*, 44, 69, 72
Grazing stance, 118, *124*
Grooming, 176–77
Ground manners, 82, 165–68
Growth plates, *126*, 130, 131
Gullet, of saddle, 159, 161

Half-round shoes, *70*, 104
Half-swedge shoes, *70*
Hand-forged shoes, 28–30, 33, *188*. *See also* Blacksmiths and blacksmithing; Hot-fit shoeing
Handlers
    farriers as, 180, 190, 197
    roles/responsibilities of, *82*, 165–68, 175–80, 182–86
Hanna, Toni, 195, 197
Hartman, Paul V., 24

Head style, on nails, 27, *27*
Heart bar shoes, 40, 50, *50*, 117
Heel-first landing, 35, 99, 107
Heels, of horse
    bruising of, 50
    bulbs, 59
    contracted, 60, 106–7, *106*
    cracks in, 96, 99, 110
    high, 108
    length of, 140
    low, *42*, 96, 116
    pads for, 41
    rolled-under, 96
    sheared, 93, 94
    support of, 49, *58*
    underrun, 37, *37*, 40, 41, 60, 108, *137*
Heels, of shoes
    calks on, *6*, 43–44, *65*, 142
    closed, 40, *40*, 49–51, *49–50*
    extensions on, *38–39*, *125*, 127
    modifications for, 39–40
High/low syndrome, 118, *124*, 150
Hind end, conformation defects in, *90–91*, *93–95*, 96–97
Hind pattern shoes, 30, *31*, 39–40, 121
Hoary alyssum, 111
Hocks, arthritis risk, 96, 97
Hoof angles, 41, 113, 137–38, *137*
Hoof boots, 58–59, *59*, 69
Hoof care, 4–19, *143*, *173*, *179*. *See also* Shoeing
Hoof casts, *16*
Hoof pads. *See* Pads
Hoof taps, 58, *58*
Hoof testers, 102, 119
Hoof wall
    sealed, during hot shoeing, 79, *79*
    separation of, 50, 60, 108, 116
    thickness of, *5*, *14*, 31, 57, 60, 81, 152
Hoof-pastern axis. *See* Hoof angle
Hoofprints, in assessing footing, 72

Hooves
    alignment of, 98
    anatomy of, 2–3, *2*, 35–36, 93
    breeding considerations, 132–34
    conditions/diseases in, 101–18
    function of, 55 (*see also* Gait)
    injuries to, 40
    moisture levels in, 7, 57, 59, 77, 79, 109
    picking of, *173*
    size of, 142
    uneven growth in, 58
Horizontal cracks, *102*, 109, 110, *110*
Horses
    looks vs. functionality of, 86
    modern uses of, 1, 63–71
    size of, 89
    in transportation history, 24
    welfare of, 171
    in WIDTH protocol, 5, 7
    wild and feral, 10–11, 14
Horseshoes. *See also* Shoeing
    accessories for, 41–44
    alternatives to, 57–59
    assessing horses for, 4–12
    fit of, *4*, *136*, *139*, 141, 146, 150–52, 181–82, *182*
    history of, 22–23, *23*, 28–30
    longevity of, 32
    loose/lost, 145, 146–49, 178–79, 183–85
    manufactured vs. handmade, 28–30, *29–30*
    materials and design of, 22–23, 25–26, 28–32, 45, 202–4
    modifications for, 32–40, 49–53, 151–52
    nailed-on vs. glue-on, 53–54
    pulling of, 140, 183–85, *183–85*
    resetting, 12, 14
    safety considerations, 10, *153*, 165, 183
    sizes of, 32

temporary, 60
therapeutic, 39–42, 46, *46–48*, 49–53
trimming and, 11–12, *12*
weight of, 9, 23, *25*, 33, 63, *63*, 65–66, 70, 79
Hospital plates, 51, *51*, 111, 115, 116
Hot plate, 79
Hot-fit shoeing, 40, 50, 75–82, *78–79*, 83, 84. *See also* Blacksmiths and blacksmithing
Hunter horses, 32, 60
Hydraulic shaping machines, 81
Hyperplasia, 108

Impulsion, 97, 160
Infections, 79, *79*, 109, 115–18. *See also* Abscesses
Inflammation, *111*, 114
Injuries
acute, 101
to farriers, 165, 175, 199
to feet/hooves, 84
related to shoes/shoeing, 44, *136–38*, 183
shoeing for, 18
soft-tissue, 120
Insulin resistance, 111
Intensity, in WIDTH protocol, 5, 6
Interbulbular dermatitis, 110–11, *110*
Interference problems, 38–39, 50, 95, 96, 146, *149*
International Association of Professional Farriers, 181, 190
International Hoof Care Summit, 21, *199*, *200*

Joints, injuries to, 7, 72. *See also* Conformation
Jumpers, 60, *71*, 97
Jury duty anecdote, 192

Keratoma, 111
Kicking, 39, 148, 170–71, 173, 174
Knees, 88, *88*, 96
Knock knees, 127, *129*
Kraus, Steven, 20–21, *47*, 192, 200, 207

Lameness
assessing, 102, 119, 163
in barefoot horses, 13
case studies, 100
caused by trimming/shoeing, 25, 136, 181
severity grading scale, 119
shoeing for, 121
Lameness exams, 119–20
Laminitis
about, 111–13, *111*, *113*
complications of, 116
hoof care implications, 9
shoeing for, 40, 42, 45, 50, 57, 121
Landing phase, of stride, 99, 107, 108, 119
Lateral, as anatomical term, 93
Lateral balance, 60
Lateral support, 62
Layton, Eugene, *46*
Leg feathers, 108
Legs
alignment of, 89–99, 123–35
anatomy of, 2–3, *3*
Leverage reduction, 62–63
Ligament injuries, 72, 86, *92*, 138, 142
Limb support, shoeing for, 62
Lite shoes, *62*
Loose horses, 176

Manufactured shoes, 28–31, *29–31*
McLane, Myron, 45, 121
Medial, as anatomical term, 93
Medial balance, 60
Medial flares, 95
Mentorships, *189*

Miller, Michael E., 17
The Mirage of the Natural Foot (Miller), 17–19
Moisture levels, in hooves, 7, 9, 57, 59, 66, 77, 79, 109, 117
Motion sensor systems, 203, *203*
Mowers, Harold, 135, 195, 197, 207
MRI imaging, 120, 202
Mud, 147, *147*, 176–77, 183
Mustad Hoofcare Group, 20, 27, 45

Nails and nailing
best practices, *18*, *137*, 141, 152, 182
vs. glue-on shoes, 25–26, 45
injury risk, *153*, 165, 183
myths regarding, 54
nail styles, 27, *27*
Natural hoof care, 4–19, 20, 54
Navicular disease
risk factors, 96, 106, *106*, 118, 142
shoeing for, 60, 113–14, *113*, 121
Nutrition, 132, 148

Osteochondrosis, 132
Osteomyelitis, 115–16
Osteophytes, 138
Outliers (Gladwell), 188
Over at the knees, 127, *128*
Overreaching, 26, *146*, 157, 164, 183. *See also* Stepped off shoes
Over-trimming, 13, *13*, 138
Owners. *See also* Handlers; Riders
micromanagement by, 100, 176
roles/responsibilities of, 1, 135, 146–49, 169, 175–81, 182–86

Pacers, 63–64, 69–70
Pad stacks, *63*, 65, 71
Paddling movement, 95, 149
Pads. *See also* Saddle pads
pour-in, 16, *16*, 104, 106, 110

as temporary shoes, 57
types of, 41–42, *41–42*
uses of, 62, 65, 114–15
Pain, horse's behavior and, 168–69
Palmar angles, 93, *93*, 96
Pastern angles, 88. *See also* Hoof angles
Patches, for cracks, *109*, 110
Patton, Ada Gates, 197
Pavement, traction on, 43
Pedal osteitis, 114–15, *114*, 118
Pendulum effect, 23
Performance, of horse, 10–11, 13, 23, 61–71, 86, 143
Perioplic membrane, 122, *122*
Pharoah plates, 52–53, *52*
Phenotypes, 86
Pituitary gland, malfunction of, 111
Plantar angles, 93, 97
Plastic shoes, 60, 202. *See also* Glue-on shoes
Plates, protective, *10*, 51–53, *51–52*, 111, 115, 116
Platt, Dr. George, 121
Plumb lines, in conformation assessment, 89–92
Polo, *6*, 9, *31*, 44, 60, 69
Posting, 149
Posting trot, 149
Propane forges, 75
Protection, shoeing for, 62
Pulling contests, 68
Puncture wounds, 51, *51*, 106, 115, *153*, 183

Quarter clips, 34, *34*, 38
Quarter cracks, 60, 93, 94, 109, *109*
Quarter horses, 7, 63–64, 100

Racing, 60, 63, 69–70, 135, 145
Racing plates, *70*, 85
Radiographs, 120, 139, 202

Radius (bone), 93
Railroads, width of, 24
Rasping, 185–86, *185*
Recreational use, of horses, 1, 83
Reining, 62, *68*, 69, *69*
Resetting shoes, 12, 14
Respect
  between clients and farrier, 176
  of horse for handlers, 165–68, 172
Riders, 149, 154, 162–64, 169, 175–86. *See also* Owners
Riding disciplines, shoe design for, 63–71
Rim-style shoes, *6*, 30–31, *31*
Ringbone, *92*, 103–4, *103*, 105, 106
Roads, width of, 24
Rocker-toe shoes, 38, *38*, 63, 69, 79
Rocket boosters, dimensions of, 24
Rockwell, Norman, 194–95
Rolled-toe shoes, 38, *38*, 63, 69, 114
Roman roads, 24
Rotational deviations, 91, 97, 125, 141

Saddle fit, 148, 155–60, *156–59*, 164
Saddle pads, 157, 161
Saddlebreds, 63, 65
Schedules and scheduling, 176, 178–79, 180
Schrage, Joe, 60
Scratches (infection), 104
Sedatives, 169–71, *170*
Shear forces, 33–34
Sheared heels, 93, 94
Shire horses, 33
Shoeing. *See also* Horseshoes
  best practices, *18*, 142–43, 145–46
  corrective/therapeutic, 10, 18, 42, 50, 94, 98, *111*, 121
  cost of, 14, 194
  defects caused by, 106–7
  hot vs. cold, 73–84
  pre-shoeing checklist, 173

schedule/frequency of, 144–47, 176
technology and, 202–4
training horses for, 165–74
Shoeing in Your Right Mind (Butler), 89
Shoeless horses, 4–19
Shoes. *See* Horseshoes
Shop skills, *196*
Shoulder, of horse, 157–58, *157*, 160
Sickle-hocked conformation, 39, 97
Side clips, 34
Side cracks, 95
Side weight shoes, 63
Side wings, on glue-on shoes, 56
Sidebone, 93, 95, 96, 103–4, *103*
Sigafoos, Rob, 45
Slide plates, 62, *69*
Snowball pads, 41–42, *42*
Sole pads. *See* Pads
Soles, 14, *14*, 81, 82, 139. *See also* Puncture wounds
Soring, 71
Spider plates, *10*
Splay-footed, 95–96. *See also* Toed-out conformation
Spooky horses, 150, 171
Sport horses, 64
Sprung shoes, *149*, 153
Square toe shoes, 38, 63
Standardbreds, 9, *9*, 17–19, 63–64, 69–70, *70*
Standing, for farrier, 165–67, 172–73, 175
Standing-under conformation, 39, 97
Steel shoes, 23, *25*, 74, 202
Stepped off shoes, 50, 54, 146–48, *146*, 151
Steroid medications, 104
Stock breeds, 64
Stomping, effects of, *14*, 18, 148
Stopping, traction needs, *6*, *31*, 34, 62
Straight bar shoes, 40, 49, *49*
Straightness, of movement, 38–39

Stretching exercises, 168, *168*
Stride. *See* Gait
Studs, 14, *42*, 43–44
Surfaces, in WIDTH protocol, 7. *See also* Footing
Surgery, for limb deformities, 86, 98, 123, *125–26*, 126–27, 130
Suspensory ligaments, 72, *113*, 138, 140
Synthetic surfaces, 72

Technology, in farriery, 202–4
Tendon issues, 72, 86, 96, 126–27, *126–27*, *128*, 138
Tennessee Walking horses, 63, 70–71, 183
Terrain, in WIDTH protocol, 5, 7–9, *8*. *See also* Footing
Thoroughbreds, 7, 9, 17–19, 63–64, 70, *70*, 134
3D-printed shoes, 53, *53*, 202–3, *204*
Thrush, 42, 117–18
Titanium, in shoes, 25
Toe grabs, *65*
Toed-in conformation, *87*, *88*, 91, *92*, 96, 97, *131*, 141
Toed-out conformation, 91, 95–96, 97, 141
Toe-first landing, 99, 108, 140
Toes, of horse
    cracks in, 109, *109*
    length of, 37, *37*, 60, 96, *137*, 139, 150
Toes, of shoes, *33*, *34*, 35, 38–39, *125*
Toe-weighted shoes, 65–66
Tools, 184
Traction. *See also* Calks; Studs
    in eventing, 66–67
    footing and, 72
    in polo, *6*, 9, *31*, 44, 60
    reduction of, 62
    shoe design/devices for, 14, 30–31, 43–44, *43*, 62
    in WIDTH protocol, 6–7
    for working horses, 68

Trail riding, *8*, 9, 59, 68–69, 70–71, 154
Trailers (heel modification), 39, 63
Trailering considerations, 148
Training, for farrier visits, 80, 81–82, *129*, 165–67, 172–73, 175
Transitioning, to barefoot, 15, 20, 54, 58–59
Treats, 167
Trimming
    for cold-fit shoeing, 82
    for conformation defects, 94
    errors in, 13, *13*, 136, 138–40
    of foals, *129*
    Golden Ratio in, 36–37, 142
    for hoof alignment, 98–99
    horses' behavior for, 165–74
    importance of, 11, *140*, 143, 152, 181
Tripping, 96
Trot, 118, 119, 149, 164
Trotters, 63–64, 69–70
Tungsten carbide, 43, 44
Turnout considerations, 39, 147–48
Tying considerations, 168, 174

United States Equestrian Federation, 65–67
United States, farrier training in, 187–93
United States Polo Association, 69
Upright feet, 106. *See also* Club feet

Valentino, John, 135
Valgus/varus deviations, 125
Ventilation, 79, 80, 175–80
Vet-farrier partnerships, *101*, 118–19, 121, 130, 192–93
Vietnam war draft, author and, 200

Warmblood-type horses, 32, 66, *66*, 77, 142
W-bar shoes, 40
Wear, excessive, 58

Web size, *6*, 31–32. *See also* Wide-web shoes
Wedge shoes, 41, 51–52, *52*, *63*, 71
Weight-bearing phase, of gait, 55
Weighted shoes, 9, *63*, 65–66
Welded studs, 44
Western riding/performance, 60, 64, 72, *156*
White line disease, 58, 60, 116–17, *116*
Wide-web shoes, *6*, 32, *32*, 66, *66–67*, 108, 114–15
WIDTH hoof care analysis protocol, 4–10, 17, 19, 20–21
Wild horses, 10–11, 14
Wildenstein, Michael, *47*
Winter hoof care, 15, *15*, 41–42, *42*
Wire fencing, shoe loss and, 147, *148*, 150
Withers, saddle clearance of, 158
Wolf's Law, 91, 138
Women, as farriers, 195, *195*, 197
Woodie, Brett, 130
Work
    shoe design for, 63–71
    in WIDTH protocol, 5, 6
Work site/setups, 169, 174, 175–80, *177–78*, 204–6, *204*
Working cowboys, 189
Working horses, 64, 65, *65*
World Blacksmith Competition, 194
World Horseshoeing Classic, *193*
World War II, influence of, 83

X axis, 90, *90*, *92*, 94–99, *133*
X-rays, 120, 139, 202

Y axis, 91, *91*, 95–99, *133*
Young horses, 118. *See also* Foals

Z axis, 96, 97, 99
Z-bar shoes, 40, 50, *50*, 110